Cornelis Petrus Tiele

History of the Egyptian religion

Cornelis Petrus Tiele

History of the Egyptian religion

ISBN/EAN: 9783337263904

Printed in Europe, USA, Canada, Australia, Japan

Cover: Foto ©ninafisch / pixelio.de

More available books at **www.hansebooks.com**

COMPARATIVE HISTORY

OF THE

EGYPTIAN AND MESOPOTAMIAN RELIGIONS.

By C. P. TIELE.

EGYPT, BABEL-ASSUR, YEMEN, HARRAN, PHŒNICIA, ISRAEL.

VOL. I.—HISTORY OF THE EGYPTIAN RELIGION.

TRANSLATED FROM THE DUTCH, WITH THE CO-OPERATION OF THE AUTHOR,

By JAMES BALLINGAL.

BOSTON:
HOUGHTON, MIFFLIN AND COMPANY,
NEW YORK: 11 EAST SEVENTEENTH STREET.
The Riverside Press, Cambridge.
1882.

HISTORY

OF THE

EGYPTIAN RELIGION.

BY

DR. C. P. TIELE.

*TRANSLATED FROM THE DUTCH, WITH THE CO-OPERATION
OF THE AUTHOR,*

By JAMES BALLINGAL.

BOSTON:
HOUGHTON, MIFFLIN AND COMPANY.
NEW YORK: 11 EAST SEVENTEENTH STREET.
The Riverside Press, Cambridge.
1882.

AUTHOR'S PREFACE.

THIS volume is the English translation of the first portion of my "Comparative History of the Egyptian and Mesopotamian (Hamitic and Semitic) Religions." It has been considered advisable not to publish more than this first portion at present; but should it be received favourably, the publication of the other portion, which treats of the Babylonian-Assyrian religion, and of the religions of Phœnicia and Israel, will, it is intended, follow.

While the present volume may be looked upon as forming by itself a separate whole, I, nevertheless, wish it to be kept in mind that it has been written as part of a larger work, and from the point of view of comparative religious history. It does not claim to be an exhaustive history of the Egyptian religion.

Owing to the progress made in Egyptian studies since 1872, when the original work was published, revision has been necessary, and numerous alterations and additions have been made. Of this thorough revision the English translation has had full advantage, and may, in fact, be considered as an amended and improved version of the original work.

I gave my sanction to the translation being made; and after having gone over it carefully, I can testify that Mr. Ballingal has throughout reproduced my thoughts with the greatest accuracy.

C. P. TIELE.

LEIDEN, 1882.

CONTENTS.

PAGE

INTRODUCTION . . . . xv–xxiii

CHAPTER I.

NATIONALITY OF THE INHABITANTS OF THE NILE VALLEY.

Antiquity of Egyptian civilisation — Origin and race of Egyptian people—Constituent elements of the population—North and South 3

CHAPTER II.

THE SACRED LITERATURE.

Greek accounts—Egyptian records—"Book of the Dead"—Magical papyri—Sacred hymns, &c. 20

CHAPTER III.

THE RELIGION OF THINIS-ABYDOS.

Antiquity of Egyptian worships — Osiris - worship—Set—Horos—Isis—Nephthys—Hathor—Thot—Anubis — Seb and Nu—The Sun myth and the doctrine of Immortality 35

CHAPTER IV.

THE RELIGION OF HELIOPOLIS.

Heliopolis—Correspondence of Osiris- and Ra-worship—Ra-Tum—Dualistic character of Heliopolitan worship—Hymns of Ra—Shu and Tefnut—Review . . . 74

CHAPTER V.

RELIGION UNDER THE OLD KINGDOM.

Memphis—Ptah-worship—Not Phœnician—Sechet (Bast) and Neith—Sekru—Animal worship—Deification of kings—Religion under Chufu and Chafra—The temples—Religion under the Sixth Dynasty—Review . . . 90

CHAPTER VI.

RELIGION UNDER THE MIDDLE KINGDOM.

Dynasties—Chem, god of Koptos—Munt, of Hermonthis—Religion of this period agricultural in character—Other worships not neglected—Chnum, Sati, and Anuka—Sebak—Hâpi, god of the Nile—Review 120

CHAPTER VII.

RELIGION UNDER THE NEW KINGDOM.

The Hyksôs—Religion under them—The new kingdom—Amun of Thebes—Amun-ra—Approach to monotheism—Chonsu—Other gods reformed after pattern of Amun-ra—Religious revolution under Amenophis IV.—Aten-ra—Reaction under Horemhib—Religion under Seti I. and Ramses II.—Apis-worship—Treaty with Chetasir—Decline of South—Increase of priestly power and of superstition—Review 141

CHAPTER VIII.

EGYPTIAN RELIGION FROM THE FALL OF THE RAMESIDS
TO THE PERSIAN CONQUEST.

PAGE

Preponderance of the North—Religion of Mendes—Of Bubastis — Sechet and Bast two forms of the same deity — Ethiopian conquerors — Pianchi — Amun-meri-nut — Religion under the Saitic kings—Town and temple of Saïs—Cambyses—Uzahor-pen-res—Oracle of Amun—Transition to Universalism 186

CHAPTER IX.

CHARACTER AND MORAL RESULTS OF THE EGYPTIAN RELIGION.

Two principal phenomena—Hypothesis of esoteric and exoteric doctrine — Symbolic-mystic tendency — Combination of monotheism and polytheism—Egyptian religion symbolic, theocratic, monarchic, polytheistic—Principal idea, life—Religion and art—Religion and morality . 216

INTRODUCTION.

My purpose is to write a chapter of the comparative history of the ancient religions, not a religious history of antiquity. The latter would perhaps be the more interesting of the two, but I do not think that the time for it has yet come, and I for one do not, at the present stage of our knowledge, feel equal to the task.[1] It would indeed be a most attractive undertaking to delineate the development of religion among the different nations of antiquity who have succeeded each other in the sovereignty of the world; or, in other words, to sketch religious thought in history. But, in order to do this, to climb painfully step by step from the lowest to the more advanced, from rude nature-worship to religions in which the moral order of the world is recognised and reverenced side by side with the natural, and from these again up to others in which moral ideas are exclusively dominant and the standpoint of nature-worship wholly abandoned,—to do this, we must first possess an historical view of the different religions themselves mutually compared, and that is what I shall now in part endeavour to give.

---

[1] I have, however, made the attempt to give an outline of such a history in a little book recently translated into English by Professor Estlin Carpenter, "Outlines of the History of Religion to the Spread of the Universal Religions." London: Trübner & Co.

As in this task I shall at first confine myself to ancient religions, I must explain what I understand these to be. The ancient religions have one peculiarity, common to them all, by which they are distinguished from the modern: they are all tribal or national religions; they are all based on particularism. Even a superficial observer will notice that religious history naturally divides itself into two great parts, two periods or ages of the world which are essentially and markedly distinct. The prehistoric period as to which we can only venture upon conjectures and hypotheses, and the study of which properly constitutes the palæontological section of the science of religion, is everywhere followed by that of the tribal, national, and state religions, during which every religion belonged, as a matter of course, to a particular tribe or tribal league, to a nation or a state, and no one dreamed of spreading it more widely. To belong to a nation, to be counted as one of a tribe, is one and the same thing as to worship the gods of the country, the national gods. Whether a separate and ordered priesthood existed or not, whether the priests dominated the princes, or the princes the priests, as soon as a state was formed, be it monarchy, oligarchy, or republic, extending like the Celestial Empire over half a continent, or, like Carthage, confined to a town and its colonies, in every case the religion of the people became the religion of the state, closely bound up with it, and by it maintained, defended, and, when necessary, imposed by force. The idea of a separation between religion and the state is utterly foreign to all the religions of antiquity. To deny the gods of one's fathers is the same thing as to deny one's nationality. The existence of foreign gods was not denied, but it was believed that they were confined to the people over whom they ruled, that their power reached no farther; and men constantly imagined as to this that the foreign gods were less powerful than their own. Usually they did not worship them, though they had no doubts about their real existence; sometimes, especially when the worshippers of foreign gods were enemies, they hated them no less than their worshippers, and looked upon them as evil hurtful beings, powers of darkness. Not unfrequently a people adopted, not indeed the religion, but the gods of their neighbours; these, however, never became genuine national gods of that people unless they first laid aside their original nationality. In no case was a place given them in the ancestral pantheon if they did not wholly alter their form, character, appearance, and not seldom, their very name.[1]

The Greeks transformed the myths of Aphrodite, Herakles, Dionysus, by introducing into them Semitic ele-

---

[1] A case which is given on a stone tablet (stèle) brought from Thebes and preserved in the Imperial Library at Paris, and which seems to form an exception to this, which is certainly the general rule, stands quite alone and rather confirms it. The prince of Buchten or Bachten (Behistan?) in Asia, whose daughter was the wife of Ramses XII., king of Egypt, besought him to send a physician skilful enough to cure his other daughter, Bent-ent-resht, who was ill of a nervous disease. When the physician had failed, he asked if his son-in-law would send him no less than one of his gods, the Theban god Chonsu, in order that through his influence the evil spirit might be driven out. This was done, and when it was proved that the disease could not resist the power of Chonsu, the Asiatic prince would not allow him to go home again. Soon, however, he had cause to regret what, in those days, must have been looked upon as a deed of violence; and when he himself, being sick, dreamed that the god of Thebes, in the form of a sparrow-hawk, sent curses from his sanctuary, he no longer withheld him, but sent him back to his old home. It is evident here that the Asiatic prince, while recognising the power of Chonsu, looked upon him all along as a foreign god; and we also see how strong the conviction was that each god belonged to a particular nation; nay, even to a particular spot. See Brugsch, Histoire d'Egypte, i. 206-209; F. Lenormant, Manuel de l'Histoire Ancienne de l'Orient, i. p. 302 *et seq.* If, as is possible, the story is only a legend without historical value, or, as Wiedemann has it, a novel, the above conclusions retain their force.

ments, but it is with difficulty that these gods can be distinguished from those that are purely Hellenic. Who would perceive in the charming, graceful Cyprian goddess the Ashthoreth of the Phœnicians; who, in the beautiful myth of her birth out of the foam of the sea, would recognise the tasteless nature myth of the Phœnician cosmogony, if ample proof did not compel the acknowledgment of their identity? The Anâhita of the Persians has something in common with the Chaldean mother of the gods Anat, but how completely has the form of this goddess been recast under the influence of the Aryan spirit! Serapis, brought by a mandate of Ptolemæus Soter from Sinope to Egypt, never obtained the full rights of a citizen in the Osirian mythology, and received homage only because people saw in his name a combination of the names of two ancient Egyptian divinities, Osiris and Apis, Asar-hapi.[1] The Asiatic god was thus obliged to assume an Egyptian shape in order to obtain the homage of the Egyptians; and, in spite of the protection of the king, even this was only grudgingly rendered. Many more examples could be adduced to prove the same thing. The national element stood in the foreground in all the ancient religions. It is true, intolerance did not always prevail. From political motives, conquerors like Darius Hystaspes, and even Cambyses in his best days, Alexander the Great, and others, paid a certain degree of worship to the gods of the nations whom they had conquered; but this was done precisely in order to show publicly that they had become the lawful lords of the country. There was no other design in it than merely to soothe the national

---

[1] See the passages in Plutarch, Pausanias, Tacitus, Clemens Al., and other authors of antiquity, in Wilkinson's Manners and Customs of the Ancient Egyptians, 2d series, i. p. 360 *et seq.* See also E. Plew, De Sarapide : Regiom. 1868, where the question is pretty fully gone into.

pride of the humbled people. This, moreover, did not happen till the time when the old conception had begun to yield, and the forerunners of a new era were beginning to show themselves. Besides, while they might as princes judge it necessary to bring an offering to the gods of a conquered people, they yet at the same time remained faithful to the gods of their own race. Darius continued to draw up his decrees in the name of the great Auramazda alone, and the Greeks were not provoked at the comedy played by Alexander in the Oasis of Ammon, for they had contrived to find in this African god a form of their own Zeus.

It was, moreover, quite natural in the common view that another nation should have another worship; that the boundaries of the land should be also the boundaries of the religion in which men found the greatest satisfaction of their religious needs. Herodotus can tell, without the least danger, about all sorts of foreign religious customs and ideas, and does not need to be afraid lest the Greeks should thereby be led into doubt, or lest the question might arise in any of their minds, Is the worship of Osiris or Ptah, of Bel or Ormazd, perchance better and more exalted than that of the Olympian Zeus and the Delphic Apollo? The Israelite himself, in whose eyes the gods of the Gojîm were, when compared to Jahveh, mere gods of clay and as vanity, never thought of making proselytes to his religion till certain neighbouring nations set him the example, and already the conception of a universal religion had begun to mature. "Your people is my people, and your god my God,"[1] was, in ancient times, a synonym, and the two went always together. As yet no one had any conception of a world-religion. Men developed, re-

[1] Ruth i. 16.

formed, modified, and enriched at need their own religion, but held by it always, and considered it as treason to the state to introduce the worship of strange gods. Thus the Romans honoured everywhere the native gods of the nations who had not been able to resist the victorious power of their sword, but persecuted all who wished to introduce strange gods into the great Roman Empire. It is true that by this time the new period had already come, and the evil could no longer be stemmed.

The new era, the second great world-period, does not begin everywhere at once: it is earlier with some nations than with others; in some it has not yet begun at all.

As particularism is the special mark of the first, so universalism is the mark peculiar to this second period. The new religions are no longer national religions but world-religions. They spring from the thought that religion is the concern not of a nation but of humanity, and therefore ought no longer to be tied down to any nationality. They speak not one but many tongues. They are not content with the allegiance of the nation by whose means they rise into being, but immediately begin to extend themselves even to utterly foreign and barbarous nations, revealing very clearly that their aim is to conquer all mankind.

And if in course of time a universal religion of this kind assumes among the people who profess it a national character, if it should even become at first, as in most cases, a state religion, the feeling of unity is never wholly lost; with all their differences in forms and customs, men feel themselves united as to the main thing. The old principle still goes on working, and reaction follows on every step of forward progress; but the new power is too strong not to be victorious, and gains ground persistently.

The revolution brought about by religious universalism is the greatest and most complete which the history of the world can show; all others, political or social, are as nothing compared to this. One religion spread over all the countries from Ceylon and Java to Siberia, one faith from Persia to Spain—in the days of antiquity such a conception would have been rejected as a chimera. The Roman was of opinion that the whole world belonged by rights to him. It seemed to him quite natural that there should be a universal empire founded and maintained by the sword, a varied medley of nations brought into subjection to the commander-in-chief of his victorious army elected by the host to be emperor; but if it had been foretold to him that the high-priest of Rome would one day in virtue of his office lay down the law for the nations and princes of the whole of the West, he would not have believed it. Can we wonder, then, that such a change did not come about suddenly, but that we can see it slowly approaching, slowly preparing beforehand, and accomplished at last only through great convulsions? The east of Asia seems to have become ripe for it sooner than the west; Europe and Western Asia sooner than Mid-Asia and Africa. Five centuries before the first missionaries of the Gospel set out from Palestine for Greece, Egypt, and Italy, to proclaim the crucified King of the Jews to the civilised peoples who inhabited the coasts of the Mediterranean Sea as their Redeemer, accordingly before the rise on the borders of the Semitic and Aryan territory of the noblest world-religion which, originating among the Semites, was rejected by them and accepted by the Aryans;—five centuries before this time that religious communion was founded in Hindostan which not only stirred the Brahmanic world, but, long before it was banished out of India by the Brahmans, already numbered by millions its adherents among the other nations of Eastern Asia. While Buddhism had thus conquered the Turanian world, and had already obtained a firm hold on the Tibetans, Chinese, and Tartars, Christianity began its conquests among the Aryans of Europe. And again, five centuries later, there arose in Arabia the youngest world-religion, a pure Semitic one, which was successful in driving Christianity, which, through the influence of the Aryan spirit, had freed itself from many Semitic peculiarities, out of the whole of the territory in which the Semites had formerly borne sway; but, nevertheless, in all countries where the higher civilisation prevailed, Mohammedanism was wholly thrown into the shade by Christianity. Still, though Islâm more than its two rivals bears the impress of the race which gave it birth, it did not confine itself to that race alone. It is essentially a world-religion. It overcame the national religion of Persia, which was the less able to contend with it on account of the people of Western Erân having been for a long time subjected to powerful Semitic influences. In the east and middle of Asia, Mohammedanism soon became a formidable rival of Buddhism, from which it wrested the dominion of the Indian Archipelago, especially of Java. It also contested the supremacy of Buddhism among the Tartars. And while it thus spread irresistibly, it produced converts among all manner of nations and races,—Arabians and Syrians, Egyptians and Berbers, Gallas and Negroes. It is to these three religions, proceeding from the new humanitarian principle, that the present and at least the more immediate future belongs. We may therefore with perfect propriety name them the *new* religions. Under the name of *old* religions, on the other hand, I understand all the others which, essentially particularistic in their nature, are peculiar to a special tribe, tribal union, or people; all religions which, though they may not yet have all died out,—the majority of them in truth still survive,—and though they still show a certain vitality, and as yet have come little or not at all into contact with the new, nevertheless begin to yield more and more before the power of the world-religions.

Book I.

HISTORY OF THE EGYPTIAN RELIGION.

"O Egypt, Egypt, of thy religion there will be left remaining nothing but uncertain tales, which will be believed no more by posterity, words graven on stone and telling of thy piety."—*Hermes Trismegistus Æsculapius.*

HISTORY OF THE EGYPTIAN RELIGION.

CHAPTER I.

NATIONALITY OF THE INHABITANTS OF THE NILE VALLEY.

THE cradle of civilisation, the spot where man first awoke to self-conscious and reflective life, seems to have been the valley of Sinear—the valley of the Euphrates and Tigris. We are, however, unacquainted with any civilisation more ancient than that of Egypt. Compared with this eldest-born among nations, all the other peoples of the world whose traditions have come down to us are mere children. The reliable history of Egypt, authenticated by monuments of the highest antiquity, ascends to a time when all the other races were still sunk in barbarism, or at least when they had taken scarcely more than the first steps in the direction of a higher development.

If we may take for granted that Manetho gives the reigns of the Egyptian kings accurately, and that the dynasties of which he tells us are for the most part consecutive, then, long before the first man, according to the common chronology and to the tradition of the Hebrews, was made by the breath of God a living soul, Egypt already stood at the same stage of development in industry and the arts at which, centuries later, it was found by the Persians and Greeks; or rather, what is said to have astonished the latter, the civilisation they found was only the fading remnant of an epoch of splendour, the commencement of which lay far back in grey antiquity. It is, indeed, the case that to all appearance the Proto-Chaldeans preceded the Egyptians in civilisation; but, however this may be, they are a race which has left such slight traces in the annals of humanity that neither its history nor that of its religion can be written. It is not till after the foundation of the Semitic empires in the valley of the Tigris and Euphrates that the history of these countries begins to be based on contemporary monuments. We are obliged to reconstruct the religion of their ancient inhabitants by an induction from that of their conquerors. The beginning of the oldest so-called Semitic [1] or rather Mesopotamian kingdom—that is, the Chaldean—is usually placed in the twenty-first century B.C., and the oldest dynasty of the Chinese does not go much farther back. In the opinion, however, of most Egyptologists, the greatest portion of Egyptian history had then been already enacted: the Old and Middle Kingdoms of the sons of Ham had already fallen, Egypt had reached its point of culmination, and its most flourishing epoch was already left behind. The religious literature of the Hebrews, venerable as it is for its antiquity, does not begin before Moses; but we possess a MS. from Thebes in hieratic characters, written several centuries before the time of the Hebrew lawgiver under the twelfth Egyptian dynasty, and the author of which may have lived at a time considerably earlier.[2] There is also reason to suppose that certain portions of the Egyptian "Book of the Dead" are older still. We

---

[1] Instead of the Semitic, I should prefer to speak of the Mesopotamian race; but to prevent confusion, I retain the old nomenclature.

[2] I refer to the papyrus named after Prisse. It contains a moral disquisition by a certain king's son, Ptahhotep, of the fifth dynasty (cir. 3000 B.C.), and the last pages of another moral writing in the days of King Snefru (cir. 3600 B.C.) Comp. Chabas, Le plus ancien Livre du Monde; E. de Rougé, Exposé de l'Etat actuel des Etudes egyptiennes (Progrès des Etudes rel. à l'Eg. et l'Orient, Report to the Minister of Instruction in France, 1867), p. 55; Brugsch, Hist. d'Eg., i. 29 *et seq.* For the date of the MS. see Ebers, Aeg. u. d. Bl). Mos. i. 147. The MS. is in the Imperial Library at Paris.

do not know exactly at what time the Vedas, the oldest existing records of the Aryan race, originated, but in any case their date cannot be earlier than two thousand years before our chronology; but even if they existed so early, they are still centuries more recent than the Egyptian work we named, and were at least ten centuries later of being written down. A relatively moderate calculation, that of Brugsch, places the commencement of the series of indisputably historical kings of Egypt in the forty-fifth century B.C. But if the reigns of the kings as given by Manetho, an Egyptian priest, who lived in the time of Ptolemæus Soter, and wrote the ancient history of his country, are added up, we then ascend to the fifty-first century B.C., or somewhat higher still. It has indeed been suggested that the royal houses named by him were not all consecutive, but that some were contemporary, reigning in different parts of the country at one time, and therefore that the number of years ascribed by him to such dynasties should be deducted from the sum-total. Brugsch likewise considers the ninth, tenth, fourteenth, and twenty-fifth dynasties as instances of those contemporary with others; while Bunsen, above all, has carried this supposition to excessive lengths in the construction of his chronology. Nevertheless, monuments discovered recently tend more and more to confirm the accuracy of Manetho, and justify the opinion that he chronicled the reigns of those only which were in his eyes the legitimate ruling houses, and that he did not take into account their rivals, whose rule only extended over portions of the country.[1] Be that as

[1] The doubts cast by Max Duncker in his "Geschichte des Alterthums," i. 12 et seq., on this high antiquity of the Egyptian state, have been removed by more recent investigations, and the evidence, growing ever clearer, of the monuments. The new so-called table or list of the kings at Abydos, discovered by Mariette, has tended to strengthen the testimony of Manetho. The list of the kings of the six first dynasties occurring there is almost equally complete with that of the Sebennyte. It contains the names of sixty-five kings anterior to Aahmes, the founder of the new empire, and seventy-five before Seti I., who erected the monument. And that it contains only a selection out of the complete list of kings is proved by the fact that of the immediate predecessors of

it may, we may look upon it as extremely probable that Egyptian history begins not later, and perhaps even much earlier, than 4000 B.C. But the style of writing on the monuments of this early period has already reached such perfection and settled form, and the pictures in the tombs of the oldest dynasties betoken a civilisation so rich and so firmly established that we are obliged to allow many centuries more of slow preparation and growth anterior to the period of which the historic evidences have come down to us. When the Egyptian nation enters upon the scene of the world's history it is already full grown. Like Pallas Athena from the head of Jupiter, it issues from the night of past ages fully equipped into the light. The brain reels in confusion when we think of the unreckoned prehistoric centuries in which its early childhood and youth were passed.

To what race and to what nationality does this people belong which thus took the lead of all other peoples of the world in the path of civilisation? Some would have us believe that it belongs to the Aryan race, others that it

---

Seti's father, Ramses I., *i.e.*, of the thirteen or fourteen kings of the eighteenth dynasty, whose existence is undoubtedly proved by the monuments, only eight are named in the table of Abydos; and thus not only the four considered illegitimate who nevertheless reigned, but also one or two others distinctly legitimate, are not noticed. C. Piazzi Smyth, the Scotch astronomer, goes further still. He places the Great Pyramid in the year 2429 B.C., in this agreeing with Osburn. If the years of the date of Ramses II.'s reign, which cannot have been much earlier than 1400 B.C., are deducted from this, there remain about a thousand years betwixt him and Chufu, the founder of this pyramid. On an inscription at Havaris, Ramses speaks of a chronology instituted by one of the Shepherd Kings four hundred years previously. This king cannot have been the first of their princes, for the institution of a chronology can scarcely have occurred before the rude conquerors had had time to receive the civilisation of the Egyptians. Accordingly, six hundred years remain, and within these six centuries the reigns of the earlier Hyksos, together with those of five other dynasties vouched for by the monuments, and at least four successors of Chufu, must be placed. Now, even if we allow for an instant that the six dynasties mentioned over and above these, and for which room must be found in this period, never existed, and this is possible, since they left behind next to no monuments, we should still feel the impossibility of what Piazzi Smyth asserts. His tactics, in truth, consist in ignoring the most powerful arguments, and in the repetition of dogmatic utterances which prove nothing. P. S., On the Antiquity of Intellectual Man from a Practical and Astronomical Point of View. Edin., 1868.

is to be considered as Semitic (Mesopotamian). It presents analogies, important traits of relationship to both, and is also distinguished from both by other characteristics no less weighty. If, as there is every reason to believe, these two races are two branches of a primitive stock, from which they were detached long before historic times, the Egyptians, whose ancestors certainly came from Asia either across the Isthmus of Suez or by passing across the Red Sea, may be the representatives of this anterior race commingled in Africa with the original inhabitants of the Nile Valley, whose own character, not differing from that of the other most advanced peoples of that part of the world, has left marked traces in Egyptian civilisation.

Up to the present time, however, the all but universally accepted opinion was that the Egyptians should be set apart as a race different from both Aryans and Mesopotamians. Proceeding upon Gen. x. 6, scholars spoke of the Hamitic race as that to which, besides the Egyptian, three other nations, or groups of nations named in that passage, belong. I can only look on the Hamitic race as being the fruit of a powerful imagination and of perverted exegesis. It was long ago conjectured that the division of the nations known to the Hebrews into sons of Ham, Shem, and Japheth, does not rest on an ethnographic basis, but on one of a very different nature: in other words, that the passage does not speak of three races which we have to distinguish from each other in speech and origin, but that here it sets, side by side, three groups of peoples for a reason other than that of language and descent. For comparative philology, which had already convincingly proved the unity of the Aryan nations from their community of speech, was in favour neither of a Semitic nor of a Hamitic race according to the division of Gen. x. There the Canaanites are counted as sons of Ham, and it is certain that all the Canaanite nations, including the Phœnicians, spoke a language closely related to Hebrew; yet, in spite of this, the Hebrews are reckoned as sons of

Shem. The same thing holds, though in a less degree, of the sons of Phut and of Cush, who are counted, in Gen. x. 6, among the sons of Ham. Both of these are, by descent and language, much more closely related to the Arabians, Syrians, and Hebrews than to the Egyptians proper. The mode in which some have thought to vindicate, not the accuracy of the author, but the traditional exegesis of Gen. x., is one of the astonishing feats by which the advocates of a lost cause usually try to save themselves. The Canaanites, though belonging to the sons of Ham, are supposed, at their immigration into Canaan, to have there fallen in with certain Semitic tribes whose language and religion they, in one word, adopted as their own.[1] The unreasonableness of this hypothesis is too great for it to find any support from an unbiassed investigator, and it really is not deserving of serious refutation. More thorough and scientific students have therefore adopted the opinion that the division of the nations in the chapter so often referred to is founded on a geographical basis. By Ham, Shem, and Japheth the ancient author is supposed to indicate, not three races, but three regions or zones; so that Ham was to him the representative of the south, Japheth of the north, and Shem of the middle of the world which was within his view.[2] Attractive as this notion is, I cannot entertain it. It fails also to remove all the difficulties. The sons of Japheth named in Gen. x. dwell indeed mostly in the north, but the sons of Ham are not always to be sought more to the south than those of Shem. The Canaanites dwelt more to the north than the Arabians and Babylonians; and though they all came from the south-east, the Hebrews and other Semitic tribes came also originally

---

[1] So, along with others, Lenormant, following Munk, in his "Manuel d'Histoire ancienne de l'Orient," ii. 246, a work that would be much more worthy of praise if the author did not look upon it as a Christian duty constantly to wrest history into accordance with the tradition of the ancient Hebrews.

[2] Thus, among others, Renan, Hist. génér. et systéme comparé d. Langues sémitiques, 2d ed., p. 40.

from that quarter. Phut the son of Ham is to be sought for more to the north than Joktan the son of Shem; and so this explanation also is unsatisfactory.

But, in my opinion, we need no longer remain in uncertainty as to what the Hebrew author meant with his division into sons of Ham, Shem, and Japheth. His meaning at once appears when we look at the nations to whom Ham is allotted as their first ancestor. In Ham, like all the other tribal fathers, a mythical personage, the black land of Egypt itself was long since recognised. Kem, or Kam, was the name given to their native land by the inhabitants of the Nile valley themselves.[1] There are next enumerated as his sons, Cush, which is the name given on Egyptian monuments to the Ethiopian nation to the south of Egypt proper, which in historic times migrated thither from the east from Mesopotamia, where the stock from which it was an offshoot still remained behind. Next comes Mizraim, the common Hebrew name for the kingdom of the Pharaohs, especially for Middle or Lower Egypt, a name the dual form of which[2] excites no surprise, whether we consider it as derived from the two great divisons of the country, or find that it signifies the two enclosures, and agree with Knobel in thinking that these are the two mountain chains that border the Nile valley, or with Ebers, that they are the double walls which, according to the most ancient monuments, protected Egypt against the inroads of barbarians.[3] Phut, or Punt as it is called on the Egyptian monuments, is a country with which the Egyptians were in many ways closely connected, but the signification of this name is somewhat uncertain: it either denotes an African tribe, or it refers to

---

[1] See Brugsch, Hieroglyphisch-demotisches Wörterbuch, p. 1451, voce *Kem*.

[2] Mizraim, as is well known, is a dual form.

[3] See Ebers, op. cit., p. 86. Even under the oldest dynasties two walls are found in existence distinguished as the northern and southern wall; the former was dedicated to Neith, the latter to Ptah. Comp. De Rougé, Monuments des VI. premières Dynasties, p. 97.

that part of Arabia which was under the rule of the Egyptians, or where at least they held some posts in military occupation. The fourth son is Canaan, at that time the region occupied by the Phœnician peoples. Now, to any one familiar with Egyptian history, it is very evident why these nations in particular are called, as distinguished from others, the sons of Ham. Mizraim is not indeed the son first named, because the author appears to travel in his enumeration from south to north, but there is no need to prove that he has full right to the name of a son of the black earth. The Cushites, or Ethiopians, were for a considerable time tributary to Egypt, and so were the Punt. Canaan also was for a long time under Egyptian dominion, and the Canaanites owed all their civilisation to Egypt, while, as will presently be seen, Phœnicians inhabited the north coast of the Delta, and even in Memphis had a special quarter of the town set apart for themselves. The sons of Ham, sons, that is, of the black Nile valley, are thus simply the Egyptians and the nations subdued and civilised by them. The division into three national groups, by the author of Gen. x., is neither ethnographic nor geographic, but—if I may be allowed the word—historico-social (*cultuur-historisch*). The sons of Ham represent the most ancient and to the Hebrews an offensive civilisation: the sons of Shem that next in succession which, though quickened and raised up under Egyptian influence, was yet a development much more independent and original than that of the peoples directly subject to Egypt. The central point of this civilisation is found in the Assyrian empire. Assur is named among the sons of Shem. All the other nations known to the ancient Hebrews, though they belonged to different races—Aryan or Turanian—were included under Japheth, and he is called the eldest son, either as being the greatest, the one whose territory was most extensive, or, and this is more likely, as being the one who had longest retained the primitive state of culture, and remained still at a stage of development long since left behind by the Hamitic and Semitic races. Into this question, however, I cannot now enter farther. For my purpose it is enough to have proved that the sons of Ham in Gen. x. can teach us nothing about the origin of the Egyptian people. This result, though negative, is at least in one respect valuable, for it removes an erroneous idea, which hampered investigations likely to be fruitful.

Accordingly, the question—To what race do the Egyptians belong?—remains open. The task of answering it must be left to comparative philology. Attempts in this direction have already been made. Benfey has tried to prove that the ordinary so-called Semitic languages are nothing but one of two branches of a family of languages, the other branch of which must be looked for across the Isthmus of Suez, and which, along with the Egyptian, embraces all the languages of North Africa, to the Atlantic Ocean. He has been followed in this by others, as Ernst Meier, and Paul Bötticher—(De Lagarde). Bunsen adopted the same view in a somewhat modified form. According to him, the Egyptians were an early offshoot from the Caucasian race, at a time when the Semitic and Aryan elements had not yet definitely separated from each other. In this way the points of agreement between the ancient Egyptian and both these branches of language, may, Bunsen thinks, be best explained.[1]

This idea is not unfamiliar to other Egyptologists as well. Besides De Rougé, who has only cursorily glanced at this subject, Brugsch and Ebers have laid great stress upon the close relationship between the ancient Egyptian and the Mesopotamian (Semitic) languages. The former

---

[1] See Renan, Langues Sémitiques, 2d ed., p. 80 et seq. Renan himself, as is well known, is in favour of limiting the Semitic group of languages to the narrowest possible bounds, even refusing to allow that the Assyrians and Babylonians are Semitic. More recent discoveries, both in Mesopotamia and in Egypt, and a closer study of the idioms of both countries, have deprived his arguments of much of their force. He has himself made concessions recently on this point.

considers it as almost certain that the Egyptian tongue has its root in the Semitic, and regards it as a fact which new investigations will more and more confirm, that this and all Semitic languages are the offspring of a common mother, whose original seat is to be sought on the banks of the Euphrates or the Tigris.[1] The latter does not hesitate to affirm that the Egyptians are a Semitic, apparently Chaldean, stock, the cause of whose wide difference from their Eastern brethren is, that they adopted from the original inhabitants of the land in which they settled not a little both of their language and their customs.[2] In spite of the determined opposition that Benfey's opinion at first encountered from various quarters, and notwithstanding that his opinions were opposed on the one side by the Hebraist Ewald, and on the other by the Aryologist Pott, Egyptologists appear more and more inclined to adopt the results of the Göttingen linguist. The question is not yet ripe for decision. One thing is certain, that the Egyptians belong originally to Asia, and are closely related to that great race, which includes the Aryans as well as the Mesopotamians. They must have migrated into Egypt long before the beginning of history, either by way of the Isthmus of Suez or across the Red Sea, and established themselves in the country between the Delta and the Cataracts. It is very remarkable that Western Asia always continued to be called among them, the holy land, the land of the gods, *Ta Nuter*. They are undoubtedly not a pure Aryan people, though some superficial investigators of history have set this down without much reflection. The points in which their customs and speech coincide with the so-called Semitic civilisation and language are far more numerous and important than the

---

[1] Brugsch, Wörterbuch, Einl. ix.
[2] Ebers, Aeg. u. BB. Mos. i. 45. Ebers declares that he has more than three hundred examples of words which, he alleges, are derived from Semitic roots, and he believes that he will by-and-by be able to support his opinion more completely. In any case, there is no lack of Aryan roots in the Egyptian, and some of them express very important ideas.

points of agreement between them and the Aryans. Since, however, sufficient light has not yet been thrown on this subject, and we do not wish to assert more than is really ascertained, I shall not as yet rank the Egyptian among the Semitic peoples, and I shall, on account of the many peculiarities of their religion, treat of it separately.

The inhabitants of Egypt, moreover, comprised diverse elements. The name Egypt, given to the country by the Greeks, and, according to Brugsch, derived from Ha-Ka-Ptah, *i.e.*, house of the worship of Ptah, or, according to Ebers, from Ai-Kaft, *i.e.*, the coast country Kaft, or the curved coast,[1] was not a native word. They themselves, as we have seen, called their land Kem, the black, in contradistinction to the red clayey soil of Libya and Syria, and they honoured the kernel of the population, the inhabitants of pure blood, under the name of Retu or Rutu, the men, which coincides with the Ludim of Gen. x. 13, who are there designated as the first sons of Mizraim.[2] To esteem themselves as the men *par excellence*, is so entirely in harmony with the spirit of antiquity, and is still so common [3] with many primitive nations, that we cannot look upon this as extraordinary. These Retu appear to have been the ruling class, the natural aristocracy. But other tribes had also settled on the black earth. To these belong the Aamu or Amu, who have been compared with the Anamim of Gen. x. 13.[4] They were certain Arabian

---

[1] Brugsch, Histoire, p. 6 *et seq.*; Ebers, Aeg. u. BB. Mos. 133 *et seq.*

[2] Ebers, op. cit., p. 91 ; De Rougé, Mon. d. VI. premières Dynasties, p. 6. Since the Egyptians, as well as the old Iranians, had no L, and as the D could only be expressed by them by the combination (NT), *Lud* is the simple Hebrew transcript of Rut. The final U is the termination of the plural, corresponding to the Hebrew IM.

[3] Comp. Waitz, Anthropologie der Naturvölker, iii. 36, 303.

[4] Ebers, op. cit., p. 101, sees in the Anamim the Amu with the Egyptian word An = nomad, prefixed : an-amu, *i.e.*, nomadic Arabs to be carefully distinguished from anukens, *i.e.*, the Nubian nomads who belong to another people. The conjecture of Ebers has certainly more in its favour than that of De Rougé, "Mon. d. VI. prem. Dynasties," p. 6 *et seq.*, who sees in the Anamim simply Anu, *i.e.*, nomads, and the name of these nomads is brought by him into connection with the names of towns, Heliopolis, Dendera, and Hermonthis, that are all called An

pastoral tribes, who, with the consent of the government, settled in Egypt so early as the time of the twelfth dynasty. Their chief places of abode were in the Sinaitic peninsula, on the Bucolic Nile branch, and in Middle Egypt between the Arabian mountain-range and the Red Sea. They appear, however, never to have mixed with the Egyptians. The Casluhim, out of whom, according to Gen. x. 14, came Philistim, seem to have lived more to the north, in that land of scorched mountains which extends from the east of the Delta to the boundaries of Palestine, and which was subject to Egypt. In the west are found the Libyans, the Lehabim, or Lubu (properly Rebu) of the Egyptian inscriptions. They are a northern tribe of the people called by the ancient Egyptians Tehennu or Temhu, and their country was on the eastern border. This people not unfrequently made inroads on Egyptian territory, and their descendants survive still in the Tuaregs, who prefer to call themselves Imoshagh, in the neuter Tema-shight, a word that recalls the old name Temhu.[1] The coast between the Libyan territory and that of the eastern Semitic tribes appears to have been early inhabited and taken possession of by the Phœnicians, and they, perhaps, are the Caphtorim of Gen. x. 14, a name which was formerly supposed to indicate the Cretans.[2] It is, at all events, certain that

in the old Egyptian. He thinks that these towns may originally have been colonies of these people. But *An* in the name of these towns has certainly nothing to do with nomads, and is undoubtedly derived from *an* = stone or pillar.

[1] See Barth, Discoveries and Travels, i. 195 *et seq*. One of their gods is *Amun*, who thus bears the same name as the chief god of Thebes and of the Libyan Oasis.

[2] This question has been very fully gone into by Ebers, Aeg. u. BB. Mos. i. 127–252. Most interesting of all are the evidences adduced by him of the immense influence exercised in Egypt in very early times by the so-called Semites. That he draws thence some rash inferences, and once or twice proves too much, is to be expected, as he is trying to support a happy conjecture in every possible way. This lucky guess is the explanation of the Hebrew Caphthor by Kaft-ur, "great Phœnicia," literally "great curved (coast) land;" for Kaft is the (later) Egyptian name for Phœnicia. We grant him willingly the rapid spread of this busy people through the north of Egypt, and acknowledge that of this fact he has collected various fresh proofs. But, what he certainly has not proved is, that the Phœnicians were already settled in Egypt before the

they had no sooner set foot in Egypt than they tried to penetrate farther and farther into it, and exercised considerable influence on the culture and even on the religion of the north of Egypt, not excepting Memphis. This influence is not, however, perceptible till under the new kingdom after the time of Hyksos, and cannot have been great before the invasion of the latter, even though we were obliged to allow that, at that time, the Phœnicians already inhabited the north coast of the Delta.

With such a distribution of population it is not to be wondered at that the north and south of the country, though mostly always united under one sceptre, were yet clearly distinguished from each other, and that not only did each of them exhibit a sharply marked character of its own, but they were also constantly in conflict as rivals for supremacy. Only by keeping this in mind is it possible rightly to understand the history of Egypt. In religious ideas, in dialect, and in customs, Lower and Upper Egypt were essentially different. The author of Gen. x. has not overlooked this; but according to his mode of regarding the two divisions of the land, they are two sons of Mizraim, that is, two different tribes, the Naphthuchîm and the Pathrusîm. The former are the Na-ptah (pronounced in the Memphitic dialect phtah), that is, "those of Ptah," the worshippers of the god of Memphis, the capital of

time of the Hyksos, though he repeatedly assures us that this was the case. Not only is that unlikely in itself, but, from the account of an officer who, in the reign of Amenemha I. of the twelfth dynasty (that of the Hyksos is the seventeenth), was sent to Edom and a district of Palestine, it appears that at that time no trace of Canaanites was found in that region (Chabas). It is true that, if with Ebers we make Abraham's visit to Egypt fall so early as under the twelfth dynasty, then we must allow that the Canaanites already lived at that time in Palestine, but this, too, requires more distinct proof. Equally hazardous seems to me the hypothesis of Ebers, p. 143, that the town of Koptos, in Upper Egypt, derived its name from the Phœnicians, and was inhabited chiefly by them, unless we accept the supposition that they migrated thither from the shores of the Red Sea, which was their first abode. We shall afterwards have an opportunity of considering the Phœnician elements in the Egyptian religion, which, according to Ebers, p. 237 *et seq.*, must have been very important.

Lower Egypt. The latter are the inhabitants of the south country P-ta-res, or, according to Ebers,[1] Pathyr(Pe-hathar)res, the southerly Pathyr, the nomos sacred to Hathor. The pure Egyptian element was always more represented by the South. The North was overrun by foreigners who were with difficulty kept in restraint by the ruling power at Memphis. The whole history of Egypt is a struggle of Egyptian nationality against the ever more and more successful encroachments of Semitic or Mesopotamian intruders who pushed their way, for the most part by the Isthmus of Suez, or by the north coast, through to the fat land which they coveted. At first, the cultivated and powerful South makes its supremacy felt by the rude North. Menes unites both divisions under his sceptre, and founds Memphis with the evident design of keeping the whole of Lower Egypt in check by means of this fortress. This was successfully done. During a period of many centuries six pure Egyptian dynasties ruled over the whole country from their seat in Memphis. Then comes a period of turmoil and confusion. A Lower Egyptian dynasty, proceeding from Herakleopolis,[2] managed to acquire the sovereignty at least of the north, and was followed by a second, also belonging to Herakleopolis. Meanwhile, in Upper Egypt a royal family, which sprang from the Theban nomos, had established itself as an inde-

---

[1] Ebers, op. cit., i. 115 et seq.
[2] It is uncertain which Herakleopolis is referred to here. There were three towns of the name all in Lower Egypt : one, Herakleopolis Magna, to the south of Memphis ; another, Herakleopolis Parva, on the most easterly branch of the Nile, in the Sethroitic nomos ; and a third on the most westerly branch. Lepsius, and along with him Ebers, exclude the first, on the ground that a royal family, whose seat was so close to Memphis, could not have reigned simultaneously with a Memphitic dynasty. This difficulty is removed, if with Mariette we make the Herakleopolitan reigns not contemporary but in immediate succession to the last Memphitic dynasty. Should Mariette's opinion turn out to be unassailable, I would in that case seek the ninth and tenth dynasty in Herakleopolis Magna. The other two places were too insignificant, and the extreme north had assuredly not obtained at that early period such influence as to make it probable that a line of sovereigns which ruled over a great part of the country should have come at that time out of one of these border towns.

pendent power, and was successful, if not in the first dynasty that reigned, at least in that which followed, the twelfth, in bringing the whole kingdom once more under its own purely Egyptian sovereignty, and in raising it to the most flourishing condition in arts and civilisation. While the dynasties that had Memphis for their seat are usually designated as the Old Kingdom, this first Theban supremacy is best indicated by the name of the Middle Kingdom.

But this brilliant epoch having now passed away, the power of the South declines, and again the North raises its head. It shakes off the yoke of the Theban power, and pays homage to a dynasty established at Xoïs in the Delta. This was, however, only the prelude to still greater humiliations in store for Egypt. Foreign hordes from Arabia bring into subjection the whole of Lower Egypt by means of the sword, and compel Upper Egypt to pay them tribute, and for four centuries the domination of the Hyksos or Shepherd Kings presses heavily upon the land.

Once again emancipation comes from the South. The Arabian kings, who had gradually adopted the civilisation of Egypt, lost, it would seem as they did so, their ferocity, and apparently at the same time their old energy as well. The tributary Theban princes venture to throw off the yoke. Aahmes, after a long struggle, is successful in expelling them, and unites all Egypt under his rule. With him begins the New Kingdom, and the third flourishing epoch of Egyptian civilisation. Under three successive royal families, the Thutmeses and Amenhoteps, the Setis and Ramesids, Thebes continued, except for a time once and again, to be the chief seat of the kingdom of the Pharaohs, which extends once more to its ancient confines, and inspires the whole of Western Asia with respect.

With the eleventh century, however, the balance inclines once again over to the side of the North. The high priests of Amun at Thebes set upon their heads the double crown; but various dynasties from the Delta contest with them the supremacy, and they are at last compelled to retire into Ethiopia, where they establish an independent kingdom. But not even then do they, the last representatives of the ancient true Egyptian power, abandon the hope of one day bringing the whole country again into subjection to themselves. So soon as the North begins to show signs of decline, or becomes divided, they hasten to the spot, obtain easily possession of Thebes and its territory, and also, after a powerful resistance, become masters of Memphis. But not for long. After a brief supremacy, they again disappear from the scene, driven back into the land of Kush. And now Tanis, Bubastis, Sais, all northern towns, give Egypt its kings; and it is a matter for congratulation when it is only native princes who fight with each other for supremacy, and not Assyrian conquerors like Esarhaddon and Assur-bani-pal, who come, and by total subjugation and dismemberment of the country, take their revenge for the hostilities carried on by Egyptian princes against their fathers. The glory of Ham has passed away, the day of Shem has come. Nevertheless, these princes, though not of pure extraction and of mixed race, adopted the traditions and customs of the ancient Pharaohs, and the Egyptian civilisation, which, under one of them, Amasis, even attains a certain brilliance. But it is only the flicker of the light before it expires. Persian conquerors add Egypt to their vast dominion, and then, after it had for about half a century enjoyed a certain degree of independence, Greeks and Romans take the place of the Persians. With the arrival of the Greeks, my history of the Egyptian religion ends. It is indeed the case that, under the Ptolemys, who did not suppress but rather honoured the Egyptian nationality, the Egyptian religion was freely exercised. Indeed at a later period magnificent temples were rebuilt or founded at their expense and at that of the Roman emperors, yet this was nothing more than an artificial revival of a past from which all life had fled. The period of the Ptolemys does not properly belong to the history of the ancient religion; but it is especially important as part of the preparatory history of the new religion, which indeed arose in Galilee, but the first moulding of which was greatly influenced both by the Greek philosophy of Alexandria and by the ancient religion of Egypt.

CHAPTER II.

THE SACRED LITERATURE.

ONLY fifty years ago nearly all that could be known about the religion of the Egyptians had to be sought from Greek sources. Besides the little that Clemens Alexandrinus tells us incidentally about their sacred literature in the fifth and sixth book of his *Stromata*,[1] nothing more was known on the subject than what Herodotus, Diodorus, and especially Plutarch, communicate. If to this we add the few fragments of Manetho's work in Josephus and Georgios Synkellos, and what has been preserved under the form of history in a single scholiast,[2] we have summed up all the sources from which formerly a dim conception could be formed of the religious worship of the inhabitants of the Nile valley. And even, supposing that the accuracy of all these sources of information was to be relied on, their accounts, with the exception of Plutarch's, are very scanty, and, considering the antiquity of Egyptian civilisation, also very recent. Herodotus allows the priests to tell him whatever tales they choose. Plutarch reproduces the myth of Isis and Osiris, with on the whole remarkable faithfulness, but he gives it in the form that was most acceptable to himself: he had no conception of the thought originally expressed by it. Moreover, the Greeks were accustomed to hellenise everything and to transfer the names of their Olympians to foreign gods, a custom which

---

[1] Stromat., lib. v. p. 237 (Pott. ii. 657), and lib. vi. p. 268 *et seq.* (Pott. 756), in Bunsen, Aegyptens Stelle, III. Urkundenbuch, p. 91.
[2] See Bunsen, op. cit., esp. pp. 58, 71.

hindered them from properly understanding the nature of a foreign religion. How slight, for example, is the resemblance between Ptah and Hephaistos, Chonsu and Herakles, Horos and Apollo, or between Neith, the mother of the gods, and the virgin Athena! A knowledge of the Egyptian religion obtained under such conditions must of necessity have been inexact and superficial, and anything approaching to a history of the religion could not be looked for.

The invaluable discovery by which the name of Champollion the younger has been immortalised put an end to this uncertainty. He found the key to the hieroglyphics, that ingenious though cumbrous mode of writing which was in common use so early as the time of the first dynasties—a key which the Greeks and Romans might so easily have preserved for the use of posterity, but which, in their indifference to everything that appeared to them barbarous, they allowed to be lost. Thus, at last, the scholarship of Europe gained access to a literature which may be ranked as one of the richest in the world.

For it would seem as if the Egyptians, proud of possessing this instrument to immortalise their thoughts and great deeds, left no opportunity of employing it unused. Books were not sufficient for them, the temples and palaces, the tombs and obelisks, common utensils or decorative objects, were all covered over with inscriptions. The whole of Egypt became in time like one closely written volume. And great as has been the industry of men like Champollion, Rosellini, Lepsius, Brugsch, De Rougé, Mariette, and Dümichen, in collecting inscriptions, there can be no doubt that as yet no more than a small proportion of all that the Egyptian monuments have to tell has been made known in the West. Yet the wealth of materials is great even now, and we shall sometimes be more embarrassed by the excess than by the want of original records.

In the case of a nation like Egypt, in which state and religion were so closely united, almost all the historical monuments and records are at the same time sources for the history of religion. To enumerate them all would in this place be impossible and unnecessary: they will be referred to in the course of our history. At present, I merely desire to say a few words about what may be more definitely called the sacred literature.

The most prominent place in this literature is occupied by the collection of sacred texts to which Prof. Lepsius has given the appellation of "The Book of the Dead," and M. De Rougé "The Funeral Ritual." In the opinion of some the original Egyptian title is found in the words written at the head of the first chapter, and which signify "chapters by the magical power of which the deceased may issue forth at will during the day and accompany the sun in his triumphal march."[1] This, however, is the title of the first sixteen chapters only, which form a collection by themselves. The opinion of De Rougé, who by "the day" spoken of in the ancient superscription, understands the eternal light, is preferable to that of Lepsius, who thinks it refers to the great day of judgment in the under-world. As will afterwards appear, the conception formed by the ancient Egyptians in regard to the fate of souls after death, is derived from what they saw daily happening to the sun, which was to them the most complete manifestation of the Deity. The sun set in the west and rose again in the east, or, put in mythological form, the sun-god conquered by the powers of darkness passed at eventide into the realm of the dead, waged there a triumphant contest with numerous enemies, and rose again in the morning with full radiance as if new born. With the human soul it was the same: in the sacred book, indeed, the soul is

[1] These words have been translated by scholars in various ways:— by Champollion and E. de Rougé, "Manifestations in the light, the light of day;" by Lepsius, "in light;" by Birch and Pierret, "the going out of the day," that is to say of life, an idea quite foreign to the Egyptians. As they say "to go out in the morning," they say likewise "to enter in the evening," that is, to set with the sun. The translation of M. Lefébure, "Chapters for going out in the day" is the most accurate.

wholly identified with the sun-god. Dying with him, it fights along with him against the evil spirits of the under-world, and after having been justified in the judgment, is born again with him and then leaves the regions of the under-world in order to accomplish as a spirit of light in his train his triumphal course in the day. "The day" must therefore be understood literally, and manifestation in the day is the beatification of the justified after the night of death and conflict, the culminating point of the ever-renewed drama.

The critical investigation of the "Book of the Dead" has been no more than commenced, but this much is evident, that it cannot be regarded as one treatise. It is a collection of documents belonging to different periods: the main portion of it was, however, in existence under the Theban kings of the New Kingdom. At a later period one or two additions were made to it, but little that was original. Of the 165 sections comprised in a MS. of the time of Psamtik I., the well-known Turin papyrus, the first 125 were collected and arranged in order so early as the time of the eighteenth and nineteenth dynasties. These 125 sections are designated as chapters (*ro*) with the exception of the last, which is called the "book" (*sha* or *shat*), and it seems to have been the first supplement to the original collection. The 40 portions added afterwards are likewise called books (*shatu*). The last four are quite modern, and may be easily recognised as different from the rest. The most ancient MSS. date from the eighteenth dynasty, the fourteenth or fifteenth century B.C., but most of them are unfortunately written with great carelessness. The text of some has even been designedly mutilated. This dishonesty could be practised without fear of detection as the tombs were intended to be closed up for ever. Also, no doubt it might not always be easy to meet the numerous demands for copies, as every person of means wished that a copy of the sacred book should be taken along with him into his grave.

These, however, are not the oldest texts which we possess of various portions of the "Book of the Dead." On sarcophagi belonging to the period previous to the reign of the Hyksos, some chapters have been found that occur in the later collection, as well as one or two portions hitherto unknown. These texts throw a clear light upon the way in which the "Book of the Dead" was originally put together and came into existence. The conjecture which had previously been made, that, in the text as given by the MSS., a distinction must be made between the original nucleus and explanatory notes or glosses added later, has been reduced to a certainty by the evidence of the sarcophagi of the eleventh dynasty, and of an earlier date. On these there occur some short explanations also, which may be distinguished from the ancient text by their difference in colour, though not in every instance with exactitude. A comparison of the MSS. shows that, originally, glosses and additions were but very sparingly added, and that there was a remarkable increase in their number under the royal families of the New Kingdom. If the tradition of the Egyptians themselves may be trusted, some portions of the sacred volume are even more ancient than the eleventh dynasty. Thus, according to the subscription attached to chap. lxiv., that chapter is said to have been discovered by Prince Har-titi-f, who inspected the temples in the reign of King Menkaura (Mycerinus) of the fourth dynasty; at which time the famous 17th chapter is said to have been already written. According to other accounts the so-called scarabean text, which in the collection follows the 64th chapter, was written in the reign of Menkaura, and the 64th chapter itself, under an earlier king, Husapti (the Οὐσαφαΐς of the Greeks), but in my opinion all this seems very improbable.[1] A strong proof of the antiquity of the

[1] See De Rougé in the Revue archéol., 1860, i. 69-99; Chabas on the Papyrus Abbott after Birch, ibid. 1859, p. 269 et seq.; especially, however, Lepsius, Aelteste Texten des Todtenbuchs nach Sarkofagen des altaegyptischen Reichs im Berliner Museum, Einl. u. 43 Tafeln. Berl. 1867.

great majority of the different parts of which the "Book of the Dead" is composed is, that in them there is found no mention of Amun or Amun-ra, the chief god of Thebes. His name occurs in the last three or four books only, but these betray their origin by many foreign words, Nubian as well as others, and likewise by their whole spirit. These were most probably written in Ethiopia, where the Theban priests of Amun had founded an independent sacerdotal kingdom, and accordingly belong to the tenth or ninth century B.C.

In all the other chapters and books, even in those which are not found in the most ancient MSS., there is no mention of this god who was so ardently worshipped by the Amunhoteps and Ramesids, and after whom kings, even of the eleventh dynasty, were named. This fact can be explained only on the hypothesis that not only those portions of which a collection was made in the time of the eighteenth dynasty, but also the books that were added later, were already written before the worship of Amun rose in the fifteenth and fourteenth century B.C. to such a height of splendour.

Hence arose the especial reverence with which the Egyptians regarded the book, and the great degree of sacredness they ascribed to it. Beatification in the day of resurrection was represented as depending on a man's knowledge of the principal chapters of it. "He who knows this book," so says a sarcophagus of the eleventh dynasty, "is one who in the day of resurrection in the under-world, arises and enters in; but if he does not know this chapter, he does not enter in so soon as he arises." And the close of the first chapter is as follows:—"If a man knows this book thoroughly, and has it inscribed upon his sarcophagus, he will be manifested in the day in all (the forms) that he may desire, and entering in to his abode will not be turned back," and so on.[1] It hence became customary for people to learn it off by heart

Lepsius, Aelteste Texte, pp. 5, 25.

during their life, in order that they might thus keep in check the evil spirits in the under-world, and that they might be assured of the blessed life. Some portions, like the 64th chapter, are expressly stated to have been written by the deity himself, usually Thot; and it was also told how they were found at or below the feet of an image of the god, where they had been deposited by the god himself.[1] However much the "Book of the Dead" differs in character and contents from the Vedas, the Zend-Avesta, the Old Testament, and other books regarded by various nations as of divine origin, it may yet be emphatically called the Holy Scriptures of the Egyptians.

On the whole, a very false idea has generally been entertained of the "Book of the Dead." Properly speaking, it is not a book at all. This arises, among other things, from the very remarkable circumstance that not two of the ancient papyri give the chapters or texts in the same order. It was not until a much later time, after the twenty-sixth dynasty, that the arrangement of them seems to have become in a measure fixed. All the ancient MSS. are thus, in fact, independent collections of texts that are similar, and no one of which has ever been generally adopted. It is consequently inaccurate to give the name of unacknowledged chapters of the "Book of the Dead" to magical texts which refer to the life to come, and which have not happened to be inserted in any one of the collections known to us. In a book that has been brought together, bit by bit, and that is made up of portions of widely different degrees of antiquity, plan or unity cannot be expected. Certain chapters (*ro, shâ*), indeed,

---

[1] Lepsius (*Aelt. Text.* p. 17, nt. 2, and p. 18) gives the following explanation of the discovery of these documents. The founding of a town began with that of the temple dedicated to the local deity, e.g., at Hermopolis with that of Thot, and the building of the temple commenced with the founding and erection of the sanctuary in which the image of the god was placed. Under the feet of this image lay the most sacred foundation (*senti*), and under it, a cavity for the reception of sacred records or papyri. When long afterwards these documents happened to be found, they were ascribed to a divine origin.

are a sort of summary of the phases of life after death, from the first successively to the last. The first chapter itself ends with the issue to the day which is the culminating point of the drama; and the same is the case in the 17th, the 64th, and some others. But some, on the contrary, present only some special points treated in an isolated way. This is especially the case with the final moment of the conflict. Others, like the 45th, include sacred texts, hymns, or prayers.

We should accordingly seek in vain for any regular order, either logical or chronological, in the "Book of the Dead," but there is nevertheless observable a certain arrangement of the material. Usually those portions which treat of analogous subjects are found conjoined, and it is possible to point out two or three large separate collections. Thus in agreement with Lepsius we find two distinct principal ones: chaps. xvii.–lxiii., and chaps. lxiv.–cxxiv. These are preceded by a small collection of sixteen chapters, forming a group by themselves, and are followed by the later additions, of which the 125th chapter is the most ancient, and these in turn may be divided into different groups. The first sixteen chapters have not hitherto been discovered on ancient sarcophagi, and they appear to be of somewhat more recent date than the two principal collections, but more ancient than the additions, chaps. cxxvi.–clxv. In these sixteen chapters, the complete drama of the resurrection is unfolded. The deceased travels through the regions of the under-world, is justified in the sight of his enemies, and already, in the 11th chapter, is represented as triumphing in the form of Ra, the sun-god. In the 15th chapter he has reached the goal, for he beholds the light, and is admitted to the fellowship of Ra and Tum to sing the praises of these gods.

The two collections that follow begin each with one of the two indisputably most ancient chapters of the whole book, the 17th and the 64th. Chaps. xvii.–lxiii. comprise again the same cycle as chaps. i.–xvi., but in a totally different form. The 17th chapter, the most important of all, is complete in itself, and represents the deceased as one already justified. To give an idea of its contents, the commencement, after the most ancient text, and without explanations or glosses, is here quoted, the translation being that of Lepsius:—

"I am Tum (the hidden sun-god), a being who is one alone;

I am Ra in his first supremacy;
I am the great god, the self-existing;
The creator of his name, the Lord of all gods,
Whom none among the gods upholds.
I was yesterday, I know the to-morrow.
There was a battlefield of the gods prepared when I spoke;
I know the name of that great god who is in that place.
I am the great Bennu[1] who is worshipped in An (Heliopolis).
I am Chem (Min) in his appearing; I have set both my feathers upon my head;
I am come home to the city of my abode."[2]

---

[1] The Bennu, a species of heron, is, as a bird of passage, the symbol of the sun-god, who disappears at night, and shows himself again in the morning. Brugsch compares it to the phœnix (φοῖνιξ), mentioned by Herodotus, and considers the Greek name a corruption of the Egyptian. Lepsius' ground of objection to this opinion appears to me rather weak. Herodotus, it is true, says he never saw a phœnix, though he must have known the heron quite well; but the phœnix he did not see is the mythical bird which is said to return once every five hundred years. The Egyptian b does not correspond, in the opinion of Lepsius, to φ; yet he himself says that the palm-tree, called φοῖνιξ by the Greeks, is also called in the Egyptian bennu (Kopt. beni, benne), and that the palm-branch (Kopt. ba, bai) bore the same name as the soul (be, ba, bai, with the symbol of the bennu-bird), and was also the symbol of definite periods of time. That Herodotus limited the phœnix to An (Heliopolis), while the Bennu was worshipped also at Abydos, is little to the point, for Herodotus happened to hear the myth of the Heliopolitan priests, which was not extensively known in Egypt. More than this, Horapollo also calls the φοῖνιξ a symbol of the sun and of the soul, which, just like a bird of passage, come home again after long wanderings. Horap., Hierogl., ed. Leemans, i. 34, 35.

[2] The way in which glosses and commentaries have by degrees fastened themselves on to this ancient text may be seen from the following example:—

Ancient text—"I am the great Bennu of An."

1st Commentary (sarcophagus of Menuhotep, 11th dynasty)—"That

This chapter is the opening one of a series, in which a certain regular order of events may be clearly traced out.

After having, in three sets of texts of similar import, told of the justification of the deceased, and, as might be expected, brought it into connection with the divine example, the justification of Osiris by Thot, a description is given next of the events that immediately follow in *Cher Nuter* (the under-world). The principal fruit of his justification is, that the use of his members is restored to him, especially of his mouth, that he may be able to utter the sacred words indispensable as a means of warding off the evil spirits, and of his heart, which is the principle of life. And now the revivified one has to enter upon the conflict. He is obliged to contend with all kinds of monsters that approach him, in the shape of snakes, crocodiles, tortoises, and especially in that of the great serpent, Refrof or Apep. He overcomes these opponents with two weapons of two kinds, a long spear that he always carries with him, and the magical power of the sacred words which he pronounces. Not until he has withstood this trial and gained the victory does he rest secure from the miseries that await the wicked, and not till then are vouchsafed to him the blessings laid up for the faithful. Both of these are next described. The worst punishment is undoubtedly the second death. It consists in this: Horos or some other deity beheads the condemned person upon the *Nemma* or scaffold; but there are also other punishments, such as being obliged to eat and drink putrid victual. On the other hand, blessedness consists in the inhalation of the pure breath of life, and in drinking of the water of life, ideas which recur at a later period principally in the Jewish

---

is the fulfilling of that which is."

2d Comment. (end of the Middle Kingdom)—"That is the fulfilling, &c. What is that? Osiris it is of An, and that which is, is the always and the forever."

3d Comment. (beginning of the New Kingdom)—"That is—An is his body, or also is the always and the forever; the always, now, is the day, and the forever the night."—Lepsius, Aelt. Texte, p. 46.

apocalyptic writings, and even in Christian symbolism. With these descriptions, the 63d chapter and the second collection is brought to a close.

The collection that follows treats in part of the same things, but in another generally more detailed form. The chapters which give a summary of the whole progress, as the extremely ancient 64th and the little less interesting 72d, here again stand first. The deceased attains again the point at which the sun is born, and thereafter An, the celestial (?) Heliopolis, where the sun as *Bennu* again sets out on his journey in the world of light. Then in the following chapters the subject is taken up of the various forms which the soul, now become a *Chu* or spirit of light, can assume. Properly speaking, it is able to disguise itself in any shape that caprice may suggest, and the principal ones only are mentioned. In a set of five chapters the union of soul and body is depicted, and the pilgrimage already described begins once more. The idea of conflict falls more into the background, and advance into the light-manifestation is here in a greater degree, but not exclusively, considered as progress in heavenly knowledge, destined to be crowned with full manifestation in the light.

The one and forty chapters with which the book concludes are deficient even in the slight unity and connection which marked the preceding collections. Some, like the famous 125th, include a number of things not referred to in the previous parts, but most are devoted to the elaboration of points which had been mentioned before. Mystical ceremonies are described, especially those having reference to objects with which the neck of the deceased was ornamented. But the chief end aimed at in these texts is to make as perfect as possible the knowledge requisite to the departed, since it is by means of that alone that he can gain the victory in the conflict which takes place in the under-world. With a view to this he is instructed as to the names of holy places, spirits, and gods, and, among other things, there is a list of no less than a hundred names of Osiris, names to which a powerful magical efficacy is ascribed.

Since every text, the shortest ones included, and at a later time the collection as a whole, had for its object to give aid to the deceased in this way, the magical words are in consequence found plentifully inscribed in connection with the dead. They were graven on the sarcophagi, written on the bandages of the mummies and on other objects, especially on a papyrus deposited by the side of the corpse. Down to the time of the twenty-first dynasty hieroglyphics were employed for this purpose, and afterwards in later times hieratic writing. But also—and here M. de Rougé's view is correct—the sacred texts were made use of in the sacred ceremonies celebrated in honour of the deceased, or rather for the salvation of his soul. This fact is attested by a great number of explanatory notes, found at the end of several of the chapters.[1]

We must not, however, over-estimate the " Book of the Dead " as a source for the history of Egyptian religion. It is, doubtless, one of the principal sources we possess for their eschatological beliefs, for the ideas which they entertained about what was to be expected in the future, but in reference to their religious beliefs it is not equally valuable. No doubt the prayers and hymns included in it possess, in regard to the latter, great value ; but most frequently it contains only short and obscure mythological speculations, which, far from helping to explain anything, have great need themselves of a commentary.

There exist a great number of texts analogous to those in the " Book of the Dead " which may well have been either not gathered into it, or not written till after the collection was closed. Of these I shall notice particularly two only.

---

[1] See chaps. xix., xx., lxiv., cxxx. (very ancient, though it certainly contains interpolations of later date), cxxxiii., cxxxvi. The titles affixed to chaps. i., xxxi., xlii., xlv., lviii., lxx., lxxxiv., lxxxix., xci., xcii., xcix., cxxxv., are likewise very instructive. Some, such as the 18th, were set apart for special days.

In the first place, the "Book of the Breathings of Life" (*Shâ an Sensen*), known to us from a manuscript of the time of the Ptolemys. Its doctrine is in perfect accordance with that of the "Book of the Dead;" it was looked upon as very sacred, and was placed beneath the left arm of the corpse, next the heart. No less holy were the Laments of Isis and of Nephthys after the death of Osiris. This, properly speaking, formed a ritual which was known only by the priests of the highest rank, and was recited at the festival of Osiris.

The *magical papyri*, several of which have been discovered, and some published and explained by scholars,[1] appear to have been composed with an aim similar to that of the Holy Scriptures *par excellence*, which we have just been considering. The "Book of the Dead" is, in fact, nothing else than a great magical papyrus for behoof of the dead, or at least it was studied by the living with an eye to the conflict and the judgment of Osiris that awaited them in the under-world. The other writings to which this designation has been given were intended, not for the use of the dead, but of the living. They are collections of ancient texts, hymns for the most part, and more modern magical formulas that had to serve here on earth as the means of warding off diseases, sickness, evil spirits, and hurtful beasts. The very existence of these formulas bears witness to a decline in the religious consciousness, but in as far as they comprise ancient fragments, they are of the highest importance for the religious literature.

Not least important are the numerous *hymns* in which the Egyptians sang the praises of their gods. Looked at from a literary point of view, they deserve to be placed in the first rank. In form, they remind us at times of the creations of ancient Hebrew poetry. Their contents, however, correspond better with some of the Vedic songs, and

---

[1] Along with others, the Papyrus Magique Harris, by F. Chabas, Chalon, 1860; and the Papyrus 348 revers du Musée de Leide, in the Etudes Égyptologiques of W. Pleyte, Leiden, 1866.

with the sacrificial songs of the Persians; they are pervaded by a spirit so lofty, by such poetic fervour and inspiration, conjoined throughout to depth of thought, that, in my judgment, they surpass at least the last of these.

If I am not mistaken, the hymns are among the most ancient products of sacred Egyptian literature. What tends to prove this is the fact of their being used, as they were in the magical papyri, as charms against evil spirits and beasts of prey, and their being even found woven into the "Book of the Dead." Not unfrequently, too, they were graven on little flat columns (stelæ), which the Egyptians were accustomed to place in their tombs. Those dedicated by the heretic Amunhotep IV. (Chunaten) to a deity by whom he caused Amun to be supplanted are by no means the least exalted. Although the hymns are occasionally obscure, as is the case with the Vedic songs, because they rather contain references to myths than explain the mythical stories, they still give us, better than anything else, a conception of the nature of the gods. And that which has been remarked in the most ancient songs of the Hindu people holds good here also, at least for the New Kingdom; the god in whose praise the hymn is sung, Osiris, Ptah, Ra, Shu, Amun, or whoever it may be, is always, for the singer, the highest, if not the only one; all the others sink into the background.

Besides these writings having direct reference to religion, which are the principal sources for our history, there are others also, such as the already mentioned moral essay of Ptahhotep, or such as the "Tale of the Two Brothers," a legend of the time of Seti Merenptah II., the son of Ramses II., which can do us service in aiding us to understand rightly the spirit of the Egyptian religion. The latter especially contains a rich store of mythological material, and, when carefully considered, is seen to be nothing else than the chief myth of the Egyptians moulded into the form of a tale.[1] The temple inscriptions likewise yield to the investigator of religious history a superabundant harvest.

[1] It is translated by E. de Rougé in the Revue Archéologique, 1852, p. 385 et seq., and by Brugsch, Aus dem Orient., Berl. 1864, p. 7 et seq. Comp. Ebers, op. cit. i. 311 et seq.

CHAPTER III.

THE RELIGION OF THINIS-ABYDOS.[1]

IT would be difficult to say which is the most ancient religion of Egypt. Some forms of religious worship are known to us as having arisen, or at least as having for the first time acquired significance in historic times. This was the case, to give one instance out of many, with Amun-worship. The institution of certain customs is recorded; for example, that of the worship of sacred animals at Memphis and Heliopolis. But whether those religions which appear first on the stage of history are in reality more ancient than those which rose to supremacy in later times cannot now be made out; this may, however, in the case of one or two, be asserted with a high degree of probability. But we can tell with certainty what religions are mentioned earliest on the monuments, and thus are shown to have reached, sooner than others, an epoch of splendour.

Before Egypt was united as one kingdom there flourished, side by side, just so many local worships as there were small kingdoms in the valley of the Nile. These different worships were not brought methodically, or, rather, they did not attain, without many struggles and at times severe conflict, to a system of polytheism, manifold at first, and extending constantly. It was later still that

[1] The author has now reasons for thinking that this form of the ancient religion of the Egyptians came originally only second in the chronological order, and that it was preceded by the religion of Heliopolis (chap. iv.), the chief god of which is Ra.

they passed into a system more monotheistic in character, towards which the Egyptian religion had a strong tendency.

The policy of those wise kings who, in the course of centuries, reigned over Egypt was not an exclusive one. They purposely rendered homage to the chief gods of all the principal divisions of their kingdom, to the gods of the north and of the south, of Memphis and of Thebes, of the Delta and of Nubia, and endeavoured to unite them into a sort of pantheon. As the result of this policy, they were enabled to exercise their power undisturbed, and rule in peace within the boundaries of their territory. Other kings, who did not adopt this policy but were zealously devoted to the god of one particular locality and to one special form of worship, and who excluded and persecuted those who were not of their way of thinking, had to experience, in serious insurrections, the consequences of their unstatesmanlike policy. Some of them even lost in this way all their power. Yet in all cases the dominant religion of the kingdom is that of the reigning dynasty, and in every case the religion of the reigning dynasty is the local worship of its place of origin.

The first dynasty that ruled over Upper and Lower Egypt in historic times is that which is said to have been founded by Menes (Mena is the name of the sacred bull of Heliopolis), a mythic personage, who is perhaps the same as Minos and the Indian Manu. Previous to his time the Egyptians are habitually called Hor-Shesu,[1]

---

[1] The reading *Shesu-Har* (*hor* or *her*) of De Rougé and Brugsch seems preferable to that of Duemichen, *Shai-her*. It may be translated servants of H. and successors of H.; since, however, the word never occurs in a royal cartouche, or accompanied by the emblems of regal power, it cannot be supposed to refer to any king, though it would not be in the least extraordinary to find the Egyptians calling their princes successors of H. the divine ruler, who had reigned first of all. But even in that case it would not be only the kings before Menes who would have a claim to the title. All kings are called by the Egyptians, not successors of Horos, but Horos. They are identified with him, a conception much more familiar to the Egyptians. By Shesu-har is undoubtedly always meant the most ancient men, or the most

worshippers or servants of Hor or Horos, while Horos[1] is always regarded as the master and creator of the Rutu, the men of higher race, of pure native extraction. It is possible, however, that, like Horos himself, the Shesu-Hor are mythical beings.

The worship of Osiris and that of Ra are the most ancient religions mentioned on the oldest monuments. They are those which in after-times prevailed most generally, and may be said to have formed the foundation of the national religion.

The worship of the Memphitic Ptah and of the Saitic goddess Neith, mentioned not quite so early, but still on very old monuments, is perhaps equally ancient, at least the latter is very probably so. There is, however, reason to think that neither of them were of purely Egyptian origin, and they were certainly not adopted into the religious system of the Rutu and universally acknowledged until a later period.

The principal ancient seat of Osiris-worship, a form of Horos-worship, is without doubt Thinis (Teni), the town from which the royal house of Mena and the dynasty next in succession take their name, Thinitic. It is situated in Upper Egypt, about sixty geographical miles to the south of Memphis, and fifteen miles to the north of Thebes, on the west bank of the Nile. Osiris is constantly designated Lord of Abydos (Abet), a place in the immediate neighbourhood of Thinis, by which it appears to have been cast into the shade; or perhaps he is thus named as lord of the district (nomos) in which Thinis and Abydos were situated. The town itself bore the sacred name, house of Osiris, and the temples that have been discovered there were dedicated to him. Hitherto the only temples known were those founded by Seti I.

ancient Egyptians, who, as the people believed, lived in the abodes of the blest with Osiris. See De Rougé, Monuments des VI. prem. Dynasties, p. 163 et seq.

[1] Horos, a god of Upper as well as of Lower Egypt, fills an important place in the circle of Osiris and in that of Ra.

and Ramses II., kings of the nineteenth dynasty, but some years ago the indefatigable Mariette discovered to the north of Abydos the remains of a much older temple, which not unfrequently crumbled to dust on being exposed to the air. The inscriptions he found testified to visits having been paid by various sovereigns to this venerable sanctuary. The other temples erected in honour of Osiris, like those at Memphis, at Mendes in Lower Egypt, on the island Phineb at Philak in the south, and in Ethiopia, are undoubtedly all of later date. At Thinis-Abydos Osiris was worshipped as the king of eternity dwelling in the west, and ruler of the kingdom of the dead. At his side there, but below him, stood Anhur, a war-god armed with a sword, apparently a form of the god who is met with at Heliopolis, and at a later period at Thebes, under the name of Shu;[1] Horos, the avenger of his father; Isis, the great mother, and the four children of the concealed (*Meschen*), which may possibly refer to the four genii of the dead. The other gods of the Osirian circle had, even in the earliest times, temples of their own in Upper Egypt. The temple of Thot at Sesennu (Ashmunein) is mentioned on the very oldest monuments. The temple of Hathor and Horos at Dendera, founded under the eighteenth dynasty, is, in a very old record found in that place, brought into connection with Chufu of the fourth dynasty and even with the Shesu-har,[2] and thus appears to have supplanted a simpler sanctuary. That of Horos at Edfu is so closely connected with it that it must be quite as ancient, although the sanctuary, the ruins of which are still to be found there, belongs to the latest period of the Egyptian kingdom. The temple at Hermonthis perhaps belongs likewise to the same time.

---

[1] Chabas, Pap. Mag. Harris, pp. 37, 40. Anhur is thus a god of the heaven or of the air, as is indicated by the name, which may easily be connected with *anhu*=embrace, include.

[2] Duemichen, Bauurkunde von Dendera, Taf. vi.

THE RELIGION OF THINIS-ABYDOS. 39

Every one is familiar with the myth of Osiris in Plutarch. With him it becomes entirely a traditionary tale, although he himself expressly warns us not to take it for history. Osiris, an Egyptian king, not satisfied with combating rude and barbarous customs in his own kingdom, travels through the world, that he may everywhere spread the blessings of civilisation. In his absence, the queen, his wife and sister, acts as regent, and firmly maintains all the institutions of Osiris, taking care to see that no infraction of them occurs. This vexes Typhon, her own and Osiris' brother, who would have liked to introduce a different and ruder law, and who now, along with some of the nobles and an Ethiopian queen, forms a conspiracy to kill Osiris. He causes a chest or sarcophagus to be prepared, made so as exactly to fit the body of his brother Osiris; whom, along with the conspirators, he invites to a banquet. As if in jest, he promises to make a present of the chest to him whom it may be found to fit. All in turn lie down in it, but of course without success; scarcely, however, has Osiris done so, when the lid is put on and fastened closely down. The chest is then thrown into the river, and floats out to sea by the Tanaïtic branch of the Nile. After some time it is stranded at Byblos, a Phœnician town on the coast of Asia, and there it gets entangled in the boughs of a tamarind tree, which grows over it so completely as to wholly conceal it. Meanwhile, as soon as tidings of the horrid deed reach them, Isis, along with Nephthys, her sister, fill the air with shrieks of despair and cries of wailing. Isis goes everywhere seeking her murdered consort, and at last discovers him in the palace of the king at Byblos, who had caused the tamarind tree to be hewn down and a pillar to be made out of it for his house. With this precious treasure she now returns to Egypt; but, while visiting her son Horos at Bubastis, she neglects to take proper care of the sarcophagus, and Typhon, hunting by moonlight, finds and opens it, and cuts the body of his brother into fourteen pieces, which he scatters over the country. But Isis manages to recover the whole of them, one after another, and causes each to be buried at the place where it was discovered. And now Horos arises as avenger of his father. He challenges Typhon and overcomes him, and afterwards delivers him over to Isis. She lets him go free again, and when Horos hears that she has done so he is filled with indignation. After having sternly rebuked her for thus yielding, he attacks Typhon again twice over, and finally succeeds in killing him outright. Osiris then becomes lord of the world of the dead, and Isis, who has continued to have intercourse with him there, brings forth Harpocrates, a child born prematurely, and lame in both legs.

We shall not occupy ourselves with the explanations of this myth given by the Greek moralist. He gives it in the form in which it was related in his time. His version thus presents, along with much that is ancient and genuine, some traits of more recent origin or of foreign derivation. Also, one part of the story is given erroneously, for Harpocrates, who is merely one of the forms in which Horos appears, is distinguished from him as a separate being. Harpocrates is the young Horos, Har pe chruti, *i.e.*, Har the child, represented by the Egyptians as sitting in the lap of his mother, with his hand on his mouth and his legs hanging down. The Greeks fancied the dangling legs were lame. At a later time he was even looked upon as the god of taciturnity, because of his hand pointing to his mouth—this, however, was with the Egyptians the sign that he was yet an infant and could not speak. The foreign part of the myth is that in which Byblos is mentioned. That part has been incorporated with the view of bringing the worship of Adonis, which prevailed there, into connection with the Egyptian Osiris-worship; just as Lucian likewise relates how, at the great festival of Adonis, a head was observed to have come ashore, which had floated thither from Egypt, and was thereupon consigned to the earth with great pomp. It was only in relatively modern times that the Egyptians ventured to navigate the Mediterranean, so that in ancient times Byblos must have been unknown to them. What is said about the sarcophagus drifting to sea through the Tanaïtic branch of the Nile cannot be original either, for that branch did not become famous in the estimation of the Egyptians till the Shepherd Kings had made Tanis (San, Hebr. Zoän) a centre of the worship of Sutech, the god who is supposed to be identical with Typhon. The division of the body of Osiris into fourteen pieces seems to have been invented as an explanation of the fact that so many towns in Egypt could boast of possessing the grave of this deity.

Nevertheless, along with those marks of a more recent period, the tale comprises elements of great antiquity, and the foundation of the myth, its nucleus, is as ancient as the kingdom of Egypt. The principal outlines of it are found recurring in various original records. In a hymn in honour of Osiris, belonging to the first years of the eighteenth dynasty, *i.e.*, to the commencement of the New Kingdom, we read as follows:—" His sister Isis has been filled with concern about him, and has scattered his enemies in a threefold rout. . . . She is Isis, the illustrious, the avenger of her brother; she has sought him without resting; she has wandered all round the world as a mourner; she did not cease until she had found him. She has made light with her feathers, she has made wind with her wings, she has made the invocations of the burial of her brother; she has taken with her the principles of the god with the peaceable heart, she has made an extract of his being, she has made (thereof) a child, she has suckled the infant in secret. No man knows where that was done."[1]

This representation is indeed in some respects different from that of Plutarch, since here, not Horos but Isis is the avenger of Osiris, and Set-Typhon is not even named;

[1] The translation is that of Chabas in the Rev. Archéol., 1857, p. 65 *et seq.*, and p. 193 *et seq.*

but in a MS. of the "Book of the Dead," which must be accounted as contemporary with the hymn just quoted, the conflict of Horos with Set is expressly mentioned,[1] and upon the sarcophagus of Mentuhotep, which dates from the beginning of the Middle Kingdom, Horos is spoken of as the avenger of his father. On an inscription of the time of King Chufu of the fourth dynasty, Osiris is called lord of Rusta or Roseti, that is, of the world of the dead, and "Horos the Conqueror" is an appellation already very common in those days. Indeed, in that portion of the "Book of the Dead" quoted in the preceding chapter, and therefore in the most ancient text of all, which was already in existence in the time of the earliest dynasties, we read that there a place of battle was made ready for the gods. In other passages, too, in the "Book of the Dead," mention is made of the laments of Isis, of her vigil on the night of the burial, and of the tears poured forth by her and her sister Nephthys. The lamentations of the two sisters have even been discovered in a Theban papyrus. "Come back," it says, "come back, god Panu, come back. For they who were thy foes are here no more. Ah! fair helpmate, come back, that thou mayest behold me thy sister, by whom thou art beloved; and thou drawest not nigh to me! Ah, beautiful youth, come back! come back! I behold thee not, my heart is grieved for thee, my eyes search for thee. I cast my eyes around (?) that thee, that thee I may behold . . . the radiant one. Come to thy beloved, blessed Unnefer, come to thy sister, come to thy wife, god Urtuhet, come to the mistress of thy house. Am I not thy sister? I am thy mother, and thou dost not draw nigh to me; the face of the gods and of the children of men is turned towards thee while they bewail thee, at the time when they see me as I wail because of thee, as I weep and cry unto heaven that thou mightest hear my supplication, for I am thy sister, by whom thou wast beloved upon earth. Never didst thou love another than

[1] Book of the Dead, xvii. 17, glosses.

THE RELIGION OF THINIS-ABYDOS. 43

me thy sister!" In the same way Nephthys, too, laments, "Ah! lordly king, come back, let thy heart rejoice, for all they who persecuted thee are here no more. Thy sisters stand beside thy bier, they bewail thee and shed tears. People turn (?) thee round on thy bier that thou mayest behold their beauty. Oh speak to us, king and our lord!"[1]

Osiris, nevertheless, according to the old monuments, comes back on earth no more. His soul is indeed united again to his body in the mystic place *Tanen*, a ceremony in which all the gods of his circle take part; his parents, Seb and Nu, his sisters Isis and Nephthys, Thot and Horos, and above all Shu and Tafnu, who watch over his heart and punish Set.[2] Osiris, however, remains in the invisible world of the departed or justified, while his soul alone, as the constellation of Orion, is displayed in full glory in the heavens, just as the soul of Isis shines forth in that of Sirius.

Such is the tenor of the myths, of which, from Plutarch's time down to our own, various interpretations have been given, though in truth one alone is admissible. If, first, we study the nature of the various gods who here play their parts, and if, especially, we set them in the light which the old monuments can throw upon them, the myth itself will be easily understood.

Osiris is a sun-god. This is indubitable and was perceived also by the ancients, although even at an early period he was made a god of the moon, a Nile-god, or even a god of wine like Bacchus. It is to be noted, however, that all these significations are really identical. The Nile, source of the fertility of the Egyptian soil, and wine, which imparts fresh life, corresponded on earth to the heavenly beverage called by the Aryans *soma* or *haoma*, and by the Greeks *nectar*, together with *ambrosia* the food of immortality, while the moon was looked upon as the reservoir or fountain-head of these celestial waters. In short,

---
[1] Dr. H. Brugsch, Die Adonisklage und das Linoslied, p. 22 *et seq*.
[2] Papyrus magique, No. 825 Brit. Mus., in the Rev. Arch. 1863, p. 125.

if Osiris is rightly regarded as a sun-god, it is the sun at night which he represents, the sun dead but risen again, and hence he is the god of the life eternal "of the length of time or of eternity," as the Egyptians say, and to him belongs by right all that gives or has life.

The signification of his name Asar, As-iri, which Lauth not long ago proposed to translate "son of the earth," is indeed uncertain,[1] but that he cannot be other than a sun-god is evident if we notice his peculiar relation to Horos, the sun-god, who at one time is identified with him, and then is called his father, and oftenest of all his son. Osiris is also designated as son of Seb, the god of the earth, and of Nu, goddess of the heavenly ocean, as grandson of Ra, the sun-god *par excellence*, who is called first in his circle, the father of fathers, and of whom it is said that he is united with Osiris in Suten-se-nen. This conclusion, that Osiris is a sun-god, is confirmed by a number of expressions used regarding him. In the hymns, his accession to the throne of his father is compared to the rising of the sun, and it is even said of him in so many words: "He glitters on the horizon, he sends out rays of light from his double feather and inundates the world with it, as the sun from out of the highest heaven." Like the sun he is called in the sacred songs, Lord of the length of time. Yet it would be a great mistake to say that Osiris signifies the sun. He is the divine being who reveals himself in the sun. One of his usual appellations is "mysterious soul of the Lord of the disk," or simply "soul of the sun." He is thus the soul of the sun, not dying when it dies, its ever-abiding vital force, which at nights is displayed in the glittering constellation of Orion, and in the morning is united again to the revivified body

---

[1] It is worthy of note that the hidden or under-world heaven, of which among the Egyptians Osiris is lord and originally also a personification, is called among the Assyro-Babylonians, *ashru* or *ashar* (which occurs so often in the kings' names), and that the signification of the word (אשר = to be good) corresponds to Osiris' surname, Unnefer, "the good being."

of the sun. He is also more definitely this, in a special character. The operation of the sun is twofold, beneficent and terrible; it quickens or it destroys life. The Greeks united both characteristics in Phœbus Apollo. The Egyptians kept them separate. They called Osiris Unnefer, that is, the good being representing the beneficent power of the sun that triumphs always over the powers of darkness, and cannot be annihilated by those injurious powers that are also exercised by the sun. That is the original physical signification of Osiris, always evidently betrayed in words and symbols even after his moral significance came more into the foreground. Becoming ever more and more detached from nature and exalted above her, he grew by degrees to be Lord of the universe (*Neb ter*), to whom everything owed its origin, who formed the sun, and who makes it rise and set, the Lord of life without whom nothing can live. How these conceptions arose out of the original natural one is self-evident, and it is equally clear how he soon became the type of the good man, of the human soul which is obliged to carry on a conflict similar to his against the powers of death, and which finds in his victory a guarantee of its own triumph, in his rising again a pledge of its own immortality. From the most ancient times accordingly, we find the dead, both men and women, represented as identifying themselves with him, their everlasting ideal.

We have given no more than the outlines of the conception of Osiris as entertained by the Egyptians. Were we to come down to details and to attend to slight variations, we should be lost in an ocean of symbolism and mysticism. As a necessary consequence of the prevalence of Osiris-worship in Egypt, a number of local legends have been incorporated with his myths. To this widespread devotion likewise he owes his manifold names, of which the 147th chapter of the "Book of the Dead," to give one instance, mentions no less than a hundred. To the same cause may be attributed the sacred metamorphoses that he, according to the old texts, underwent, and the mysterious forms he assumed. It would appear that so soon as his worship had established itself in any one place, Osiris took the form of the deity whose ancient seat it was, and the sacred animal of that particular town or district was consecrated to him. Thus, at Heliopolis and at Abydos, he is represented as the migratory bird Bennu, which appears to have been originally a form of the Heliopolitan god Ra. After the amalgamation of Osiris and Ra worship this form was bestowed upon the former as well.[1]

At Memphis, among other forms he appears to have assumed that of a certain species of ape, and also that of a *nechta*, *i.e.*, a mighty one, a giant of seven cubits, who was concealed in a chest eight cubits in height.[2] It was most likely at Memphis, too, that he was imaged as a pillar beginning in the lowest and ending in the highest heaven, a conception which is undoubtedly referred to in that feature of the myth, as related by Plutarch, where the King of Byblos causes a pillar to be made in his palace out of the tree which had grown around the sarcophagus of Osiris. In fact, we possess delineations of Osiris as well as of Ptah answering to this description. On a post upon which is graven a human countenance, and which is covered with gay clothing, stands the so-called Tat pillar, entirely made up of a kind of superimposed capitals, one of which has a rude face scratched upon it, intended no doubt to represent the shining sun. On the top of the pillar is placed the complete headdress of Osiris, the ram's horns, the sun, the ureus-adders, the double feather, all emblems of light and of sovereignty, and which in my judgment must here have been intended to represent the highest heaven.[3] The Tat pillar is the symbol of

---

[1] See above, p. 28, nt. 1.
[2] Chabas, Pap. mag. Harris, p. 116.
[3] See the plate in Wilkinson, M. and C., 2d Series, Suppt. Pl. 25 and 33, No. 5. Mariette, Abydos, I., Pl. 16.

durability, immutability. This representation of Osiris, which its rude and simple character without trace of art proves to have been one of the most ancient, must apparently be held to be symbolical of him as "Lord of the length of time or of eternity." Elsewhere again he was a *nemma* or dwarf with two heads, one of a sparrow-hawk, the other human, very evidently a symbol of his twofold being as sun-god and type or king of men.[1] All these varied transformations, which are found in all mythologies without exception, are nothing but the ancient forms of a deity which in later times, after the deity had come to be represented usually in human shape, were regarded as being forms he could still assume at pleasure. Here, as in other mythologies, these various forms have given rise to or have helped to embellish all sorts of legends. In the Osirian myths they have been employed chiefly for the purpose of carrying on the conflict with Set, who in seeking the body of his brother is again and again mocked by finding himself face to face with a totally different shape. Set likewise, as might be expected, transforms himself into the shape of his sacred animals—into that of the crocodile, for example. In this respect, however, he is outdone by Osiris, who by this device constantly succeeds in escaping persecution; or, to express it differently, the symbolism and mythology of the good sun-god was in Egypt infinitely richer than that of the violent evil one, and his worship prevailed much more extensively than that of the latter.

For I venture to consider it as certain that Set, the enemy and brother of Osiris or of the more ancient Horos, is likewise a sun-god, although Plutarch says that those who consider Typhon is the sun are unworthy of being listened to. In spite of his unamiable character and

---

[1] The sparrow-hawk, as is well known, is in Egypt the emblem of the sun. The emblem is made still plainer by the scourge, token of lordship, in the dwarf's hand, and the sun circle with the double feather between the two heads.

hideous shape, he is one of the most interesting figures in the Egyptian pantheon, for he has had a peculiar history. In turn revered and hated, invoked and persecuted, he was at last so much detested that his very name, where it occurs on the monuments, was wherever possible expunged or chiselled out. At no time was he regarded as a good deity. Even in the oldest myths he is the great enemy and adversary of Horos, and plays the unenviable part of traitor and murderer; and though finally he is not actually killed, he is nevertheless overcome and severely chastised, all which is not calculated to increase the reputation even of a divine being. Yet, though never a beneficent god, he was not detested in ancient times. He possessed temples and was worshipped, no doubt mostly out of fear. At a relatively late period warlike kings still named themselves after him. Homage was paid to him in Lower as well as in Upper Egypt, of which he was the special god; and the kings who united both these countries under their sceptre were looked upon as the incarnate Horos and Set, as being images of the one as well as of the other. They are frequently depicted, even in comparatively recent centuries, as standing betwixt these two gods, as anointed by them with life and power, or as receiving instruction from both, from Set no less than Horos, in the art of handling their weapons.

It is, indeed, the case that Set received more homage from foreign peoples who came into contact with Egypt than from genuine Egyptians. The Shepherd Kings, or at least one of them, selected him from among all the gods of Egypt as the object of exclusive worship. In the south, at Ombos, which must be reckoned as in Nubia, he was looked upon as the local deity, and derived from that town his most usual designation. He is also not unfrequently called the god of the negroes. Was he then perhaps, as has sometimes been asserted, a foreign god, one of the so-called Semitic gods, introduced from Asia? The truth is precisely the contrary of this. From the most remote antiquity Set is one of the Osirian circle, and is thus a genuine Egyptian deity. His place in the ranks of these gods is clearly defined; he constantly stands, even so early as the time of the first dynasties, betwixt Isis and Horos, with his wife Nephthys, forming thus along with her the complementary pair to Osiris and Isis. Even strictly Osirian kings, who neglected other gods, such as Ptah, worshipped Set. Among these were Chufu, Chafra, and Pepi. In Lower Egypt he was originally worshipped at Memphis only, the royal residence of the Upper Egyptian kings, and under the fifth dynasty, which was distinguished by the orthodoxy of its Osirianism, he possessed a temple in that town. His being called the god of the Nubians and Negroes, who adopted the Egyptian civilisation, and with it the Egyptian mythology, must be explained by the fact that the gods whose worship was most popular there had more in common with his character than with that of Osiris. When the Egyptians established themselves in Nubia, and looked through the list of their gods for one to whom this new portion of their kingdom might appear peculiarly to belong, none was found so suitable as Set. It was the same with the Hyksos, the character of whose god, beyond doubt warlike and devastating, allowed of his being identified most easily with Set, though both at that time and ever afterwards he remained the special god of Upper Egypt. This high favour in which he stood with foreign conquerors may perhaps have contributed to make the Egyptians regard him with steadily lessening reverence; it is at any rate certain that various reasons combined to bring about the persecution to which at a later time he was exposed, and the erasure of his name. In the first place, growing civilisation and the softening of manners made the people, and the cultivated priesthood in particular, zealously hostile to the service of a god so barbarous, just as in Israel we see the prophets entering the lists to combat the worship of Moloch;

secondly, there was the influence of Persian doctrine, with its dualism, for it is remarkable that the aversion to Set became conspicuous just after the time of the Persian conquest; and lastly, the influence of the Greeks, who could as little tolerate the gloomy death-god on the banks of the Nile as in their native country, where they always looked with a certain degree of abhorrence on Hades and his temples. This influence, however, was not felt till a much later period. In remote antiquity there can be no doubt Set was a sun-god. This is evident from his being properly the complement, not the adversary only, of Horos the sun-god. Like him, Set is found on the deck of the bark of the sun, ready to ward off the serpent of darkness, with which, by a curious fatality, he was one day destined to be identified. Like Horos, he is god of war and executioner in the under-world; and he would never have been raised, as god of Upper Egypt, to the level of Horos, god of Lower Egypt, had he not corresponded to him in general significance, however much he differed from him in character. As sun-god he is sometimes called the great lord of heaven, and the spy.[1] In contrast to Horos, the sun-hero from whom proceed life and fertility, and who is to be dreaded by none save those who are friends of darkness, and in contrast especially to Osiris, Unnefer, the good being, the good nature-power, the beneficent though concealed sun-god, his position was just like that of Melek, the fire-king, the severe Semitic god, who was worshipped in Juda also, in contrast to the luxurious life-giving Canaanite Baäl; or like Çiva in contrast to Vishnu. He was the personification of the sun's terrible desolating power, of the sun as devouring fire, the god of exterminating war, with all its terrors. Hence he speedily was made god of death. Elevated soon a little above nature, and conceived of as more human in form, he grew to be not only the fell adversary of Horos, the lord of light, but also the being who causes all that is evil in nature—

[1] See Brugsch, Zeits. d. Morgenl. Gesellschaft, vi. 253 et seq.

THE RELIGION OF THINIS-ABYDOS. 51

earthquakes, scorching heat, tempests, thunder and lightning, pestilential vapours that pollute the air and the water, and even mount up towards the moon, in order to make her and all that glitters in heaven dim and dark. It is he who wounds, or puts out, or swallows up the one eye of Horos, after which it is handed over to Ra, the sun-god highest in rank, that he may heal it. This, as Plutarch correctly explains, is a reference to a total or partial eclipse of the moon.[1] All plagues (*neshni*) proceed from Set;[2] and, accordingly, the animals sacred to him are beasts of prey, and consequently unclean animals—the hippopotamus, the crocodile, swine, and the monster with stiff ears, peculiar snout, and tail erect, which is the hieroglyph of this god. Finally, after having been completely dissociated from nature, apparently, as I said, by Persian influence in the first place, he became the evil principle in the creation, and in the moral world as well. It was at this stage that his name began to be removed and his images supplanted by those of Thot and Horos. Even on the tomb of Seti I., father of Ramses II. (Sesostris), the king's name was altered into Osiri.[3]

The lot of his rival Horos, usually Osiris' son, and avenger of his father, was totally different, for throughout the course of centuries he remained one of the most honoured of the gods of Egypt. In a sense, it may be

---

[1] See Zeits. für Aeg. Sprache u. Alterthumskunde, 1868, p. 33. The B. of the D. (chap. xvii., glosses 17 and 18) expressly says that the eclipse of the moon takes place during the conflict between Horos and Set.

[2] See ibid., 1868, p. 27.

[3] The name of Set is not yet thoroughly explained. It is perhaps connected with *sat* = flame, and with *sati* = ray of the sun and phallos. The Greeks called him Typhon, a name which, in the opinion of some, is to be discovered in the Egyptian *Tebku*, the god of Teb, where special homage was paid to him. Teb is the hippopotamus, Set's sacred animal, and the sacred name of the town is derived from it. In any case the Greeks must have got the name Typhon from the Phœnicians, who identified Set tebhu with their god of storms (*Ziphon*). Much has been done to explain the myths and history of this god by W. Pleyte, in his "Religion des Pré-israélites ; recherches sur le dieu Set," and in his "Lettre à M. Th. Devéria." Comp. also the smaller work of this author, "Le dieu Set dans la barque du soleil."

said of him as of Baal (as regards whom, proof of the assertion we make will be found in Book III. of this work), that his name was not so much that of a definite deity, as the common title given to a particular class of gods. In support of this opinion, we can adduce the following facts: we rarely find the name of Horos used without attribute or epithet; nearly every locality has its particular Horos, designated by a special surname:—thus Harhut at Edfu, Harsamto and Ahi at Edfu and at Dendera, Harmachu, he who is Ra, Harkamutef, he who is Chem and Harka, the young one, son of Chem and of Ament, at Thebes, &c.,—in fact, one frequently sees several different Horos deities represented side by side on the monuments: moreover, some divine beings, like the star Sirius (*Harsapd*), have the title of Horos bestowed upon them when they are masculine; and in later times at least, the name of Horos in the plural is always used as synonymous with the *nuteru*, the gods. The signification of the name of Horos accords perfectly with this use of it. *Har*, or *Her*, means really the most exalted, the Highest, the Lord, accordingly the principal divinity, the god considered as king of the country.

Three classes of Horos gods are to be distinguished: the first includes Horos the old (Hor-ur) brothers of Osiris and of Ra; the great Harmachis (Harmachu, Horos on the horizon), of Heliopolis; Horos Amun, and the ithyphallic god Hor Chem. The second is composed of the various sons of the preceding, in particular, the famous son of Isis (Har-se-ise), the avenger of his father, just as is Har-hut, the god of the winged bark of the sun at Edfu, the executioner of the judgments of Osiris in the under world, the king of the kings after whom, correctly speaking, no king reigns, since all the kings are only his lieutenants. Lastly, the third class is that made up of the infant Horos gods (Har-pe-chruti). Ahi and Samtoti, the youthful gods represented in the flower of the lotus, and which are very modern, having been, as Dr. Pleyte believes,

THE RELIGION OF THINIS-ABYDOS. 53

borrowed from India in the centuries immediately before our era, belong to this category.

As god of the visible sun, he is father and brother as well as son of Osiris, for in truth, the sun at night may equally well be called a son of the sun that shone the day before, as father of the sun that rises next day. Thus both sun-gods may be also conceived of as a pair of brothers, and this occurs not unfrequently in other mythologies. Horos is accordingly as *Har-oer*, Horos the great, the elder, son of Seb like Osiris, and husband of Isis or Hathor; he is found, however, most often as son of Osiris, and Isis or Hathor, and is called Har-pe-chruti, the infant Horos, the young, scarcely born sun at its first rising again in the morning. The Egyptians did not find these conceptions inconsistent with each other; they felt, on the contrary, that the elder and the younger Horos were one and the same, that the new-born sun, though apparently another than that they had seen die, was not in reality a different one, and they expressed this feeling of their identity in the mythological paradox, "Horos, (or Min, or Chem), husband of his mother." Horos also is a warrior god who, standing on the deck of the sun-bark, contends with the serpent Apap, the demon of darkness, or, in the character of avenger, with his father's enemy Set. At one moment he is seen brandishing his spear, at another he hurls his trident at the snout of the hippopotamus, one of Set's disguises,[1] and again he is armed with a sword ready to behead the wicked upon the scaffold (*nemma*) in the kingdom of the dead. But, notwithstanding this, he, equally with Osiris, is a good deity who fights against darkness only, and the pious need not be afraid of him. Formidable to his enemies, the enemies of his beloved Egypt, for his sparrow-hawk always hovers aloft over the head of the Egyptian kings as they go forth to battle, he is yet a guardian to his worshippers, and speaks as a

---

Zeits für Aeg. Sprache u. Alterthk. 1868, p. 18.

father to the king, whom he calls his beloved son.¹ "I make you," thus he speaks to the king—" I make you a terror to evil-doers, and spit before you on the hearts of your enemies."² But he is likewise the beneficent creator of the full harvest, the lord of the grain. His beauty, especially that of his countenance, is frequently celebrated. Hence he is represented as the Sphinx (*hu*), whose face, turned eastwards under its broad projecting head-dress, is the radiant sun, and whose body in the form of a lion is emblematic of his divine strength. As the winged sun's disk—a representation found in Egypt as well as in Babylon and in Assyria, from which latter country it was introduced into Persia—he is named *Hut*, the great god, the lord of heaven; and he imparts "life, vital power, long life, health, and all good fortune, as the sun in eternity." In this form he was worshipped even in the most remote antiquity, especially at Edfu (Hut).³

It would be inaccurate to regard Horos when without any attribute as being the god of the sun, and it would be more inaccurate still to mistake him for the sun itself deified. He is very far from being identical with Ra, whose name is oftenest used to designate the sun. The sun and the moon were called the eyes of Horos. He must, therefore, be regarded as the god of the light, the token of life. The conflict with Set, in which he interposes as avenger of his father Osiris, or as Marshal of the armies of his father Ra-Harmachis, has furnished an inexhaustible subject to the poets, painters, and sculptors of Egypt. This is not the place to describe and explain the myth as it has been found delineated at Edfu in a series of pictures, and since its discovery made generally known through

---

¹ Thus in the inscription on the sphinx at Gizeh, "The majesty of this god speaks with his own mouth; like a father with his son, so he speaks: Behold me, my beloved son Thotmes (Thotmes IV., eighteenth dynasty), I am thy father Haremchu." Brugsch, Reiseberichte aus Ægypten, p. 335.
² Duemichen Bauurkunde von Dendera, p. 13.
³ De Rougé in the Rev. Archæol. 1861, iv. 198.

the admirable publication of M. E. Naville. In its
essence it was unquestionably a nature-myth, but of the
most exalted kind, in which the actors are not simply
natural phenomena deified, but are already nature-spirits,
a sort of abstraction and personification of the powers of
nature. Of this kind is the mythic conception of the
conflict between the light and the darkness, between life
and death. Day and night succeeding each other, the sweet
revivifying warmth of spring followed by the scorching
heats of summer, all contributed features to the picture.

From a remote period, however, this nature-myth was
for the Egyptians the mere outward form of a dogma,
which was the very foundation of the faith they cherished,
faith in the triumph of light and life over darkness and
death, faith in the eternal order. They found a pledge
of this faith in the changing phenomena of nature, and in
the regular succession of the kings, the representatives of
Horos on earth.

An historical application of the myth was made, there
can be no doubt, in very early times. The struggle maintained by the kings in their effort to unite all the divisions
of Egypt under one sceptre, the wars carried on against
barbarian invaders, or against foreign powers, were all
referred back to the celestial drama. There is to be found,
however, no particular and definite historical fact under-
lying the myth, it simply expresses the lasting antagonism
between the pure Egyptian race and foreign races. Yet,
while this is the case, we must not suppose the origin of
the myth is to be found in this struggle: the truth is, that
the myth was, in the course of centuries, so modified as to
reproduce the features of this national struggle.

Side by side with the three sun-gods stand three goddesses who, from the nature of the case, differ from each
other even less than the three gods to whom they are
assigned as wives and sisters. These are Isis, Nephthys,
and Hathor.

Isis with a thousand names, as she was afterwards

called, enjoyed in the later centuries of the Egyptian kingdom, especially under the Ptolemies, greater honours than all the other gods, with the exception, perhaps, of Hathor. It was then that the beautiful, much frequented, and often described temple, situated on the island of Philak, was dedicated to her. At that time, too, her worship found its way to other peoples, so that she with her little Horos on her bosom became the model for the *Madonna col bambino*. An attempt has been made to prove from this that her rank was higher than that of her husband,[1] an idea that, at least as regards the most ancient, purely Egyptian period, is utterly untenable. In ancient times the place she occupied was rather in the background, and before long she was cast into the shade by other goddesses, such as Hathor, Mut of Thebes, Sechet of Memphis, and others; or else was worshipped merely in combination with these. Yet we know with certainty that she already had, even under the earliest dynasties, temples of her own. Her name (As) gives no clue to her nature, for whether this is understood to mean " the ancient," or whether we suppose, as I think is much to be preferred, that it signifies " the exalted, the worthy of being revered,"[2] both meanings are too general to give us any information about the nature of this deity. After their usual fashion, the Greeks have compared her to some half-dozen of their own goddesses, but especially to Demeter, Persephone, and Hera, a clear proof that she is not to be altogether identified with any one among them all. Still, these comparisons are not quite without foundation. As wife of Osiris, the god of the kingdom of the dead, or, to take the name given to her most frequently, as " Royal consort of Unnefer," she is

---

[1] This is asserted by Sharpe, Hist. of Egypt, i. 23.
[2] Mariette (Rev. Archæol. 1866, p. 85) explains *As* by παλαία. The word does actually occur with that signification (see Brugsch, W. B., p. 120); but in the instance referred to has not the chair for determinative. With this determinative, at least with a person seated, it signifies "adorned," and "worthy of reverence, exalted." And since the hieroglyph of Isis is a chair, the latter signification must certainly be chosen.

herself called "Mistress of Shetu," one of the designations of the kingdom of the dead, and in this respect she corresponds to Persephone. With Demeter, mother-earth, she has this in common, that she is "the great divine mother," and goddess of fertility. As mother goddess she wears her coif in the form of a vulture, a bird which was looked upon as the emblem of maternity; or in place of a human head she has that of a cow, a symbol that needs no explanation;[1] and she is also called *Oerhaku*, "the great power," the nature-power of conception and birth deified in her person.

It is now impossible to tell precisely to what natural phenomena the character of Isis at first referred. Originally she was a goddess of fecundity, the goddess *par excellence*, as wife of the supreme god and mother of the god Horos, the avenger of his father. In common with all the Egyptian deities of a certain rank, she was regarded as mistress of heaven, daughter of Ra, and she shared with Horos the title of Lord of the two worlds, and his emblems of celestial power, the solar disk, horns, and ureus adder. She was accordingly a goddess of heaven, sister, daughter, mother of the sun-god, and in respect of these titles may be likened to Hera-Dione, the Juno of the Italians, who, as goddess of the nocturnal heavens and of the moon, is wife of Zeus or Jupiter, originally god of day and of the bright heaven. As goddess of night, her head is the moon.

It is almost impossible to draw a sharp line of distinction between Isis and her sister Nephthys, who is called likewise mother goddess and goddess of heaven, and she too

---

[1] The opinion of Wilkinson that she owes her cow's head to her identification with Hathor, is refuted by an ancient myth which relates how her son Horos, in order to punish her for her mildness towards Set, smote off her head, and how Thot gave her a cow's head in place of it. The myth points to a combination of Isis with Set; in other words, it proves that, before the Osirian mythology became fixed, Isis was in some localities regarded as consort of Set, and in that character was represented with the shape of a cow. She, likewise, is found under the form of a female hippopotamus, a form which is pretty common even down to later times, and which marks her as the wife of Set.

wears the vulture hood and the sun's disk, with the horns on her head, and also is called "mistress of heaven," and it is said of her that she bestows fulness of life and joy.[1] Not unfrequently she is confounded with Isis, who, in one instance, has been discovered wearing on her head the hieroglyphic emblem of Nephthys.[2] And while on the one hand Isis is sometimes found designated as wife of Set, Nephthys, on the other hand, is said to have become by Osiris the mother of Anubis, whom Isis in her turn brought up; so that before the Osirian mythology was fixed, we see that Nephthys was regarded by some of the worshippers of Osiris as the lawful wife of this beneficent deity, and it is perhaps in connection with this that she is called *Nebt-ha*, i.e., " mistress of the house."

The well-known fact may be repeated here that nearly all the myths about the adultery of the gods sprang simply from this, that in different localities the principal deities were found coupled with different consorts. One among these, she who was most honoured, or the goddess of the ruling tribe, was by and by declared to be the lawful spouse, while the others sank to the rank of concubines.

Nephthys never shared the evil fame of Set her husband, the god of death. Along with Isis, she bewails the murdered Osiris, and watches over the beloved dead with outstretched wings.[3] While, accordingly, she is named guardian of the dead, it is in a favourable sense. She presides at the close of life, but it is a close which leads to victory.

The signification of Isis and Nephthys as nature goddesses comes out with somewhat greater clearness in the description of the divine ship of Horos. It is said there that the yard is the goddess of heaven (Nu), and that Isis and Nephthys are the two extremities of this yard. They must therefore be considered as the two extremities of

---

[1] Pleyte, Lettre à Devéria, p. 17.
[2] Wilkinson, M. & C. Suppl., Pl. 34, No. 2.
[3] Brugsch, Die Adonisklage u. das Linoslied, p. 23.

heaven, the two horizons, whether the east and the west, or the north and the south, or, as that which is quite the same thing, the morning and evening twilight.

The name Nephthys (*Nebt-ha*), "mistress of the house," was undoubtedly understood originally in a physical sense, the house being that to which the sun returns at the end of his course, that is, the nocturnal heavens; but afterwards Nephthys became, like Isis, the exalted, a symbol of the wife of kings, the heavenly type of the Egyptian matron, whose usual designation was "mistress of the house." This moral signification appears to have secured to her a place in the Osirian pantheon beside Isis, to whom, as a nature goddess, she so entirely corresponds.[1]

Another goddess of the Egyptian pantheon, Hathor, in quite as great a degree as Nephthys, resembles Isis, and was in a much greater degree identified with her. Though no definite part is assigned to her in the well-known myth of Osiris, we must nevertheless consider her in this connection. That she was sometimes confounded with Isis is not astonishing, since she had in common with her a form with a human or with a cow's head, the coif being adorned sometimes with the very emblems of Isis; and also the form of a cow. Hathor too is the mother and nurse of Horos, and at the same time his wife. Among the names by which she is designated in her principal temple at Dendera, that of Isis occurs frequently, and she is there even called "Hathor who is Isis at Dendera," although it is to be noticed that these inscriptions at least belong to a later period; but, at any rate, she was placed on a line with Isis at an early date. With Nu likewise, of whom we shall speak presently, she had not a few points in com-

---

[1] The explanation is well known that makes Nephthys goddess of the desert between the Eastern Nile bank and the Red Sea, Set the desolating wind of the Libyan desert, Osiris the Nile, and Isis the earth. But how in that case is it conceivable that Nephthys should have been represented as the sister of Isis, and as grieved at the death of Osiris? It is certain there is nothing on the monuments to justify this view, which is a mere intellectual conceit, originating at a time when the primary signification of the myths was not understood.

mon; for example, she is said, like Nu, to have been "She who brought forth all the gods," and seated in the heavenly sycamore, she pours out the waters of life. If it be asked whether this intermixture of deities is of ancient date, I would answer that in my opinion it is not, and that the conception according to which she is goddess of love and beauty, of joy and of song, has equally little claim to antiquity. That conception is, indeed, not foreign to her nature, but it appears to have arisen from the circumstance that the Greeks regarded her in the same light as their Aphrodite. Her worship prevailed so extensively as to supplant that of Nu, Nephthys, and Isis; and we may take for granted that the peculiar attributes of these goddesses with whom she had so much in common were insensibly transferred to her, for this was a process very usual in Egyptian theology. She too, like the majority of Egyptian goddesses, is mistress of the visible heaven and of the invisible. She is not, like the mourning Nephthys, the guardian of the dead, but rather goddess of the heavens by day, bathed in the pure bright sunshine, and of the heavens at night, glittering with the mild light of the stars, the fertile and fertilising mother, bestower of pleasure and of good fortune.

In this character she is the first-born of the beginning, the nurse who satiates gods and goddesses with her gifts, and fills Egypt to overflowing with her benefits. It is she who, as Nub, the golden one, first receives and greets the sun at his rising and at his setting, that is, at his birth and at his death. Mother of the young god of the sun, she bears likewise the name of daughter or child of Ra, the sun-god in general, the creator. Hence, as Horos is called the golden god, she is called golden goddess. In Egypt there is presented at sunset and sunrise a spectacle so magnificent that it can scarcely be imagined by those who have not witnessed it. "The western horizon," to quote the words of Ampère, "is a furnace of molten gold, the stems and foliage of the palm trees are likewise gold, and through this dazzling glow the purple tints of the hills can just be perceived. The sky and the Nile become in turn rose-coloured and violet, like the colours of an amethyst, then the light dies away."[1]

The moral significance of goddess of beauty and of love, of joy and of the pleasure of life, of song and of stringed instruments of music, was evolved naturally from the physical signification, although, perhaps, the influence of the Greek spirit may have tended to bring this aspect into greater prominence. It was very natural too that even in the most ancient times she was worshipped as patron saint at mines, whether they were dug[2] to obtain red copper or precious stones, for there could be found for such works no patroness so suitable as the goddess who from her dark womb brought forth to the light the golden sun.[3]

Besides the three pairs of gods already mentioned, two other deities also belong to the Osirian family. Usually they stand alone without any consort.[4] These are Thot and Anubis.

Thot (Thuti or Thui) had, from the most remote antiquity, his principal temple at Sesennu (Ashmunein) in Upper Egypt, a town mentioned on the monuments of the very earliest dynasties as being sacred to him, and the sacred appellation of which (Sesennu, Ashmunein = eight) is derived from the eight gods of creation who were

[1] Ampère, Voyage en Egypte et en Nubie, p. 296.
[2] Brugsch, Wanderung nach den Turkisminen und der Sinai Halbinsel, pp. 12, 74, 80. According to Brugsch, the mines there, which so early as the time of the kings of the eleventh dynasty were worked out, were not, as Lepsius considered them to be, copper mines, but turquois mines. If he is right, the blue gems taken out of the mine were a fitting image of the blue heaven that would seem to be dug out from the masses of dark clouds, represented by the mountain.
[3] Though Mariette and Maury (Rev. Archæol., 1862, vi. 133, and Rev. d. deux Mondes, 1867, p. 189) regard her as the nocturnal, or, as they call it, the heaven of the underworld, I believe this to be incorrect. It would at least leave unexplained various attributes of Hathor, about which there is no difficulty according to the explanation I give.
[4] It was not until he had become Thot, the thrice great, Hermes Trismegistus, that at Troja, near Memphis, at Philak and at other places, he was coupled with Nehemanus, or Nehemau, one of the forms of Hathor. See Lepsius, D. Götter der vier Elementen, taf. iv., No. 13. Brugsch, Reiseberichte, p. 45.

worshipped there along with him. As to his nature there is no room for doubt. He bears the moon's disk between two horns on his head, and on that account, and for other reasons, he must unquestionably be regarded as god of the moon. Moon deities of the male sex are not uncommon in other mythologies—in the Germanic and Roman, for instance; and among the Babylonians and Assyrians, Sin, the god of the moon, occupied a very high rank. Accordingly we find Thot has a place in the bark of the sun, where the principal light-gods were grouped together. He is " King of Eternity," and in that character holds in his hand a palm branch, the symbol of the year, and upon it marks occurrences of importance, or the periods of time. That the moon-god should also be god of time, and thus of eternity, is not to be wondered at among a people who at first were acquainted only with the lunar year. In reference to this a peculiar myth exists. Thot, so it is related, invented draughts, and won from the moon the five intercalary days that at a later period were added to the lunar year.[1] Thot, by this time no longer the moon itself regarded as a divine being, but distinct from it, and become now the god of science, wins from her the five days she would not give of her own accord. In other words, the improved mode of reckoning time was ascribed to the god who invented all the arts and was the fountain of all knowledge; and since he was so closely connected with the moon, it was fabled that he had won from her these five days by gaming.[2] As God of the moon, Thot is likewise governor of the four winds— the winds, that is to say, of the night—just as the sun-god brought forth the four winds of the day " by the fire of his mouth." Ancient peoples conceived of the wind as

---

[1] See Birch, Rev. Archæol., 1865, ii. 57.

[2] I cannot satisfactory explain why Thot, in particular, instead of or along with Seb, is placed at the head of the gods of the earth as Horos is at the head of those of the heaven. All we know is, that the Babylonian moon-god Sin also was commonly named " the protector," or " the illuminator of the earth."

being the breath of the creative, light-giving god, whether revealed in sun or moon, and Thot as well as Ra is creator. Yet, although this natural signification was never lost sight of, a moral significance also was attributed to Thot even in the most remote antiquity. He was the god of knowledge, of letters, of priestly culture, the only culture Egypt had, and accordingly god of the priests *par excellence*. The connection between these qualities and his lunar character is easily understood. Science began with the observation of the heavenly bodies and the computation of time, and for these studies no more suitable patron could be found than the god of the moon, who, with her peaceful light, rules the stillness of night. All work demanding more than common skill and intelligence was consecrated to him. Thus, he was worshipped in combination with Hathor and Horos-sophd at the mines in Sinai. As inventor of all arts and of writing, he was master of the divine word, the writer who composed or inspired[1] the holy scriptures. He was the founder of libraries, and it was he who bestowed their significant names on the kings. He was the lawgiver, too, whose laws were immutable. In the under-world he filled the post of advocate and justifier of the good, who, through his pleading, gained an acquittal at the judgment throne of Osiris, who had once himself been in like manner acquitted through the advocacy of Thot.[2] This may, perhaps, have originally had a natural sense; the god of the moon, which receives its light from the invisible sun, may easily, in poetico-mythological language, have come to be looked on as the justifier of the sun-god, the pledge of his beneficence, the instrument of his revival. Thus Thot became in general the justifier of all who think themselves injured or disowned. "The god Thot," so exclaims the scribe Hui in his pleading (*Papyrus Anastasi I.*), " stands as a shield behind me."[3] Along with him worship

[1] See Book of the Dead, xviii. 24. für Aeg. sprache, &c., 1868, p. 1 *et*
[2] Rev. Archæol., 1863, viii. 105. *seq.*, and Lauth, Moses der Ebraër,
[3] Compare De Horrack in the Zs. p. 84.

was rendered, even in the remotest antiquity, to the goddess Safech,[1] the mistress of libraries, represented as a woman adorned almost always with a panther's skin, the dress of the higher priesthood, and bearing on her head an emblem that seems to mark her as goddess of the starlight. As far as I know, however, she is never spoken of as wife of Thot.[2] The animals sacred to him were the ibis and dogheaded ape. He is often represented under the latter form, which is also assumed by the eight gods (the Sesennu) who form his retinue. He, in common with these animals, bears also the name of Asten, or Astennu. This was an animal which was regarded in Egypt, for what reason we do not very well know, as the symbol of the equality of day and night, and generally of equilibrium, of equality. It is for this reason that Asten is constantly represented seated upon the beam of the sacred balance precisely above the index, in the psychostasias as well as in the temples.

From the first, very great honour was paid to Thot, and as the power and influence of his patrons the priests increased, and the country became more civilised, the favour he enjoyed augmented steadily. From great he rose to twice great, to thrice great, and when the name and image of Set were obliterated from the monuments, it was most frequently Thot who took the vacant place. At the time, too, when a new religion, the universal religion that took its rise in Palestine, began slowly to supplant the ancient Egyptian one, Hermes Trismegistus was the god in whom, more than any other, men gloried, and under his name a sort of theosophy was propagated which had no little influence on the formation of early Christian doctrine.

A god of much less importance, and who was very speedily cast into the shade[3] by other deities is Anubis

---

[1] Comp. Lepsius, Aelt. Texte des Todtenbuchs, p. 3, n. Her name must be written as in the text, and not, as it usually is, Saf.

[2] Other gods of libraries and literature are Atmu of Thebes (Brugsch, Reiseberichte, p. 294 *et seq.*); Ma, Goddess of Righteousness; and Pacht, the wife of Ptah, the mistress of thoughts (ibid., p. 264).

[3] The conjecture of Brugsch, that he anciently occupied the place taken

Anup (from *an* = to conduct). He is, as his name imports, the conductor of the dead, the god of mummies and of embalming, and he may always be recognised by his jackal's head. Thus, he may be seen ("Book of the Dead," chap. cxvii.) conducting the dead to the western gate *Sta*. In the tombs (*e.g.*, tomb No. 32 at Qurna) he is frequently found depicted as a guardian standing beside the mummy. One of his most usual names is Ap-heru, guardian of the ways, that is to say, of the heavenly pathways over which the dead pass towards the abode of Osiris. He is brought into connection with the Dogstar which occupies so prominent a place in the Egyptian mythology and chronology.[1] Perhaps he is nothing but this star personified as a divine being. Among other nations also, as is well known, Sirius, the most brilliant of the fixed stars, was worshipped as a god, and among the Hindoos, Persians, and Greeks, it was held in the highest estimation. It is a star peculiarly fitted to be regarded as keeping vigil over the body of Osiris and as conductor to the regions of light, and it was indeed called the soul of Isis. According to the common tradition Anubis was a son of Osiris and Nephthys, whence it appears that in the localities where homage was paid to Osiris and Nephthys as divine consorts, he usually occupied the third place in the divine triad of father, mother, and son. He is, however, also designated as a son of Osiris and Isis, or of Set and Nephthys, and in connection with these pairs he appears likewise to have filled the place of son. Like all gods of light he is son of the sun.

All the gods of the Osirian circle are descendants of common ancestors, Seb and Nu, whose precise signification is difficult to define. But if, instead of taking each of the names which have been given to them into consideration by itself, we comprise them all in one view, a satisfactory

by Osiris, while in no way proved, has not hitherto been confirmed by the most ancient monuments.

[1] See Chabas, Pap. Mag. Harris p. 101.

explanation is reached. It is accordingly proved beyond question by a very great number of texts, that Seb is a god of the earth or a personification of the earth, who even became completely identified with it at a later period. But the earth is here looked upon as material substance, durable, lasting, eternal, existing for ever. For this among other reasons, King Menkaura is called, upon a sarcophagus, offspring of Nut and flesh of Seb. Seb is therefore the most ancient of the gods, " Lord of the length of time, of eternity,"[1] and he is hence constantly named the most ancient sovereign. It is no doubt on account of this that the Greeks have compared him with their Kronos, who likewise was the king of the golden age of old. It is however incorrect to designate him, as Lepsius and to a certain extent Mariette still do, as the god of time, which neither he nor Kronos was. Upon various tombs Seb is represented as recumbent, while Nut, goddess of heaven, forms above him as it were an arched vault, exactly similar to the representations of Ymer the German giant of matter, and Audhumbla the cow of heaven. His ordinary symbol is however the goose, that according to Egyptian tradition laid the egg of the world.

His wife *Nu* or *Nu-tpe* is likewise called " She who brought forth the gods." She has this in common with most of the Egyptian goddesses, that she is regarded as a goddess of heaven. Like Hathor, she too sits in the heavenly sycamore and pours forth the waters of life into the hands of a soul that refreshes itself with them, or she even pours down a stream of all sorts of gifts, such as flowers and fruits upon her patrons. She is undoubtedly the goddess of water regarded as a cosmogonic principle, of the heavenly ocean, who gives water to the souls of the departed usually identified with the stars, and in fertilising dew she causes all kinds of blessings to come down on the earth.

At night, when even the moon is invisible, all that is

[1] So Champollion Monumens, Pl. CLXII.

in the universe, all the gods of the luminous heaven are at rest (*emhotep*) in peace. The heaven rests upon the earth like a goose brooding over her egg. The earth-god alone continues to reign. The mistress of the heavenly ocean alone shares his vigil, and reveals herself in the clear starlight, continuing all the night through to bestow her benefits ; all the other gods are hidden. Thus must it have been, thought the Egyptian, once in the beginning of things. Then there existed no others, save the eternal god, the god of everlasting substance and the eternal waters that covered and overflowed all things. But just as each morning from the marriage of these two the gods of the clear daylight heaven are born, so it happened before the ages; so before Osiris came into being, or Horos, or any one of the gods, did Seb the father of them all bear sway.

With this mythology is connected the doctrine of immortality, which in no other ancient people is so fully developed, or occupies so prominent a place in the theological system, as among the Egyptians. It is indeed the case that the doctrine did not arise out of the mythology, but was merely brought into close connection with it. So soon as man relinquishes the standpoint of instinctive belief, he begins to reflect, to reason, to seek a basis for his faith. The first pledge of renewal of life after death was discovered in what men saw happen to the sun every day and every year. He too died, and he revived. And was not he a living being ? Had not he become a personal deity ? Were not men his children ? Thus the Egyptians reasoned, and not only they but others as well, and among them the Hindoos, so that this mode of reasoning appears to have been, from remotest antiquity, peculiar to the whole Caucasian race, and not special to the Mesopotamians or the Aryans; unless it be met with, which I am not aware of, in other races likewise.

It is at all events certain, that the belief in immortality, the hope of life eternal, was in no other people more deeply rooted than among the Egyptians. Diodorus truly observes, "The Egyptians call the dwellings of the living inns, because in them they live but a short time; the tombs of the dead, however, they call eternal abodes, since in Hades they continue to live on in a limitless eternity." Hence the Egyptian was filled with anxiety about his grave more than about anything else. For example, a certain Saneha, who lived under the first kings of the twelfth dynasty, had been banished, but had had the good fortune to be well received at the court of a neighbouring—probably Libyan—prince. There he rose to the highest posts of honour, and, with his family, was at home. He lived in luxury and overflowing abundance. But the thought that he must die there, that he would not be carried to the grave in his native land, and would thus fail to secure a new birth and eternal power of changing his shape; this thought oppressed him and made him look out anxiously for leave to return home. It was given, the king remembered him, and desired his return, holding out as one of the strongest inducements the same consideration, "Think upon the day of your burial, the journey to Amenti, for you have already reached middle age." He promises that the interment shall be splendid. Saneha, on his part, does not hesitate, but leaves everything, even his very children, behind him in order to erect without delay a magnificent tomb in preparation for his approaching death. It is no wonder then that a hope so lively left its impress on the teachings of their faith, and became fixed as a dogma. The Egyptian expressed it in this way—The deceased, provided he had lived piously, as a child of light, becomes Osiris. Like that of the sun-god, his shade sinks gently down in the West, while his soul ascends to heaven, and his body is laid in the tomb. Next, it depends on what happens to himself, that is, to his shade, whether his soul shall be reunited to his body and he shall thus revive again to life. He enters that world which at one time is called "the hidden" (Amenti), at another "the reversed world of the double righteousness" (Set-i or Set-mati), and again "the land of rest" (Teser), or also Cher-nuter, "the divine under-world." There, as a sinner, he must be judged. The judgment, however variously it may be described, in its principal features amounts to the following:—first, it is ascertained whether the deceased is Osiris, or in other words, whether he is related to the divine good being. Ma, the goddess of truth and righteousness, or Horos himself, conducts him within. His soul is then weighed on the divine balance by Anubis, Horos, and Thot. The last mentioned records the sum total, and, if it be possible, justifies the soul. Finally, he is brought by Horos before Osiris, who, seated upon his throne of judgment, with the hell-monster before him, the four genii of the dead close by, and surrounded by the seventy-two judges, gives a verdict. Should it be one of condemnation, the soul has to undergo the second death, and is delivered up to annihilation. One of the gods—either the terrible Set, or Horos, or it may be one of the serpents, Sapi or Apap, demons of darkness, or the benevolent Tum, the hidden sun-god, in fact another Osiris—cuts off his head. The punishment did not, however, end with the execution, which, it would appear, did not extinguish consciousness. At least, he is next cast into the everlasting flames. A never-ending death seems to have been the conception of the punishment of hell entertained by the Egyptians. This punishment was likewise personified in the female demon Auai, a name that would seem to have been suggested by the sound of "weeping and gnashing of teeth." We have already noticed other modes of punishment, as for instance that of being torn and devoured by an evil spirit and then transmuted into its excrement. There were many such punishments, and it would appear that there was a difference in the penalties, according to the different sins of which men had been guilty, for hell had seventy-five compartments.

The deepest misery was frequently expressed by saying that the condemned see not the light, and are no longer kept in remembrance. To sit in everlasting darkness—

a phrase that irresistibly recalls the outer darkness of the Gospel—and to be forgotten, were the most dreadful ideas to the mind of the good Egyptian, the friend of the light, who his whole life long esteemed no effort that he could make too great, if he could thereby immortalise himself.

Yet he who, on the other hand, was not condemned, did not, on account of that, escape henceforth from all conflict: he was obliged to be purified in battle and cleansed by fire. He must pass through fifteen or more portals, at which the most terrifying trials awaited him. Monsters attacked him, he was menaced by dangers, nets were laid to ensnare him; at one time he was obliged to travel through desolate tracts where nothing grew, and which were under the dominion of seven evil spirits; then he had to sail over the heavenly ocean, and in his voyage was—just as they were who sailed in the bark of the sun—perpetually in danger of falling overboard and being drowned; sometimes he was caught in the mazes of a labyrinth. But if he kept steadfast and fought bravely with the sacred spear, and repeated the magical words of power from the sacred books and hymns, he reached at last the happy fields, the aalu-fields, where a lordly banquet was served up to him. There he could labour again as he once did on earth, cultivating the soil and gathering in a fabulous harvest. There he is illuminated by the glory of Osiris, and bathes himself in contemplation of the god of light. There, too, he may, as a spirit of light (*chu*), accompany the sun-god in his bark, sailing over the heavenly ocean, or at night (as *sahu*) he may sparkle in the firmament as a star. He is now one of the pious (*amhu*), the faithful (*hesu*), the wise (*akeru*), the rich (*asu*). Accordingly, to be with the deity and to be like him is, even in this, the oldest development of the doctrine of immortality, what constitutes salvation.

It may perhaps excite astonishment that in this doctrine no mention is made of the metempsychosis, nor of a distinct resurrection of the dead out of the tomb—dogmas that have

THE RELIGION OF THINIS-ABYDOS. 71

been hitherto ascribed to the Egyptians on the authority of Herodotus. According to the Greek historian, the soul of the departed is said to have passed into an animal, and after having gone through all the ranks of the animal world, it was at the end of three thousand years reunited to the human body. On the monuments, however, next to nothing has been discovered that can be said to confirm this account. In the tomb of one of the Ramesids indeed there is a representation that might suggest such a doctrine. The departed, after having been judged by Osiris, is being removed under the form of a pig, the unclean animal, upon a bark guided by two dogheaded apes, the animals of Thot, the whole being under the superintendence of Anubis. Apparently, the deceased is being taken to the place of torment, and not, as is usually believed, to the earth.[1] This representation is, however, unique, and is assuredly symbolical. Herodotus probably formed a false idea of the well-known Egyptian doctrine of the metamorphoses of the dead. According to the Book of the Dead[2] the deceased may assume all sorts of shapes—that of a sparrowhawk, an adder, a crocodile-headed god—in order by this expedient to trick his enemies, exactly as we learn from the myths Osiris used to do. Not until after this is the soul, which always accompanies the shade in the form of a sparrowhawk with human head, reunited to the body. But all this happens in the kingdom of the dead, not on earth. It is quite possible that the father of history mistook the doctrine taught by Pythagoras among the Greeks for a genuine Egyptian one. Perhaps, too, at a later period there may have arisen among the inhabitants of the Nile valley a dogma of the soul's incarnation evolved from the ancient eschatology. If so, that dogma is certainly not ancient, and their original doctrine of immortality is nothing but a mystic representation arising out of sun-worship. Just as the setting of the sun was for them a separation of the

---

[1] See Wilkinson, M. and C. Suppt., Pl. LXXXVII.
[2] Book of the Dead, chap. lxxxix.

body and the soul of the radiant god, and his rising a reunion of the two, so, they believed, was likewise the future lot of man. With the sun-god he in like manner rose again to life, to life in a higher sphere.

Meanwhile, much in the faith of the ancient Egyptians still remains obscure. The study of the Book of the Dead, a study still in its infancy, will assuredly cast new light on many points. Thus, for example, it is still customary to speak of the underworld, the subterranean heaven, but I have very great doubts whether *Cher Nuter* is really properly a subterranean tract, and I should be much more inclined to recognise in it the highest, the hidden heaven. I am not, of course, a stranger to the idea that the matter must be represented as follows—the sun-god and they who, like him, die, sink into the tomb, enter in the west the kingdom of the dead, the hidden heaven, and make their way thence, not beneath the earth, but above the visible heaven, in the opposite direction, towards the east. There is a great deal to be found in confirmation of this conception in the representations and expressions on the monuments, yet on this point I do not venture to speak with certainty, but await a solution of the problem from a closer investigation of the sources.

The myth of Osiris is in any case sufficiently clear. It sprang from the soil of nature-worship and always remained rooted there; yet it had, even in the earliest historical times, an ethical signification. Osiris is, unquestionably, the sun-god who dies every day and falls a prey every evening to the demon of darkness, the serpent Apap. Bewailed by the goddess of heaven, his sister and consort, he revives each morning in the youthful sun, the serpent-slayer, the avenger of his father. In the night, unseen by mortal eye, the conflict takes place between the youthful Horos and the powers of darkness, for it is only after the battle has been fought out that he can in the morning proceed on his journey. But the earth keeps vigil, and with her the celestial watchman Sirius, while the moon-god displays himself as substitute for the sun-god, and as the living pledge of his return. That is the simple nature-ground from which the myth arose. Afterwards, when the actors in the drama were conceived as being in a greater degree human, the place of the serpent Apep was taken by Set, the god of the scorching sun heat, who had by this time become the god of all violent natural phenomena in general, and among them of death. Hence, by a natural transition, he was regarded as the murderer of his brother, and the great foe of the youthful sun. As agriculture rose in importance in the Nile valley, the myth was undoubtedly likewise applied to the change of the seasons. It is, for instance, often brought into connection with the periodical inundation of the river. But the purely natural element of the myth belongs to the prehistoric period. When we first become acquainted with Osiris he is already more than a nature-god, he has already become a type of man dying and reviving again, and at the same time the supreme hidden god, lord of creation, who reveals himself in the sun, and in other beneficent natural phenomena. Already, in the consciousness of the ancient Egyptians, this myth is the expression of their faith in that triumph of life over death that is to be seen in all that exists, in the course of the sun, and in the returning fruitfulness of the earth. It was on this faith in the victory of life over death that they based their hope of immortality. But, besides, the myth expressed also their faith in the triumph of good, of virtue. They who, while they lived on earth, had been like the good deity and obedient to his commands, would, when, like him, they died, overcome with him, and after the victory reign with him in the abodes of light.

CHAPTER IV.

THE RELIGION OF HELIOPOLIS.

A PLACE even more renowned than Abydos is Pa-ra, the city of the sun, or as the Greeks translated it, Heliopolis. It lies a little to the east of the Nile, and not far from the spot where Memphis was built. Its usual name among the Egyptians and Hebrews was An, or On, a name borne also by two towns in the south—Hermonthis and Dendera.[1] To this place, according to the Hebrew narrator, the wife of Joseph, Asnet, or Asnath (Exalted Neith, or simply Isis-Neith), is said to have belonged; she being called a daughter of Potiphera (Peti-p-ra, dedicated to the sun-god), priest of On.[2] At a later time On became almost completely a Hebrew town, and, in fact, the religion of this locality must, more than that of any other, have agreed with that of the ancient Hebrews. In Egypt also, Heliopolis was held in the greatest esteem ; coronation ceremonies took place there as at Memphis, and the kings who were crowned there had the special

---

[1] An signifies "pillar, stone." The name may thus have been given to the towns on account of some remarkable structure, an obelisk perhaps, but it is more likely that the reference here is to a sacred stone, an aerolite that would be kept hidden in the innermost sanctuary. The spot in or near Heliopolis where this object of the greatest mystery was kept veiled from the eyes of all except the king, who beheld it at his consecration, was called "Ha-benben, the house of the two pyramids or obelisks." Or is An, which occurs as the name of a person, and then represents the supreme god, the name of the deity himself? In any case it cannot be mere accident that the name An is borne by the three cities where the victorious Sun or Light-god, as Ra-har-em-chu, Har-munt, and Har-hut was the local deity. An or Ana, which in the proto-Babylonian language signifies "heaven," has nothing to do with Egyptian word, nor has the god Anubis (Egyp. Anup) the least connection with it.

[2] Gen. xli. 45.

title bestowed on them of Haq-an, sovereign lord of On. The priesthood of Heliopolis was regarded as an exceptionally learned one, and this town appears to have been the cradle of the entire sacred literature. The religion that had its seat there was no less ancient and venerable than that of Osiris, and, like it, prevailed at a later period throughout all Egypt. Upon the same extremely ancient monuments on which we read the names of Osiris and Isis, there occurs in brotherly union with these that of Ra, the chief god of On. The place he takes in the Book of the Dead is in no way less honourable and important than that assigned to Osiris. They are there confounded with each other; now the one, now the other being the greatest; now the one, then the other being mediator. Yet from the remotest antiquity there is not the slightest trace of any jealousy having ever existed between these two closely related worships. It was felt even then that the two were one under a diversity of form; or rather, for that is saying too much, it was felt that the two were one in spirit and form, and differed only in some names and trifling idiosyncrasies.

The myth of Osiris might be described as more Semitic in character, while that of Ra is more Aryan. In every point Osiris corresponds to the beneficent sun-god of the Semites, to Adonis or Thammuz, killed by the consuming god of the summer sun. Ra, on the other hand, is like all the Aryan gods of the light and of the sky; he fights against the demon of darkness, the serpent Apap, who, properly speaking, is not a god in the same way as are Indra, Apollon, and others. These analogies ought not, however, to lead us in any way to imagine that foreign elements were introduced into the religion of the Egyptians, or to think that they may have adopted the myths of a people anterior to them in history. It would be more accurate to regard the two conceptions as two different ways of expressing the same mythological struggle, each being, the one among the Semites, the other among the Aryans, a development of one principal myth. Each people found the germ of this myth in a primitive myth which they severally took over from their common ancestors at a time anterior to the period when the race to which both belong divided into two distinct families. The myth was afterwards developed by each people under the action of special influences which determined its peculiar drift and the mould into which its ideas have been cast, the influence of climate being especially noticeable. In this way both the resemblances and the points of difference which have struck historians are alike fully explained.

The correspondence between Osiris and Ra worship in their forms is evident enough. Horos, the divinely personified being common to both systems, is represented in the Osirian mythology under two forms, namely, as Horos the elder, father and brother of Osiris, and as Horos the child. The Heliopolitan visible sun-god is likewise split into two persons. Ra, in a narrower sense, god of the sun by day, and Harmachis (Har-m-achu) the rising sun-god, the sun-god appearing to view on the horizon. Ra and Horos had the same symbol, the sparrow-hawk. Atum or Tum, repeatedly called god of An, was in reality identical with Osiris, and in the vignettes of the "Book of the Dead" is confounded with him (17, 34, and elsewhere). Shu, the god of An, as he is most commonly named, we find again at Thinis as Nunhur. The difference between the two seems to have been this, that while at Abydos, the place of honour was occupied by the dead or hidden god Osiris, at Heliopolis, on the other hand, it was Ra, the self-revealing god, who took the chief place, how great soever might be the honours paid there to Tum also. Hence the doctrine of the resurrection took a more prominent place in the Osirian theology than in that of Ra, although the "Book of the Dead" shows that Ra worship was brought into connection with this doctrine in very early times.

But the contents of the two systems are even more in accordance than the forms. This is seen among other instances from the above-quoted seventeenth chapter of the "Book of the Dead." I believe I do not err in considering Heliopolis to be the place where the original text of this chapter was composed. The gods mentioned in it belong to this locality. An is the goal of the pilgrimage of the deceased, and the ideal towards which he strives is to reach this city, the holy city. De Rougé is, however, of opinion that here the heavenly An is referred to. It is a matter of course that the deceased, as always happens in Egyptian eschatology, becomes identified with the deities, so that properly it is he, not they, who speak. But it is very possible that the ancient text was originally composed with another object than to serve as a magical formula for the departed; it may have been simply an inscription in the temple of the sun-god. However that may be, it at least makes us acquainted with the genuine Heliopolitan theology of the olden time. In this respect let us now see what may be learnt from it.[1]

"I am," thus speaks the deity, or the deceased identified with him—"I am Tum, a being that is alone." This does not as yet amount to an expression of monotheistic doctrine, for it simply means, Tum is the being who once, before the creation, existed alone. Tum, as his name imports, is the still concealed or imprisoned god,[2] in a physical sense the sun-god in the darkness of night, not revealing himself, but alive nevertheless, and who on this account is frequently likened to the setting sun. In a

---

[1] Comp. Lepsius Aelteste Texte des Todtenbuchs, which includes a commentary on this portion which I have mainly followed.

[2] I cannot agree with Pleyte's explanation; *who is not*, Theol. Tijdschrift, 1869, No. 3, p. 243. *Tum* or *Tem* certainly signifies *not*, but that is the abstract signification which gives here no proper sense. "The god who is not" would have been to Egyptians an impossibility. The root denotes to shut up, to separate, to hide, and from this the name must be derived.

cosmical sense he is the god who, before there was diversity in the creation, reigned and was alone in the fathomless abyss, or rather who was the soul of it. On this account he is, in another passage of the Book of the Dead (78, at the end), called "the first of the gods, the only one who does not change." " I am," thus continues the deity, " Ra in his first sovereignty," that is to say, Ra as the first ruler over all that exists, and as such, " the great god self-existing, the creator of his name, the lord of all gods, who is upheld by none among the gods." This god comes to view out of darkness and concealment, and is the same as the hidden god, only, inasmuch as he reveals himself, he bears another name. He is not created, but exists of himself. He himself creates his name, that is, his being, and because, as we read in another passage, all the gods are said to be only manifestations or members of Ra, he is Lord of all the gods. In this character he is symbolically represented by the beetle (choper), an emblem which is proved to have been a very favourite one among the Egyptians, by the innumerable scarabæi in every sort of material that have come down to us. This symbol implies the idea of change of being through transformation; and since the transformation here referred to is that of Tum into Ra, he is under this form frequently called Tum-ra-choper, the hidden one, who alters his form to the revealed one. Another frequently recurring emblem is " Ra in his egg." The egg is the world-egg, a conception found in other mythologies likewise, and signifying, in fact, chaos. The Egyptians looked upon Ra as its germ, the motive-power who, by moving himself, was the original cause of motion. This corresponds to the signification of his name; Ra denotes creator, for it must be derived from a root which means *to make, to create.*

Thus, as in America and other places, he is the soul of the sun, regarded as creator of the universe. To the popular conception he was the visible sun, the sun by day born in the east, and passing into union with the west.[1] But, as is proved by his name, the cosmogonic conception of him is the more ancient. It can be easily explained how he is called the divine ruler, or the first ruler of heaven, inasmuch as, not dependent on any of the other gods who all rank beneath him, he passes undisturbed on his way through the heavens.

Thus he finishes his appointed course, but he does not die for ever; "he was yesterday, he knows the morrow;" the past and the future are his. Now, however, begins the conflict. God himself has made ready a field of battle in the sight of the gods; at his command it is set in order. This is a rough mythological expression, for it is God's will that his various manifestations should be at strife with each other; rejuvenescence, renewal of life, in which the idiosyncrasy, the being of the deity, consists, cannot take place but through conflict.[2] The battle-field is the land of the west, Amenti the portal of the kingdom of the dead, or the kingdom itself as a whole, and there is the proper abode of the great deity, whose name is a mystery known only to himself. For in this sense the words are to be understood, which are uttered by the deity or by the deceased identified with him. "I know the name of the great god whose abode is there." The interpreter, who would have us understand from this that the name was "spirit of Ra," comes certainly nearest to what the ancient author meant to indicate. For now the deity becomes "the great Bennu, who is honoured in An." Bennu is the soul of Ra (*Bennu ba en Ra*), and was therefore, when the mythologies of Abydos and Heliopolis were commingled, regarded often as a form of Osiris. The sun-god, after his setting, has now become a *soul*, and as, in his glory in the heavens, in his glittering body, he was represented as a sparrow-hawk, so in his concealment as a soul in the realm

---

[1] Brugsch, Reiseberichte, p. 38.
[2] *Nuter*, the generic name for the gods, signifies, according to E. de Rougé, "the self-rejuvenating ones."

M. Lepage Renouf is of another opinion. See his Hibbert Lectures, p. 93 *et seq.*

of the dead he is represented by the Bennu-bird, the heron, which, as a bird of passage, is a symbol of immortality and of return to life.[1]

This is expressly stated in the sentences that follow: "I am Chem in his appearing, whose two feathers are set upon his head." Chem is the ithyfallic god, the special god of masculine generative power. He is the youthful new sun-god, regarded as self-begetting, and as husband of his mother, a mystic expression indicating that in all his forms the deity is one and the same, and constantly renews himself by virtue of his own never-dying force. Hence it is that this form of the deity, offensive to our modern ideas of chastity, is here identified with Ra, and in the Osirian mythology with Horos, son of Osiris and Isis, and later at Thebes with Amun.

Thus he has at length arrived at his divine abode, "in the sun-mountain of his father Tum." Thence he set out, and thither at last he returns home, but only to set out again from it in a never-ending circuit.

This is now described in the continuation of chap. xvii., so far as it is possible, conjecturally and by analogy from what goes before, to discriminate the ancient text from notes and additions.

From this continuation it appears that the sojourn with Tum is for the sun-god a mode of purification. The great hidden god takes away all his sins and makes him clean; in other words, by this return to his essence the sun-god perpetually renews his body and his purity or radiancy. He next proceeds onward in his path from Tum towards the blessed heavenly fields. He says, "I am a soul and its twins," or, "My soul is becoming two twins." This means that the soul of the sun-god is one, but, now that it is born again, it divides into two principal forms. Ra was worshipped at An under his two prominent mani-

[1] This heron appears to have derived its name from a word signifying "to be of the masculine gender," and is called also *bennu-cheper-tesef*, the self-begetting Bennu. Brugsch, Hier. dem. W. B., p. 397. If this be correct the symbolism may be different from that indicated in the text.

festations, as Tum the primal god, or more definitely, god of the sun at evening, and as Harmachis, god of the new sun, the sun at dawn.

The Ra worship of Heliopolis had a distinctly dualistic character. Upon two door-posts, which still remain there, Brugsch read on one side the praises of Tum, on the other a record of homage paid to Harmachis. The name of the sanctuary already referred to, Ha-ben-ben, the two pyramids, is likewise in close connection with this. Harmachis (Har-m-achu), usually, in the popular conception, the morning sun in contrast to Tum the evening sun, is "Horos on the horizon," or "Horos radiant," as his name imports, and therefore the sun-god as he appears shining in glory. His emblem, the sphinx with a lion's body and human head, is well known. It is the symbol of reasoning power,[1] of power enlightened and disciplined by reason.

As victor over the powers of darkness, the sun-god is next found crowned as a king. "It is I," thus he exclaims, "who have received the double crown with delight; it is I on whom the burden has been laid of ruling over the gods in the day when the world is set in order by the lord of the universe." Then, as ruling prince, as king of the day, he comes forth from the kingdom of darkness into that of light, and as god of the day he is likewise "he who exterminates plagues and rules the course of the seasons," and likewise, he appears to be "the divine beetle, the self-creating one, whose substance exists by itself."

The beetle (chepra, or choper) is a very common representation of Ra. In chap. xv. of the "Book of the Dead" he appears as king, with the full name of Ra Haremchu Chepra, and upon his head, which is adorned with the

---

[1] As the visible sun-god in general he is called *Har-m-achuti*, Horos of the two horizons, and this name is thus given to Tum also whenever he is thought of as the evening sun. See Brugsch, D. Aegypt. Gräberwelt, p. 35, in the hymns quoted there.

double crown, he has the goddess Neb-un, mistress of being, that is, the divine ureus-adder, the symbol of sovereignty. There, too (xv. 19, 20), he is a god both beneficent and dreaded—beneficent towards the good, dreaded by the wicked; for he is the righteous one, and he passes through the heaven along with Ma, the goddess of righteousness.

We must, however, guard very carefully against taking Ra as being simply the sun. It appears from the hymns addressed to Ra, included in chap. xv. of the "Book of the Dead," that at the most remote period it was already usual to distinguish betwixt the god and the manifestations of him. In that chapter he is seemingly identified with the sun; his splendid rising, for example, is referred to; but, in point of fact, a careful distinction was made between the being who was an object of worship and his visible representation. The sun's disk was called "his," "his emblem." He journeys *in* his disk, and is designated as the ancient unknown one in his mystery (xv. 46). Even when men look at him, what they behold is nothing more than the reflected rays of his glory; even before men's eyes he still walks in his mystery. That there existed a full conviction of the unity of the deity, even when he was called by various names, is proved by collective names, such as Ra-haremchu-chepra, and other similar ones. This is, at least in Egypt, no new doctrine resulting from later theological speculations. It is found occurring on the very oldest monuments. Indeed, the position that fetishism and the worship of natural objects and phenomena as such is nothing but the vulgar corruption of an originally much purer religion, nowhere appears to receive more striking confirmation than in these ancient Egyptian records. But although the facts on which this argument is founded are correctly interpreted, and the Egyptian religion at its first appearance is already far above animism proper, I cannot agree in the inference. It is indeed the case that the most ancient

Egyptian religion, so far as it is known to us, is at least simpler than it was in later times. We should, however, infer too much if we on that ground came to the conclusion that the worship of natural objects as living beings, through whose power natural phenomena are produced, is a corruption. Such worship is in all cases the original form, and it must also be the ground from which the Egyptian religion originally sprang. It is already a symbolic religion, as far back as we know it, but the symbols are all reformed fetishes. The degeneration which may be perceived in the Egyptian religion is a retrogression to the earlier standpoint, a revival of what seemed dead long ago, just what may be observed in all the higher religions.[1]

To give an idea of the worship of Ra, I quote here from the hymns in chap. xv. of the "Book of the Dead," according to the arrangement of Lefébure and after his translation:[2]—

"Hail, thou who art come as Tum, and who hast been the creator of the gods!"[3]

"Hail, thou who art come as soul of the holy souls in Amenti!"

"Hail, supreme among the gods, who by thy beauties dost illumine the kingdom of the dead!"

"Hail, thou who comest in radiance and travellest in thy disk!"

"Hail, greatest of all the gods, bearing rule in the highest, reigning in the nethermost heaven!"

---

[1] See my Outlines of the History of Religion, p. 8 et seq.

[2] E. Lefébure, Traduction comparée des hymnes au soleil composant le xv⁰ chapitre du Rit. fun. Ég., p. 123 et seq. Lefébure divides the lines 29-33 into couplets, and arranges together the five first and the five last halves. His important work has also been made use of in reference to the immediately preceding part of the text.

[3] So Lefébure. Birch (in Bunsen, Egypt's Place, pt. v. p. 170) translates "*created by the creator of the gods.*" Lefébure's translation is to be preferred. In other passages Tum occurs constantly as the creator. Comp. "Book of the Dead," i. 17, var., cited by Brugsch, Wörterbuch, voce *Kema*. Likewise "Book of the Dead," lxxix., at the beginning where it is said: "Maker of the heaven, creator of the beings produced out of the world, who makes all kinds (sorts) of forms of existence, calls the gods into life, creates himself lord of life, who fills the gods with fulness of life."

"Hail, thou who dost penetrate within the nethermost heaven (tiau), and hast command of all the gates!
"Hail, among the gods, weigher of words in the kingdom of the dead (chernuter)!
"Hail! thou art in thine abode (nest) creator of the nethermost heaven by thy virtue!
"Hail, renowned and glorified god! Thy enemies fall upon their scaffold!
"Hail! thou hast slain the guilty, thou hast destroyed Apap (the serpent of darkness)!"

It is impossible to read this song of praise in any degree attentively without seeing, what also results from all our former statements, that Ra-Tum and Osiris are not really different, and that the Heliopolitan mythology is, in fact, the same as that of Abydos. And naturally so, for, as we saw, the Osirian myth, too, was originally a sun-myth. Perhaps it was only at a later period that it was associated at Heliopolis with eschatological doctrine through being commingled with the southern myth, and in that city it may originally have had a more cosmogonic character, as among the Asiatic Mesopotamians.

The two remaining chief gods of Heliopolis whom I cannot leave unmentioned are Shu and Tefnut, and they too are cosmogonic beings. They are the two lion-gods of whom it is said in the "Book of the Dead," chap. iii., that they light Tum as he comes out from his place in the heavenly ocean. An invocation in chap. xvii. is thus translated by De Rougé, "O Ra in his egg, who shines through his disk, who glitters on the horizon, who . . . . hast an abhorrence of remaining stationary, who walkest on the supports of the god Shu! Thou who hast not thy second among the gods, who brings forth the wind by the fire of his mouth, and who lights up the two worlds by his brightness." That this last phrase applies to Shu and not Ra is evident from a passage at the commencement of chap. lv., where it is said, "I am Shu who, in advance of the light, drives or compels the winds onwards to the confines of heaven, to the confines of the earth, even to the confines of space." This has the same signification as the image elsewhere employed where the dogs, symbolical of the winds, follow him swiftly.

Shu is the cosmic heat and light principle, the world-egg within which Ra is said to be,[1] and hence he is likewise called the abode of the sun. This is expressed symbolically by saying that he is found in the centre of the bark of the sun (hur sek ti). This centre point is regarded as the quickening creative power. In other not less important texts he is without doubt the god of the air, the atmosphere, and as such he is depicted as supporting the heavens, a form mentioned below. He is also ("Book of the Dead," lxvii.) he who opens the gate, the gate leading to the place where the bark of the sun is. For this reason he, like all the gods of Heliopolis, is moreover the son of Ra begotten by Tum, but born in fact without a mother, for it is said of him that he begot himself in the womb of the goddess of heaven. He is the lord who came forth alone from the heavenly sea, Nun, over which in the beginning the quickening breath of the deity passed.[2] As the principle of creation he is uncreated; with the beginning of his existence the sun began to exist. He is the life-giver, and like all the gods that are to be taken as representing the first cause, has the marvellous designation bestowed on him of young-old, an expression by which the Egyptians sought to indicate eternal youth. It is easy to understand why he was identified with the goddesses Oer Hakau and Ma, the Great Power and Righteousness, for he is distinctively power which manifests itself by operating in matter. By him righteousness and truth reign; in short, by him, Order, of which Ma is the personification, reigns in the creation. The root whence his name is derived has a twofold signification, first that of scorching, and secondly that of stretch-

[1] Chabas, Pap. Mag. Harris, p. 96.   [2] Pap. Mag. Harris, 23, 53, 54.

ing out, growing. Both of these correspond to his nature: as the vital glowing heat of the universe he is the scorching one, and he is the outstretcher in virtue of his being the one who lights up the vault of heaven and "divides the waters which are under from those which are above the firmament."[1] In the latter office he is depicted as a man who with uplifted arms supports the vault of heaven in the shape of a woman bending forward and supporting herself on her hands and feet, and this symbol forms the determinative emblem of the root of *Shu*. Hence it is that Ra the sun-god goes on his props, for in the symbolic representation, this deity travels along the back of the goddess of heaven. ("Book of the Dead," xvii. 24, and 34 glosses.)

That, seemingly at a later period, Shu was united with Ra, and thus made like most other Egyptian chief gods into a sun-god is natural enough, for the germ of the world-egg is in fact the sun. He thus became, as the god of the scorching sun-heat, as the dread sun-god, most closely related to Set; and the ass, the animal of Set, which is also called *Shu*, appears to have belonged to him as well.[2] In the mystic language of the Egyptians this is expressed as follows :—" Shu has fused himself into the substance of his father Ra, whose enemies he seeks to destroy," or " the Self (*Ka*) of Shu unites itself with that of Ra;" in other words, Ra, as destroyer of evil powers, as the dreadful god is endued with the character of Shu. He wears then the form assumed by Ra the chastiser, that of a male cat. For the same reason he is identified with Horos-tem, Horos of the sword, and is represented not only as a war-

---

[1] Book of the Dead, xcviii. The deceased as he reaches from earth to heaven compares himself to Shu.

[2] A play upon words such as this is very common in Egyptian symbolism. Thus Shu is also called *Kai-Shu-ti*, " who erects two feathers ;" Shu also signifying feather. It is now scarcely possible to say whether some real attribute of the god is indicated by this name, or whether it is a mere play on the sounds of words. The two feathers are a common ornament of reigning gods. The name Kai-Shu-ti may perhaps have some connection with that of the mysterious deity Kai, who so early as the sixth dynasty was placed at the head of the gods.

god with lance and horns, but likewise as chastiser of the wicked in the under world ("Book of the Dead," xc.)

The wife of Shu is Tefnut or Tef. By her he effects the birth of all things. Like him, she is generally depicted as a lioness or as a cat, a form very common with the goddesses of northern Egypt. These facts lead us to infer that she too was a nature power. Her name, signifying "humidity, foam," also bears witness that this must have been her original character. She is the ocean out of which all that is came into being, personified as a living divine being. She is the cosmic water, or more precisely, the foam that has risen on its surface through the agitating motive power of the glowing Shu, whose breath the winds are. Like her the Aphrodite-Astarte of the Cretans was born of the foam of the sea. Tefnut, however, usually appears in a form that would lead us to a totally different conception of her nature. This is the ureus-adder, the symbol of regal power on the heads of princes and gods, and the common emblem of all female deities. Thus Shu is said to have his wife as protectress upon his head,[1] which can refer to nothing but this. In this instance, however, Shu is already identified with the sun, for in his usual character he wears only an ostrich feather on his head. Tefnut is likewise usually called "the only one upon the head of her father," that is, of Ra the sun-god as creator. On the surface there seems to be no connection between these two representations of Tefnut. The ureus on the head of the sun-god is emblematic of light. Whether it occurs as the goddess Neb-un, the mistress of being, or as Neb-anch, the mistress of life, or as Sechet, it denotes always "the sparkling," or "the sun's disk in his wrath," and is thus a personification of the scorching glow of the sun.[2] The serpent was emblematic of the moist warmth as well as of the withering

---

[1] See Pap. Mag. Harris, p. 24.
[2] Lefébure, chap. xv. du Riteul, pp. 28, 29. A very apt comparison is made by this scholar between the Egyptian deity referred to here and the Hebrew *serafs*, whose name signifies "the consuming ones."

heat of fire or the burning rays of the sun. Tefnut is accordingly the feminine aspect of Shu, the god of heat and light, and hence unites in herself both attributes. As wife of Shu the germ of creation, she is the foaming water; as wife of Shu the scorcher, she is the enraged puffed-up adder whose sting is deadly. Thus she is the productive and destructive power of nature combined in one being. As *tef* means also "to vomit," she is not unfrequently pictured as a lioness vomiting flames.

Such are the principal gods of Heliopolis called by the Egyptians the "lords of An." They present to us an aspect slightly different from that of the gods of Thinis. Their character of nature-gods comes indeed a little less clearly into view with the gods of this circle than with those of the Osirian circle. The myth of Heliopolis represents the conflict between light and darkness, but in it Ra himself takes more the part of a king, general of his army: the warrior-god in the strict sense of the word is a Horos of a lower rank. At the time of the commencement of the new year, the combat has come to an end, and Apap pierced through is thrown down into the sea. This victory is, however, neither decisive nor final; the conflict begins again without ceasing. Every morning, even when Ra is mounting into his bark, Apap makes an attempt to stop him, but in vain. Four times a year the opposition of the demon of darkness is made with redoubled energy, and Apap contests the right of Ra to be king, but on each occasion is victoriously repulsed.

It would be a mistake to see here nothing but a poetic representation of the conflict between light and darkness in nature. What we have here was at the first an article of faith among the peoples of antiquity. They did not know with scientific certainty that every day darkness must give way to light, that the apparent course of the stars is subject to fixed laws and to annual revolutions. The life of the sun, renewed each morning, was in their eyes a miracle, a result of the superior power of the gods of light. And although the phenomenon was daily renewed throughout the course of innumerable centuries, its permanence was not believed in or relied on, except by virtue of an act of faith, of which the myths are the expression, the dogmas.

From remote antiquity the myth of Ra was associated with the hope of immortality by resurrection, an idea which is moreover found attached to similar myths in other mythologies, as for example to those of the Hindoo mythology. Chapter xvii. of the " Book of the Dead," one of the most ancient texts known, furnishes proof of this. According to chap. cviii. 11, of the same book, the deceased will know the mysterious force by which the power of Apap is broken. The good and the wicked in this world and in the other are divided into two hostile camps, the soldiers of one fighting under the leadership of Ra, those of the other placing themselves under the orders of Apap. Hence the significance of the myth was not exclusively physical, for with ancient peoples, physical order and moral order are not clearly distinguished. While light and darkness were thus with the Egyptians not purely symbols, they were nevertheless used by them, as they are by us, as synonyms for good and evil.

CHAPTER V.

RELIGION UNDER THE OLD KINGDOM.

THE seat of what has been called the Old Kingdom of Egypt was Memphis. This town (Mennefer, the good abode) is traditionally said to have been founded, or at least extended and fortified, by Menes—that is to say, by the ancient dynasty of which this name is the personification—with the view of holding the barbarians of the north in check. The god of Memphis was Ptah, or, as it was pronounced there, Phtah, and hence the town is designated likewise Ha Ka Ptah, the place of the worship, or of the soul of Ptah. There is reason to suppose that a deity of this name was already worshipped in that district before the Thinitic kings made it their seat, but from that time forward this god occupied a high place in the Egyptian religion. It may be regarded as certain that the predecessors of Menes already exercised a general authority over Upper Egypt, before they were in a position to unite both lands under one sceptre. Hence, no doubt, the religion of their seat, Thinis-Abydos, became the prevailing one in the south. In the north, Heliopolis, with its essentially similar theology, was from time immemorial renowned for its antiquity, and for the learning of its priests. But now the day of Memphis had come. Heliopolis was, indeed, not cast into the shade altogether. The monuments show that the Thinitic kings brought their own Osiris worship thither as well as to Memphis, but they would never have ventured to pass over the principal deity of the new locality in which they had established themselves, nor to deny him the highest honours there.

Accordingly, a tradition which is to be depended on informs us that Menes was likewise founder of the magnificent temple at Heliopolis dedicated to Ptah. This temple was situated on the white or southern wall, a structure which, like the northern wall, under the patronage of the goddess Neith, was, it would seem, a fortification not unlike the wall of China, and had been erected with the same object. Ptah was hence often called "the holy one of the white wall," or, simply "Ptah of his southern wall." As at Heliopolis, the kings were consecrated, and the festival of the union of the two countries was celebrated in his sanctuary and under his patronage. We may, at least, take it for granted that so early as the founding of Memphis this festival was already instituted, though we have no account of its celebration previous to the time of Pepi of the sixth dynasty. It is strange to find Ptah often entitled bearer of the white crown, the crown of Upper Egypt, and I can only explain this as having come about through his identification with Osiris-Sekru.

It has been remarked that a more spiritual and more moral significance has been attributed to Ptah than to the other gods. If there be any truth in this, he must have gained it by means of the priests, for originally he was, like so many others, a cosmogonic deity. The signification of his name is, "he who forms," not, as is constantly asserted, "he who opens."[1] In accordance with this is a delineation of him, in which he is represented as busily engaged in drawing a child."[2] Accordingly, the Greeks compared him rightly to their Hephaistos, the god of the cosmic fire, as creative formative power. One of Ptah's usual names is Totunen, or Tanen, which, it is thought, denotes likewise "he who forms," though, in the opinion of some, it means the earth.[3] It is certain that Tanen

---

[1] From *patahu* = to form, of which the derivative signification must be "to model," and not from *pathu* = to open. Brugsch, W.B., p. 527 *et seq.*

[2] In Wilkinson, M. & C. ii. i. 249.

[3] So Lefébure, chap. xv. du Rituel, p. 95.

also occurs as a surname of other gods, as well as alone by itself. Ptah, as god of the hidden fire operating in the world, may very well be called god of the earth, and the green colour given to him on the monuments favours this explanation. Sometimes it is said that he is invisible. Every deity came into being after him, the great hidden one, and his image is not known. He is hence represented emblematically as a mummy concealed in its chest.[1]

In his character of "he who forms," he bestows new flesh and new limbs on the deceased;[2] as creator of the world he establishes all that is born, procreates and makes all things that are. The gods are said to have come out of his mouth, men from his eye. If I rightly understand this metaphor, it signifies that he quickened into life the higher world, the world of gods, or, as it is otherwise expressed, all that is made, by his word, but that he created men by means of his eye, the sun. Horos-Ra was usually looked upon as being the creator of men *par excellence*, that is, of true Egyptians. We encounter here the same intermixture of purer and more sensuous representation that is found in all myths of creation, even in those of the Hebrews. Side by side with expressions such as "thy spirit is to be revered for its creations," are found others grossly materialistic, like "with thy hands thou hast set in order created things in the heavenly ocean." The appellations of Life-giver and Creator of phenomenal forms which he bears belong likewise to the same set of ideas.

It is difficult to decide whether all these attributes were, from the remotest antiquity, ascribed to Ptah, and whether, as was afterwards the case, he was then placed on an equality with the supreme deity, the first created or uncreated, who brought himself forth and formed his own members; and whether, at a period so early, he was con-

---

[1] For this and the following passage compare Pleyte, Een lofsang aan Ptah, an article from De Evangeliespiegel, printed separately.
[2] Pap. Mag. Harris, p. 25.

ceived of as god of the under-world, who reveals himself in things visible. This is not impossible. The most ancient portions of the "Book of the Dead" contain ideas in harmony with this, and it is quite conceivable that the priests of Memphis, even at an early period, transferred these to their god. In the earliest times, however, he certainly was not yet connected with the sun, as he came to be in more recent times to which we must apparently relegate the epithets of "Lord of the long times," "The honourable, golden, beautiful, and of comely face," that are bestowed upon him in the time of the nineteenth and twentieth dynasties. The appellations, however, which mark him as god of order and righteousness, and likewise of truth, are undoubtedly ancient and primitive. He is lord of the ell (*ma*) that serves to secure *suum cuique*, and the high value of which must have been especially felt in a land like Egypt, where every year the inundations obliterated the boundary-marks between the fields. He is always very closely connected with Ma, goddess of righteousness and truth, whose name is the same as that of the ell, and derived from the same root, and he wears her emblem on his head.[1]

As the invisible shaper of the universe he is necessarily, in virtue of his office, endued with the dignity of god of justice; and when we find it said of him in later times that he is come to give beneficent laws to men,[2] or that he is the holy god who loves good, and establishes thereupon his mighty supremacy,[3] we can see that these are ideas that have been logically evolved from the main conception.

The relationship between the Egyptian Ptah-worship and the Patek-worship of the Phœnicians was long ago recognised, so that, in later times at least, the two were confounded with each other. This is seen, for instance, in

---

[1] As lord of things that are true and righteous, he is, like Thot, invoked by any one who desires to justify himself. See Lepsius, Zeits., 1868, p. 2.

[2] Inscription at Sararieh, near Memphis, cited by Brugsch, Reiseberichte, p. 87.

[3] See Pleyte, *op cit. ad sup.*

a passage of Herodotus (iii. 36), where the Greek historian tells how Cambyses paid a visit to the temple of Hephaistos at Memphis, with the intention of seeing the image of the god. By Hephaistos, Ptah is undoubtedly meant. And what kind of image did he then see? It was, says Herodotus, like the Pateks which the Phœnicians carve upon the prow of their ships; it was, that is to say, in the form of a dwarf.

In this Herodotus was quite correctly informed. The name of the Pateks and that of Ptah are the same. Genuine Egyptian images of the latter are found likewise in the form of a dwarf, a form in which other gods of Egypt are likewise not unusually found. It is significant too, that the so-called Tyrian camp, the Phœnician quarter at Memphis, was just over against the very south wall on which the temple of Ptah was erected.

Was Ptah-worship, then, a Phœnician cult adopted by the Egyptians? That idea has been entertained, but it is assuredly erroneous; for long before the Phœnicians inhabited Egypt, perhaps even before they had left their original home in Mesopotamia, Ptah was worshipped at Memphis. The case is as follows: The Egyptians often celebrate the beauty of the countenance of Ptah, and represent him as a youth; but the antiquity of this mode of representation is not proved, and the idea may well have resulted from his being confounded with the sun-god. It is, at all events, not the only conception that was formed of him. The Kabirs, the eight brother-gods of the Phœnicians, who likewise had their temple at Memphis, and who are the same as the Pateks, are called by Herodotus the children of Ptah. The Egyptians, however, mention only one son of Ptah—Imhotep, that is, "I come in peace,"[1] the final peace, namely, of the justified; or, perhaps, "I come with an offering." He is a personification of the sacrificial fire, and of the worship regulated by the sacred book (hib), and

---

[1] E. de Rongé, in the Rev. Arch., 1861, iv. 202, considers this a more correct interpretation than the alternative one.

he is always represented with this book upon his knees, and the texts designate him as the first of the Cher-hib, a class of priests who were at the same time choristers and physicians, for the sacred hymns were believed to have a magical power as remedies. This god is shown by a king's name of the fourth dynasty to have been worshipped in Egypt at a very early period, though his worship does not seem ever to have taken a prominent place. The Greeks call him Asklepios, but likewise the Eighth, thus showing that they regarded him as one of the Kabirs. These eight brother gods are the same as the companions of the architect Chnum, but are to be distinguished from the eight companions of Thot, who apparently represent the four cardinal points. There is no doubt that the worship of Ptah as god of plastic fire, and of the eight brothers who, in the character of cosmic deities, were represented in the form of dwarfs, flourished at a very remote period in the country where Memphis was founded by Mena. The Thinitic kings allowed this worship to remain undisturbed, and, at least at Memphis, certainly did not make much alteration in its form. But while this was so, there arose a more purely Egyptian conception, giving to the god a human form, and making of him, along with the northern goddess Sechet, or along with Ma and with Imhotep, who is nothing else than a fiction of the priests, one of those triads that are so favourite a form in Egyptian theology.[1] The Phœnicians adopted the ancient unreformed Ptah worship, either because in their own mythology they already had something similar, or for other reasons.

Along with Ptah, the two goddesses Sechet (Bast) and Neith filled a prominent place in Lower Egypt even in very ancient times. Both are frequently mentioned under the first dynasties, and at Memphis temples were dedi-

---

[1] Lepsius thinks that Ptah, as the more spiritual deity, should be distinguished from Ra, the more physical, *Aelt. Götterkreis*, p. 40. If this be right, it is true of this particular form of Ptah only.

cated to both, as being deities of importance in the north. The priesthood of Neith was, like that of Hathor, exercised by princesses of the blood-royal, the same person being generally priestess for both goddesses. The chief seat of the worship of Neith was Saïs, and she appears to have been especially revered by the Libyan portion of the inhabitants of Lower Egypt.[1] Sechet was the favourite goddess of the Aamu or Arab tribes, and was worshipped most of all at Bubastis, under the name of Bast. She was even looked upon as the wife, or the specially beloved (*aa meri*) of Ptah. Reference will be made further on to both goddesses.

Sekru (the slain, the killed ?), whose name occurs in the most remote antiquity, may very probably have been a form of Ptah as god of the under world. He was afterwards associated with Ptah and Osiris as Ptah-Sokar-Osiris (Ptah-sekru-asar), yet he was worshipped at Memphis as a separate deity. Besides him, we also find mentioned, under the old kingdom, Chnum, the god of the waterfalls, whence, even at that early period, stones were conveyed for the colossal buildings of the Memphitic kings. Munt, the god of Hermonthis, with whom we shall meet further on, is also supposed to be mentioned as of this period.

If Herodotus is to be trusted, an important modification of Egyptian worship took place under the second dynasty, for he relates how at that time, under King Kaiechos (Kakau), the sacred animals were first worshipped. How extensively this worship was destined to prevail is well known. The very name of Kakau (the images or genii, a word of which the bull is the symbol, and with which it is synonymous) tends to confirm this assertion. It was, in fact, the name given to the bull Apis.

The name, however, of Menes, Mena, suggesting Mnevis, the white or fawn-coloured bull of Heliopolis, would lead

---

[1] Does the symbol that accompanies the Aamu under Abisa, sculptured on the tomb of Chnumhotep, and which coincides with the hieroglyph of Neith, refer to the worship of this deity by that tribe ?

us to suppose that the worship of animals was already practised before the time of Kakau, and that what he introduced was nothing more than the worship of Apis. Binothris (Binuter, a divine spirit whose symbol is a ram or he-goat) comes in the list of kings after Kaiechos (Kakau), whence it may be inferred that just as the latter raised the worship of the bull of Memphis to the rank of a state religion, so his successor gave the same position to the ram of Mendes. At all events, we must not come to the conclusion that these princes themselves instituted the worship of animals. No king, however powerful, would be able to impose customs such as these, had they not been already deeply rooted in the national habits. Kaiechos and Binothris doubtless did no more than grant their royal sanction to these forms of religion which already were popular. The whole tale has, moreover, an extremely unreliable look. Mena, Kakau, Binuter, are, in my opinion, mere inventions as kings' names. In reality, they are the principal animals, symbols of genii and spirits of gods that have been transmuted into kings. In all the peoples of antiquity there is visible a tendency to incorporate mythological tales by degrees into their history. This process has been raised to the dignity of a theory by Euhemerus, but it is not a mere invention of his. In virtue of it, no sooner were the symbolical animals we refer to looked upon as kings than the opinion began to prevail that one of these had introduced the worship of animals into Egypt. The he-goat and the ram are emblems of reproductive power, and are symbolical of God the creator. Chnum, too, wears rams' horns as his head-dress, and represents, as is well known, the creator as the sun who produces the wind, or the spirit breathing on the cosmic waters in order to fertilise them.

Animal worship soon became very general throughout Egypt. In later times no place of any importance in the country was without its sacred animal, which was treated with all reverence, was fed and cared for, and after death was carefully embalmed and entombed. At Hermopolis (Sesennu, Ashmunein), the town of Thot, the ibis, his animal, was held sacred, and, considering the great homage paid to this god of the priests, it is not to be wondered at that ibis mummies have been discovered both at Memphis and Thebes, the seats of empire, and at Abydos, the town sacred to the dead. In the same way the dog-headed ape (kynokephalos), the symbolic animal of the eight companions of Thot, was held sacred at Hermopolis and Thebes. Where the worship of Anubis prevailed—as, for instance, at Kynopolis—jackal mummies are found, and at Butos those of mice and sparrow-hawks, symbols of the goddess and of the god (Horos) revered in that locality. Considering the wide spread of the worship of Horos, sparrow-hawk bodies are, as a matter of course, found in other places also. To the cat, the animal of Sechet and Bast, of Tefnut and Ra, especial sacredness was ascribed. The story of Diodorus is well known. A Roman soldier at Alexandria, having unfortunately killed a cat, was murdered by the furious populace, in spite of the efforts of the king to rescue him. The sacred animal of the Thebaid was the ram; that of Eileithyia the vulture; of Herakleopolis the ichneumon; of Lykopolis or Sioot, the wolf. Where Set was worshipped, there the hippopotamus was likewise revered; and in the various places where Sebak, the crocodile-headed god, had temples, as at Ombos and at Krokodilopolis on the lake of Moeris, in the Fayoom, homage was paid to the crocodile. Herodotus tells how, in the last-mentioned place, this animal was adorned with crystal and gold ear-rings and rings on its fore feet, how it was fed with meal and with sacrificial flesh, and how at its death, after being carefully embalmed, it was entombed in a sacred sarcophagus. Everywhere else, he remarks, the crocodile is hunted and killed, which must have been especially the case at Edfu and Dendera, but here he is preserved. Indeed, from what Strabo tells us, we may believe that the animals, through this constant attention, became quite tame. He himself was a witness of how the crocodile was fed by placing within his mouth the sacrificial offerings, which he appears to have swallowed down with an air of calm resignation.[1]

The most important worship of this kind was however in all periods that of the three animals before referred to, the Apis of Memphis, the Mnevis of Heliopolis, and the ram of Mendes, and especially of the first. That the two bulls were not rivals, or, to put it in another way, that the two were not symbols for the same thing, is evident from the fact that the same person could be simultaneously priest of Apis, Mnevis, and of a sacred heifer, the worship of which is several times mentioned in the time of the Old Kingdom.

It would even appear that Apis, before being conducted to his temple at Memphis, stayed first a considerable time, forty days, at Heliopolis. It is impossible to make out whether so early as under the first dynasties the four sacred bulls were worshipped, of which mention is made in the time of the Ptolemies, namely, besides the Hapi bull and Urmerti, which is Mnevis, two others of uncertain signification, Temur and Abekur. It is certain that so soon as under Chufu (Cheops) of the fourth dynasty, we read of a priest dedicated solely to the service of Apis, and besides, under Chafra we hear of a bull, Zasepf, "who appears at his hour," and of whom it is told naïvely enough that the favourite of the king Merisanch was priestess.[2]

Mena or Mnevis, as representing the again reviving sun, and being thus sacred to Ra-harmachis, was light-coloured, white or yellow. Hapi, on the contrary, as "the again reviving Ptah," and consequently a symbol of the unseen hidden god, was dark with white spots, which had to resemble the winged sun's disk, and the resemblance of a beetle, emblem of the creator, had, it was said, to

---

[1] See Duncker, Geschichte des Alterthums, i. 53 et seq.

[2] De Rougé, vi. prem. Dynasties, p. 59 et seq.

be under the tongue. The symbolism is evident enough. The god who by day reveals himself in the brilliant sunlight passes the night in the dark abyss; and, unseen, works on there as creator of himself and of all things: or, to translate from mythological to theological language, the Apis bull is the living image of the god who brings light out of darkness and life out of death. Hence he also carried a golden disk between his horns. Afterwards he was very naturally associated with Osiris and more particularly with Ptah-Sokar-Osiris. He may thus be more definitely described as an image of Ptah in his form of Sekru, and between Sekru and Osiris there was essentially no difference.[1] He is often called Son of Ptah, and this is to be understood in a literal sense, for the Apis was born in a supernatural manner. Ptah in the shape of a sacred flame, a heavenly ray of light, impregnated the specially selected cow, which remained nevertheless a virgin, and even after the birth of the divine son brought forth no second calf. Here we have a grossly sensuous form of that doctrine which the Egyptians and peoples kindred to them clothed in various forms, and which was destined to be transformed by the speculations of the early Christians into charming poetry. The birthday of the holy son of the god was celebrated at Memphis with great pomp and rejoicing. It was a time of salvation and peace on earth when even the beasts of prey harmed nobody. But the concern about the dead Apis was greater still. When he, to use the orthodox expression, united himself with Ptah in the house of times without end, to remain henceforth and for ever in the place of eternity, a great and general mourning took place, and the care bestowed on his corpse was not a whit less than beseemed a son of the deity. The service of the dead Apis seems however to have flourished only in later times. If not inaugurated under the eighteenth or

---

[1] Compare the name *Nefer-ka-sekru*, which *it is possible* to translate, good bull of Sekru, and which occurs so early as under the second dynasty. De Rougé, *Op. cit.*, p. 24.

nineteenth dynasties, it then at least soared to an extravagant pitch, and continued to rise until it reached its climax under the Ptolemies.

Many endeavours have been made to explain the animal worship of the Egyptians, which has always been regarded as quite an isolated phenomenon. Yet the matter is far simpler than has been supposed, and the phenomenon is by no means unique. All mythologies teem with animal symbolism, and examples of sacred animals revered while living are pretty numerous. Cows and oxen were worshipped not only in Egypt, but among the Romans also, and are still in the present day worshipped by the Hindoos. By Celts, Germans, and Slavs the horse was regarded as sacred, and a number of these animals were kept at their temple, and they adorned them exactly as the Egyptians used to adorn Sebak's crocodile. From 2 Kings xxiii. 11 we know of horses and chariots of the sun that were kept in the temple at Jerusalem, and from Herodot. i. 189 we likewise know of the four white Nisaæn steeds of the Persians, which had a similar significance. The Germans likewise preserved cats carefully, because they, as well as weasels, were animals skilled in magic. They also, like the Normans, made offerings to the wild birds, in order to induce them to spare the grain and the cattle. So too, in Holland, long ago the punishment of death was meted out to any one who killed one of the sacred swans kept at the expense of the State. Reverence for the stork, those at the Hague and others, springs from the same superstition. The geese of the Capitol, too, are famous all over the world. They were kept there as symbols of domesticity and fruitfulness in honour of Juno, a benefit which they requited by saving the city.

The worship of sacred animals has, however, in no case attained, in the religion of any civilised people known to us, a development so extensive as that we find among the Egyptians. In as far as we can judge of it—for as yet the monuments of the earlier centuries are few in number—

this form of worship became more prevalent rather than less so as time went on. Yet we must not infer that animal worship in Egypt was an innovation, and still less are we to regard it as progress onwards. The explanation of it lies in the tendency, usually denominated fetishistic, but more properly animistic, which led men to see in animals, distinguished for beauty or strength, or by the services they perform, or by the injury they do, or by their form, their colour, or by any other specialty, the incarnation of powerful spirits, whom it is good policy to worship in order that their anger may be averted or their favour gained. These ideas must likewise have prevailed among the Egyptians in the most remote antiquity, and this assertion will not appear so unaccountable if we accept what seems to be now established by significant traits connected with the ethnology and philology of the country; namely, that the colonists or conquerors who came from Asia, and who formed an aristocratic ruling class in Egypt, found in that country an African people whom they subdued, and with whom they became intermixed. In no other way could they so naturally have adopted ideas of the kind we refer to, for nowhere else does the worship of animals prevail so extensively as among African peoples.[1] A popular belief, so general and so deeply rooted, was destined, in one form or another, to take its place in the religion of the state, and that is what actually happened. It is in animism, therefore, that the origin of the worship of animals among the Egyptians is to be sought. It soon, however, became necessary to try to establish a harmony between it and the more elevated ideas that in process of time were attached to the chief gods. Several sacred animals were identified with these gods themselves, others became the living images of the

---

[1] Nor is this the only mark of a close affinity with the strictly African religions. Under the same head comes likewise the deification of the kings, the unity of kingly and priestly dignities, the general practice of circumcision, the mode of burying the dead, the use of a panther skin as a royal and priestly vestment, &c.

gods. Mysticism and symbolism were the bridge by means of which the passage was effected from a lower to a higher and purer religion. The worship of animals having once become naturalised in the official religion, and having, by the help of all sorts of mystic explanations, taken on a varnish of apparent profundity, the tendency to multiply symbols and allegories, and also the nature of the hieroglyphic mode of writing, led not only to the multiplication of the number of sacred animals, but also to an increase of zeal in cultivating this worship. Animals that had not hitherto been worshipped were elevated to the rank of sacred animals, because their names resembled those of the gods.[1]

No less characteristic of the Egyptian religion than the worship of the sacred animals is the deification of the kings. This, too, dates from the time of the Old Kingdom. Even at that early time their public worship was established. Chufu and Chafra, the two great kings of the fourth dynasty, appear to have inaugurated this custom officially; for although it is true that some of their predecessors, like Mena, Teta, and Snefru, were worshipped as gods, the last named at the mines of Sinai, it is uncertain whether the worship of them dates from their own times. Chufu (Cheops) was undoubtedly worshipped as a god under one of his immediate successors, and had a priest set apart for him, and the sons of Chafra exercised the office of the priesthood of their father. The same is told us of Ratutef, Menkaura (Mycerinus), Tatkara or Assa, Useskaf, Kaka (of the fifth dynasty, to be distinguished from Kakau of the second), after whom a domain was named "Invocation of the spirits of Kaka" (Kaka-uas-bin); and, in short, the same may be said of all the princes who were of the least consequence. Not

---

[1] I have given proofs of this assertion in an article in the Theolog. Tijdsch., 12th year, pp. 261 *et seq.*, to which I must refer here so as not to be obliged to go into these points at greater length. Comp. Pietschmann, Zeitsch. für Ethnologie, 1878, p. 153 *et seq.*

only were special sepulchral temples built beside their pyramids, but, while they still lived, sanctuaries were erected of which they themselves were the deities. This deification of men prevailed so extensively as to cast the worship of the gods into the shade, and so as to thrust some of them altogether into the background. Thus Una, a high state official under three kings of the fifth dynasty, declares that in the reign of Merenra, in connection with four work places, or levies arranged for vast works, he had built as many holy places, in order that the spirits of this king, the ever-living Merenra, might be invoked "more than all the gods."[1] This continued all through the centuries. The sanctuaries of the kings were upheld with a steadfastness exactly like that with which the service of the gods was maintained, and their priests succeeded each other in regular order. Under the twentieth dynasty, for example, we find, still firmly established, priests of Cheops, Cephren, and Rathoïses (Ratutef), of the fourth, and under the Ptolemies, a priest of Snefru of the third dynasty.

This worship of the kings was not instituted by the state; it was not an official worship contrived by despotic power in order to lend a greater sanctity to the office of king, but with the Egyptians it was an article of faith, as is visible in everything. The Egyptian religion was the first civilised expression of a faith in the unlimited sovereignty of the deity. The king—it is an application of the very same principle from which the worship of animals proceeded—the king was much more emphatically than the sacred animal the son of God, of the living God, the incarnation of the divine being on earth. Thus, some centuries later, a servant of Amenemha I. and Usertasen I., by name Sancha, who had fallen into disgrace with them, speaks as follows in his autobiography,[2] referring to the king: "Let god be gracious to him whom he has removed, whom he has banished to another land;

[1] See De Rougé, op. cit., p. 143.
[2] Goodwin, The Story of Sancha: Lond. and Edin., 1866.

let him be mild as Ra." Having obtained permission to return, he is almost mad with joy. He falls on his face as if in adoration before the majesty of the king. He cannot believe it is true. "The great god, the equal of the sun-god, mocks me!" he exclaims; "thy majesty is as Horos, the power of thy arm extends over all lands." "I live," he testifies afterwards, "by the breath which thou givest; I love Ra Horos fondly, the image of thy noble shape." Admitted to the royal presence, he is elated beyond measure. Again he falls upon his face. "The god," so he relates, "spoke amicably to me. I was like one brought out of the darkness into the light. My tongue was dumb, my limbs refused their office, my heart was no longer in my body, so that I knew not whether I lived or if I was dead." Deification of humanity can go no further.

The worship of the kings was hence only a consequence of the way in which they were looked upon by the people, whose view, again, may easily be explained from the character of the Egyptian religion. As every good man at his death became Osiris, as every one in danger or need could by the use of magic sentences assume the form of a deity, it is quite comprehensible how the king, not only after death, but already during his life, was placed on a level with the deity. The kings, in fact, sat on the throne of Horos, of Tum, nay, they were themselves the living Horos, sons of Ra the creator, revelations of and substitutes for the gods on earth. Just as their servants took their names with some addition or modification, so they took those of the gods with or without addition. Between a conception such as this and distinct worship there is but one step.

In this apotheosis of the kings, the inclination of the Egyptian people to materialise everything is once more strongly manifested. What took place with the worship of animals happened in this case also. The mythology presented the gods symbolically under the form of animals, and this was represented to the senses in the worship of animals. The theology or doctrine of the state, if it be permissible to speak of such a thing as existing among the Egyptians, made the kings into substitutes of the deity, and thus invested them with a divine character. This was represented to the senses in the worship of their persons. The doctrine was called in question by nobody, nor did any one take offence at its practical application. The people believed in it quite as firmly as the kings, who did not feel themselves overwhelmed by the homage paid to them, but received, on the contrary, with perfect complacency, the incense which was burned before them by their worshippers.

Another reason for the worship of kings was the idea which the Egyptians had of the state. The state was for them still a pure theocracy, and corresponded in that respect closely to that of China. As in China, the emperor alone, as son of heaven, offers sacrifice to the supreme deity, so in Egypt the temples were properly nothing but the houses of prayer for the kings, into which it was lawful for none but them and the consecrated priests to enter. The idea of theocracy that prevails among all the Mesopotamian peoples, including the Asiatics, was deeply rooted among the Egyptians. Religion and state were with them not united, they were actually one. There is no distinction between the two. God rules, the king is his son, that is to say, is God himself, his incarnation. His rule is therefore wholly absolute. This is the period when the true unadulterated *droit divin* held sway, as yet undiluted by any rationalistic speculation. In Egypt no restraints, not even the slightest, existed to fetter absolutism. There was nothing, for instance, like the prophetic schools of Israel and seers controlling God's anointed by the word of God. It seems to have been impossible in the case of Israel to uphold in its full strength the fiction that the king is as the deity. By the idea of the covenant the Israelite theocracy became, so to speak, a constitutional government, and it preserved this character quite independently of the consideration whether god's vicegerent on earth were a king or a high priest, until at last it received from Jesus its spiritual completion, and an end was put to all fiction. But pure, absolutely sovereign, divine rule is to be found in Egypt in a greater degree than in Assur and Babel, or even China itself.

The complete identity of religion and state among the Egyptians comes out also in what we know of their priesthood. A few words may here be appropriately said on this subject. The various priestly orders were as innumerable as the temples and cults, and even were it possible to do so, it is not part of my plan to enumerate the designations of the priests of each particular deity. The same person, moreover, could act as priest to several, to as many as six or seven gods. The priestly names that occur oftenest are *ab*, the pure, *ak*, one who enters, *i.e.*, into the temple; *hon*, the servant or prophet, a title bestowed on both men and women. Priestesses were also called *chen*, helper, and *suau*, consecrated to the deity. Mention is also made of male and female choristers (*hes*).[1] The *sabu-n-per-aa*, magicians of the great house (pharao), appear to have been the king's special temple priests, but it is only in later times that they are heard of. The office of *sem*, the leader, the head one, is extremely ancient, and was filled by the priesthood of Ptah at Memphis. A panther's skin was the vesture of this office, and he who filled it wore, like the god himself, his hair arranged after the fashion of a youth with a lock or plait depending on one side of the head. This was one of the most honourable priestly dignities, and was oftenest held by princely personages, sometimes by the king himself. At a later period the high priests of Ptah found their rivals in

---

[1] Interesting information on the subject of the priestly offices will be found in an article by Jacques de Rougé, in the Rev. Archæol., 1865, i. 373 *et seq.*

"those who opened the gates of heaven in Apet," the high-priests of Thebes.¹ The chief priests of this order, but not all of them, were appointed by the king. Frequently the son succeeded the father, and the daughter the mother in the priestly office, though no fixed rule is observable, and there is, at least, in the Old and Middle Kingdom, no trace of hereditary succession or of caste. Oftenest it is the sons of kings, and seemingly heirs-apparent by preference, who fill the most important priestly offices; for instance, a son of Snefru was the Sem of Ptah, a post filled many centuries later by Chamûs the son of Ramses II. When men of ordinary descent were exalted to this lofty position, it was, in most cases, owing to their being married to princesses. The renowned Ti, who lived under the fourth dynasty, and whose tomb yields so rich a harvest to the antiquary, appears to have risen to his high spiritual dignities solely because his wife Neferhotep-s, who filled at the same time the offices of priestess of Hathor and of Neith, was a princess of the blood-royal. Chua, another *parvenu* of the time of the fifth dynasty, a courtier of Nefer-ka-ra, Ra-meri, and Mer-en-ra, gained the office of "head of all the dignities of religious affairs," seemingly a kind of high-priest's substituteship, solely because he was the king's father-in-law, and because his wife belonged to the royal family.² These personages, moreover, were not exclusively priests, but filled secular and even military offices as well as their spiritual ones. Ti, whom we have just referred to, was not only "commander of the holy prophets," *heb*, or soothsayer, "head of the secret of divine words," and "of the secret of the house of worship," "head of the offerings," and "of all purifications," and besides all this, special priest of Ra, and of one of the forms of Horos; but, while fulfilling the religious duties attached to these dignities, he still found time to fulfil the more secular ones of "one of the con-

¹ Jacques de Rougé, Rev. Archæol., 1865, ii. 328 *et seq.*
² E. de Rougé. VI. Dynasties, pp. 95, 97, 132.

fidants of the friendship of the king," "head of the gates of the palace," "private secretary of his master in all his residencies," "head of all the public works of the king," grand architect therefore; besides this he was "head of the royal scriptures," "secretary for all the decrees of the king," governor of various places, and, perhaps, over and above all this, master of the Royal Hunt. Chua combined with his high ecclesiastical office that of commandant of various towns and of commander of the grandees of the north and of the south of the kingdom.

When war seemed imminent the king himself commissioned all his servants, the priests as well as the others, to undertake the drilling of the soldiers, who were levied from all parts of the country.[1] In a word, the priestly offices were state functions, the highest, it may be, and the most honourable, but which did not differ at all in kind from that of commander of the troops, governor of a district, architect, and chamberlain. In fact, both kinds of office were, for the most part, filled by the same persons. This was the case in every period of Egyptian history. An inscription, discovered in one of the islands at the cataracts in Upper Egypt, mentions a certain Amenhotep seemingly of the time of the eighteenth dynasty, who was overseer of the bulls of Amun, royal scribe, and at the same time bowman of Upper and Lower Egypt, his majesty's stall-master, prince of Kush (Ethiopia), governor of the southern districts, and, to crown all, warrior and singer to the king.[2] If there existed a learned class (*cher-chetu*), entrusted with the preservation of the holy scriptures and magical books,[3] it was certainly not distinctly marked off. It could be spontaneously chosen, and, of course, only men of education could think of entering it; but in order to be

---

[1] E. de Rougé, VI. Dynasties, p. 128.

[2] Brugsch, Reiseberichte, p. 274. In the time of Nektanebos, the last Egyptian king, a district governor of Upper Egypt still discharged sacred offices in various temples, and is director of the treasury, priest of Ra and Horos. Brugsch, Recueil des Monuments, i. 10. Comp. Pl. VI.

[3] Chabas, Pap. Mag., Harris, p. 175.

qualified, it was not necessary that a man should belong to a particular tribe or to an exclusive caste. Various writings are in existence, drawn up by contented scribes, who, seeking to persuade others to follow their own example, dissuade them from the choice of a military career. Of these, an example is the famous Papyrus Anastasi I., which I do not, like the learned editor, consider a grave reality, but rather look upon it, with De Rougé and Brugsch, as a work of fiction. The only things binding upon those who had accepted the priestly dignity, and consequently on the kings, above all, were; first, the observance of special cleanliness, one means of attaining which was shaving the head bare, and a symbol of which was the white linen clothing, the only thing they were permitted to wear, besides the panther's skin, while discharging their functions; secondly, they were obliged to abstain from the use of certain kinds of food, especially from fish and beans.

Egyptian history, such as is confirmed by contemporary monuments, begins properly with Snefru and his two successors, Chufu and Chafra; but even at that period it is visibly inconsistent with the traditions that have come to us through the Greeks and even with those of Manetho. No princes ever displayed so much religious zeal as these three, and especially the latter two. Snefru was careful to see that the mining at Sinai for turquoise and copper was carried on under the guardianship of religion. Chufu and Chafra erected many monuments, and among them various temples. Yet Herodotus relates that they were extremely irreligious, that they shut up temples which were not again thrown open till the time of Mycerinus (Men-kau-ra), the king who came next or next again after them. According to him also, their memory was in all times execrated by the Egyptians. With the positive proofs of their works in honour of the gods before us, we should have been inclined simply to reject the tale of the historian, had it not been confirmed by a remarkable fact. The

magnificent statues of Chafra, made by his own order, and
which are excelled in beauty and artistic merit by Greek
workmanship alone, have been found lying shattered in a
well, into which they must have been violently thrown,
and where, as is indicated by sure signs, they have lain
since a very early time. It would hence appear that at
his death there must have occurred some outburst of
popular fury or of party hatred against him, which, however, must have been speedily appeased, for the cartouches
that bear the names of both kings are not, as is usual in
such cases, chiselled out, and the religious worship of their
persons by a special priesthood continued without interruption. What could have been the cause of this revolt?
The Egyptians could hardly have called kings godless who
devoted so much work and so many treasures to the gods.
Nor could they have been looked upon as sacrilegious who
restored the fallen temples in fresh splendour, and placed
the gods again on their forsaken seats. To account for it
by the pressure of the severe forced labour that must have
been exacted for the erection of buildings so colossal appears to me far too modern an explanation, and one little
in harmony with the spirit of the time and of the people.
The ancient Egyptians were no democrats, and nothing
seemed to them more natural than that the possessions
and persons of his subjects should be at the disposal of the
king their master. Men-kau-ra, too, and his successors,
though their pyramids are not so large as those of Chufu
and Chafra, walked in the footsteps of these, their predecessors, without hindrance. Dr. Max Büdinger[1] has, I
think, succeeded in solving one part of this difficult problem, by exposing the error into which Herodotus has
fallen through confounding the pious kings, founders of
the pyramids, with the Hyksos kings, who desecrated and
pillaged the temples, and by establishing the certainty
that the herdsman, Philetes or Silites, mentioned in the
same passage, can be no other than the shepherd king

[1] Zur Egyptischen Forschung Herodots., Vienna, 1873.

Salatis. This does not, however, explain the shattered statues, but only that since the religious worship of the two kings suffered no interruption during several centuries, this act of vandalism must certainly be attributed to hostile kings, perhaps to the Hyksos themselves.

The gods whose worship Snefru had transported to Sinai, were for the most part Upper Egyptian, Hathor, Thot, and one particular Horos, though in this last a local Horos must be recognised, a stellar deity who was already worshipped in that portion of Arabia. Divine homage was likewise paid there to Snefru himself. But Chufu went to a greater length. All the buildings founded by him, and among them the awe-inspiring pyramid at Gizeh, exceeding all the others in size, were, so far as we know, intended exclusively to glorify his own person, and the Osirian and Heliopolitan gods who were so closely akin to each other. The great sphinx erected by him is the image of Harmachis the visible sun-god, to whom likewise is dedicated the little temple between the fore feet of the monster. In the neighbourhood he founded or restored sanctuaries of Osiris and Isis which were still standing in the time of Psammeticus. If these were already in existence, and were only restored by him, as we are led to suppose from the contents of the inscription discovered there,[1] this shows that the temples of these gods had fallen to decay, and that he caused a revival of their worship. He is said to have restored the magnificent temple at Dendera, which in its present form was built in the time of the Ptolemies.[2] This temple was known to have been dedi-

---

[1] The inscription, as translated by E. de Rougé, runs thus:—" Invenit templum Isidis ; dedit sacrum prædium de novo ; reposuit deos in sede ejus." De Rougé, VI. Dynasties, pp. 46, 47. A restoration is here evidently hinted at.

[2] The inscription first brought to light by Duemichen is in his translation as follows :—" The laying of the foundation, the great of Dendera, a monumental restoration carried out by the King of Upper and Lower Egypt, lord of both lands (Ra-men-cheper), son of the sun, lord of diadems (Thut-mes), after it was discovered in ancient writings of the time of King (Chufu)." The parenthesis indicate the royal shields or cartouches.—Duem. Bauurkunde

cated to Hathor, who was originally a goddess of the south. So far as I know, there is an account of the founding of only one temple by Chafra, but in self-glorification he far excelled his predecessor. Although it is not unlikely, it cannot be shown with certainty that the pyramid betwixt that of Chufu and that of Menkaura, the second largest, is his. There is, however, no question that in the titles which he assumed, the apotheosis is far more strongly expressed than in the case of preceding kings. He calls himself "Horos, lord of the heart," or "commanding heart," "the good Horos, the great god," and he is the first who designates himself "son of the sun," "son of the creator (Se-Ra)." His wife, or favourite Merisanch, was curiously enough priestess of Horos and Thot, and of a certain bull, Zasapf, which seems to have been different from the Apis, although in the time of Chufu the worship of Apis was certainly carried on. One of his sons was appointed by him high priest of Thot at Hermopolis and priest of the king's own temple. We find in the reign of this king next to no trace of the worship of Ptah, the god to whom homage was paid at Memphis in order to conciliate the northern portion of the kingdom.

The worship of Ptah seems to have been restored by Ratutef (Rathoïses), and Menkaura (Mycerinus) was a zealous worshipper of this god, though at the same time he did not neglect the worship of Osiris. His successors followed in his steps, and the worship of Ptah seems even

v. Dend., p. 15. Another inscription referring to the restoration of the same temple by King Pepi of the sixth dynasty, seems to place the foundation at a time still further back. It runs thus:—"The account of the foundation of the great Denderah has been found in a writing inscribed on the skin of the . . . . beast at the time of the worshippers of Horos; it was found in the inside of a brick wall of the southern house in the time of King (Ra-meri), son of the sun (Pepi), &c."—Duem., *op. cit.*, p. 19. Since the worshippers of Horos are supposed to be anterior to Menes (Duemichen translates it, "successors of Horos," but with a point of interrogation), De Rougé conjectures that already in prehistoric times the temple was in existence. With Wiedemann I doubt whether the temple really existed before Thutmes-Ra-mencheper.

at last to have gradually cast into the shade that of Osiris, until once again in the great Merira Pepi of the sixth dynasty it found a valorous champion.

While we are speaking of the fourth dynasty whose most famous king, though called a desecrator of temples by posterity, nevertheless employed himself in zealously building and restoring them, it may not be amiss to say a few words about the Egyptian temples in general. The plan of this work does not allow of my giving a detailed or even a superficial sketch of them, I shall therefore merely notice a few points in regard to their arrangement. In details they often differed greatly from each other, but in a general way they may be described as being everywhere alike. That in the course of centuries no essential alteration was made on their plan is proved by the inscription in the temple of Denderah just referred to. From it we see that when restoring a sanctuary such as this, the Egyptians consulted carefully the old records and plans, in order of course that they might deviate from them as little as possible. The larger temple-buildings were usually placed within a walled-in space which enclosed the propylæa formed of sphinxes *couchant*, the sacred trees, and the fish-ponds. It was on these ponds that the mysteries of the journeys and conflicts of the gods on the heavenly ocean were acted, and they no doubt also served for the manifold lustrations. After entering the precincts and passing through between the rows of sphinxes a second portal was reached, flanked by gigantic pylons or side towers, upon which, in most cases, might be found sculptured and painted great feats of war or religious representations. Obelisks, gilt needles of stone, the symbolism of which belongs to solar worship, were very commonly found erected on opposite sides of this entrance, or further within the building, and statues of the kings were similarly placed.

On festal occasions, gay streamers floated from high masts that overtopped even the pillars. A lofty portal led next into a wide fore-court, open to the sky, but surrounded by a pillared corridor on three or four sides. After passing through one or more of these fore-courts a lesser enclosure was reached, the roof of which, higher in the middle than at the sides, was supported by pillars. This seems to have been a sort of fore-court for the priests, for immediately adjoining it was the holy of holies, which on three sides was surrounded by lesser halls and apartments, each one being set apart for some particular rite. Offerings of incense were presented on the left, substantial offerings on the right. The holy of holies was low, small, and mysterious. There stood the sacred ark, the emblem of the hidden deity. This was a sort of chest half covered over by a veil or curtain, and, like the sacred boat upon which it was placed, it was adorned with the symbols of life, endurance, light, and fertilising power. It ought apparently to be distinguished from the mystical chest, yet in many respects its signification is the same, and on days of festival it was carried round in procession outside the temple by a number of the priests. Often, winged figures are found upon it, recalling the cherubim of the Israelitish temple. Within the ark was the image of the deity, which no one had ever beheld, though other images of the gods were conspicuous in the temples, and were also carried round in processions. Processional voyages were often made on the river with the ark; thus, for instance, on the first of the month Pachons a great festival took place at Edfu, the town sacred to Horos in his form of winged sun's disk. On this occasion Hathor of Denderah came thence to Edfu in her sacred bark Neb-meri-t, or Peset-to-ti (*the mistress of love*, and *the illumination of the world*), and Horos went forth on his bark to meet her. Hathor stayed some days in the city of Horos, during which great feasts were celebrated in honour of both gods.[1]

Each Egyptian would seem to have had his own particular chapel where he performed his religious duties.

[1] See Jacques de Rougé, Rev. Archæol., 1865, ii. 208 *et seq.*

The temples themselves could be entered only by the kings and priests, but the fore-courts were probably open to the people. On all sides the walls were eloquent, covered as they were with images and hieroglyphs. Everything was arranged with the greatest splendour and expense, but everywhere there was a feeling of mystery, of impressiveness, of seriousness. The temples of Egypt were grand and awe-inspiring, rather than pleasant and alluring like those of Greece. They were built on a colossal scale, their style was severe, and light was sparingly admitted. In one word, they were in perfect keeping with the principal idea of the religion practised within them, and expressed, above all, the notions of durability, eternity, and the sacred mystery of the gods.

With the sixth dynasty we find some alterations again taking place in the state of religion. If, under the successors of Chafra, Ptah reassumed the rights of which he had been deprived through the preference given by this king and his predecessors to Osiris and Ra-worship, rights he was destined not again to lose, it was now the turn of Osiris, whose worship had certainly for a time been neglected, to raise his head. The sixth dynasty is usually called a Memphitic one, and it really appears to have had its seat in the city of Ptah, yet with at least as good a right as the two first dynasties it might be called Thinitic, for with Teta, the first king of this dynasty, the centre of gravity of the kingdom seems to have shifted from the Heptanomis to the Thebaid, from Memphis to Abydos. The tombs of Gizeh and Sakkarah are now sealed up, those of Abydos are laid open.

The great man of the sixth dynasty, whose prolonged reign has left behind various memorials, is Pepi Merira, the successor of Teta. The monuments bear witness to the extent of his territory. Inscriptions cut by his orders are found at Tanis, a town situated on the eastern branch of the Nile, and even at this early period a place of importance, though it was at a later period that it was destined to play a more prominent part. But in the east likewise, at the mines of Sinai, in the south on the Upper Nile where he caused an inspection of the mines to be made, and at the centre of the country at Abydos, traces of the reign of Pepi have survived. He was wise enough not to throw any obstacle in the way of the worship of Ptah. This is seen from the fact that in his reign the festival of the union of the kingdoms under one sceptre, a festival sacred to Ptah, was celebrated. He seems, however, to have been himself a zealous partisan of the southern form of religion. He calls himself on the royal cartouche "Son of Hathor, the mistress of Denderah." That operations were conducted at her temple under his orders, is shown by the inscription above referred to (p. 112). He seems not to have been of royal descent, but was married to a princess, who in right of her mother must have been the proper heir to the throne, and whose children reigned in succession to each other, although another wife was the favourite. Ra-meri-anch-nes, as the mother of these future kings was called, was daughter of Chua the divine father, which was a designation given to the non-reigning princes of the reigning family. This personage was likewise a priest. He is buried along with his wife Nekabet at Abydos, which was most likely his native place. Nekabet was specially devoted to the worship of Osiris. Upon her tomb she is called daughter of Thot, of Horos, and of a goddess who, like Hathor, was represented under the form of a cow (Kabeba, Kubebe ?), but her chief title is "the consecrated to Osiris of the Amenti, Lord of Abydos." The influence of these royal personages was undoubtedly the cause of the revival of Osiris worship, and of the preponderating influence of Thinis-Abydos in the reign of Pepi. The principal ministers of this king and of his son Merenra are likewise expressly designated "consecrated to Osiris." The extraordinary deification of the person of the king (p. 103), carried under Pepi to such a height, must unquestionably be ascribed to the same influence, since it was connected closely with the worship of Osiris. It is also noticeable that while the princesses still filled the office of priestess of Hathor, they no longer combined that of Neith with it, as used formerly to be done. On the other hand, traces of the worship of Chnum, god of the cataracts, a southern and probably also Theban chief god, are discoverable.

It is thus impossible to deny the preponderance of the south during the reign of Pepi and his successors. The question arises, whether the name Imhotep, borne by one of Pepi's successors,[1] and which indicates Ptah worship, and whether likewise the name of Queen Nit-aker-t, signifying Neith the Wise, an appellation of one of the last royal personages of this dynasty, do not afford proof of a reaction and of a revival of the northern forms of worship. This question cannot be answered with certainty. The whole history of Egyptian religion bears witness, however, to this, that although from time to time the worship of Osiris and Ra may have been cast into the background by newer forms of adoration, they were as often restored; their importance and influence increased steadily, and the two religions being combined into one, forced their way everywhere, and ended by keeping the upper hand of the rest.

A view of the religion of the Old Kingdom has now been placed before us, though in a summary form. We can, however, see from what has been adduced that Osiris and Ptah, sometimes distinct, sometimes confounded, were the principal gods during this epoch. The worship of Horos, or, to be more precise, of the various gods who bore in common the designation Hor or Har, that is to say, the worship of the visible gods of the light and of the sun, seems to have been more ancient. But these visible gods were nevertheless not displaced to make room for others; their worship went on uninterruptedly; only certain other

[1] See De Rougé's VI Dynasties, p. 149.

gods were elevated to a rank above theirs. These were the gods of the hidden light, and of fire in its cosmic and mysterious operation. This fact testifies to a certain degree of religious development; worship is rising from the visible towards the invisible, from that which is perceptible by the senses to the superior power, the cause of phenomena.

It is remarkable, also, that in the tombs of this epoch it is not, as was usual at a later period, always Osiris who is represented as guardian and protector of the dead, but Anubis frequently fulfils this office. This is natural enough, for as yet Osiris was not the god with whom each of the departed became identified; the king alone became Osiris at his death. Neither do we as yet find in the tomb-temples those representations of different gods, so numerous at a later period, but rather we find extreme sobriety in the treatment of religious subjects. The titles given to the dead are, it is true, for the most part religious ones; but theology is still very simple. It may hence be inferred that although the religion of the kings and of individual worshippers was rich and profound, the power of the priests remained still strictly limited.

CHAPTER VI.

RELIGION UNDER THE MIDDLE KINGDOM.

At the end of the sixth dynasty there begins a period of confusion and uncertainty. The kingdom seems to have been rent into different portions, and the sovereignty exercised by various royal families which were, alternately or simultaneously, Memphitic and Heracleopolitan. It is impossible to decide absolutely as to the religion of this period, of which the duration is uncertain. It is not till the time of the eleventh and twelfth dynasties that light breaks in again and there is greater clearness, but again in the time of the thirteenth the light dies away, soon to be wholly extinguished through the influx of foreigners. The Middle Kingdom may be defined best as the period of the sovereignty of the following three dynasties, that of the Mentuhoteps and Antefs, that of the Amenemhas and Usertesens, that of the Sebekhoteps and Neferhoteps.

A mere glance at the composition of these names shows us that the gods who now attain supremacy are entirely different from those who formerly filled the highest place. Osiris and the gods of his circle, especially Ra and the deities associated with him, always continue to be celebrated in the tombs and on the sarcophagi, but in other respects their worship appears to be on the decline and to be confined to particular localities. This is the case with Ptah in a still greater degree. So far as I know, there is, in this period, no trace whatever of homage being paid to him. His worship was certainly continued at Memphis, but beyond that it had no influence. With the exception of a few whose worship for special reasons prevailed to a certain extent, and to whom reference will be made afterwards, the gods who now stand out as chief among all were Munt or Mentu the local god of Hermonthis (Anres, southern An), Chem or Min, the god of Koptos and Chemnis (Ekhmin, Panopolis), and Amen or Amun, the god of Thebes. These towns were all, with the exception of Chemnis, situated in the immediate neighbourhood of each other. The exaltation of these gods is natural enough, for they were the local gods of the Thebaid. The three royal houses also, under which they attained the highest honours, were native to this district, and accordingly have been designated Theban. We shall find, however, that these gods differed in name only from the earlier ones and from each other, and that the religion continued to be essentially the same as before.

The Antefs and Mentuhoteps of the eleventh dynasty, who to judge from their names must have sprung originally from An in the south, the town of Mentu, had fixed their chief seat at Koptos in the valley of Hamamât, close by the rich stone quarries that have been discovered there. They adopted, as their principal god, the god of that locality, Chem, who, in an inscription of the time of Mentuhotep III., is named "god of the mountainous tracts."[1] At first they seem to have ruled over only a portion of the country, no more probably than the Thebaid, but by degrees their kingdom became more extended. Already, under Mentuhotep II., they were masters of the south (inscription at Konosso near Philak), and the last kings of this dynasty had brought the whole of Egypt, with perhaps the exception of the Delta, under their sceptre. It seems to have been at this time that the town of Thebes, destined to reach in aftertimes such a height of splendour, was founded.

The first king of the twelfth dynasty was called, after the god of Thebes, "Amun," and his famous successor, Usertasen I., laid at Karnak (Thebes) the foundations of that

[1] De Rougé, VI Dynasties, p. 6.

huge imperial temple of Amun that was still in existence in the time of the Hyksôs, and after having been at a later period destroyed was restored by the twentieth dynasty. These kings, like their predecessors, paid homage to Mentu and Chem. Thus, Usertasen I., in a temple at Wady-Halfa in Nubia, dedicated to Chem and Amun, says that Munt as god of the Thebaid had assured to him the sovereignty over certain Nubian tribes.[1] The same may be accepted as holding good with regard to the princes of the thirteenth dynasty, at least at Taaud (Krokodilopolis), a place of which the peculiar worship was much favoured by this dynasty. Munt and Amun have been found, Munt being designated as god of the Thebaid.[2]

The god of Koptos, best known by the name of Chem, is commonly represented "in the form of his power," as the Egyptians expressed it,[3] that is, in the form of a mummy; or, if the expression be preferred, *en gaîne;* ithyfallic, with one arm uplifted and bearing a scourge, and with the high double feather on his head. These emblems proclaim him as god of fertility and as the divine ruler, and his name, admitting of the double pronunciation Chem and Min or Men, corresponded to this twofold signification, since Chem appears to signify the ruler, and Men the fertiliser.[4] He is the hidden male nature-power, the creator represented as fertiliser of the world, hence at agricultural festivals he had the first place. An opening flower or some similar symbol is usually placed beside him.

Chem, however, appears to be nothing else than a peculiar form of Horos. He is several times named Chem, the conquering Horos, the son of Osiris, or the son of Isis, and he is even called the avenger of his

[1] Champollion, Monumens, Notice, p. 36.
[2] Champollion, *ibid.*, p. 292.
[3] Jacques de Rougé, Rev. Arch., 1865, ii. 333 *et seq.*
[4] Lepsius doubts the antiquity of the pronunciation Min, which Brugsch seeks to set up as the only one. Consult, however, Lefébure, chap. xv. du Rituel, p. 50 *et seq.*, and the passages adduced there from Burton and Lepage Renouf. The pronunciation Chem is certainly original, but Men seems to be not less ancient.

father, and in a single instance—namely, in the temple of Thot, where he makes up the triad with Isis and Horos—he is placed on an equality with Osiris. He is the expression, the personification of the dogma of the unity of father and son, of Osiris and Horos in the divine triad, for his favourite appellation is, "husband of his mother." As the seed which impregnates the earth becomes, when it is shot up to a stalk, the son of the earth, or as the sun at evening sinks down into the bosom of the earth in order to impregnate her, and in the morning seems to come forth from her as her son, so did they conceive was the operation of the eternal nature-power regarded as a divine being by whom the universe is regulated.[1]

But Chem has generally been called also a form of Amun. This is not quite correct. The truth is, he is essentially the same as this god, or to express it better, both of them are forms in some respect modified of the same divine conception. For we must certainly assume that Amun or Amun-ra, the great god of Thebes, as conceived of by the priests in the time of the eighteenth and nineteenth dynasties, was not the original deity of that name. His name Men or Min is not an abbreviation of Amun, but a surname added to that one, the first letter of which was pronounced soft. The attributes of Chem are for the most part the same as those of Amun. In several representations Chem is called simply "Amun-ra, king of the gods," whence it appears that even in the time of the Old Kingdom men were conscious of their unity. Amun too is called almost always, and even in the sanctuary of his great temple at Karnak, "the husband of his mother." The lofty feathers of Chem which are mentioned in the most ancient text of chap. xvii. of the "Book of the Dead," are a distinctive mark of Amun.[2]

[1] Lepsius, Aelteste Texte des Todtenbuchs, p. 52.
[2] The two lofty feathers, the symbol of sovereignty, seem to have essentially the same signification as the ureus serpent. See Lepsius, op. cit., p. 52.

One of the significations of the Egyptian root *men*, is "to impregnate, beget," hence it naturally came about that homage was paid to Amun as the god who by impregnation secures the continued existence of the universe. But in Egyptian, Amun likewise signifies "the hidden one," and since the life-giving power of nature is hidden, this idea could quite well be considered as finding expression in the god Amun. This aspect of him became probably, through the speculations of the priests, the favourite one. Accordingly, he was regarded as the invisible highest deity, and gradually this conception of his being came more into prominence. I think, however, there are good reasons for accepting this purified conception of the god as belonging not to this period, but to a later one. We must regard this as the form assumed in later times at Thebes by the god of the Thebaid, yet without the loss of his original character, at least in the public worship.

Munt or Mentu seems, at first sight, to differ widely from the other deities of this period whom we have mentioned. Usually he is a god of war, and as a rule he has the human form with a sparrow-hawk's head, and on his head the sun with ureus, and the two feathers of Amun. He is called Lord of the Thebaid as well as Chem and Amun. Equally with him, Amun as Amun-ra is often depicted with a sparrow-hawk's head, and is, like Munt, also a god of war. There is no doubt that Munt, like the more ancient Amun and Chem-min, is essentially the same as Horos the elder.[1] At Hermonthis (a name which, perhaps, originated in the combination Har-Munt, Horos-Mônt) he was worshipped as the father of Har-pe-Chruti, the child Horos in seven forms.[2] It has been believed by

---

[1] Ebers asserts that he is in no respect different from him, and seems to propose that his name should be read in that way. See Aeg. u. d. BB. Mosis, pp. 141, 250, Zeits., 1868, p. 71. He promises to give his reasons for this assumption afterwards. He has tried, vainly as I think, to prove that Min or Chem is a Phœnician and not an Egyptian deity.

[2] Champollion, Monumens, Notice, p. 293 *et seq.*

some that the week of seven days was known among the Egyptians as early as this; and could this be proved, we should be inclined to suppose there is a reference to it under the seven forms of Horos. Horos was also, as is well known, sometimes a violent deity, god of death, and a war-god. The Mentuhoteps named themselves after Munt, yet worshipped Chem exclusively, a proof that the two were simply forms of one and the same god. Saneha, a servant of the princes of the twelfth dynasty, whose autobiography has been already referred to, says that when among the Tennu, the Berbers or Libyans, he devoted the concubines of his conquered enemy to Mentu. The meaning of this is unmistakable. There appears accordingly to have been, at least among the Libyans, unchaste practices combined with the worship of Mentu. That being so, he cannot have differed essentially from Chem, the ithyfallic god, and from Amun; and in this report we find another proof that Munt was properly the chief deity of the Middle Kingdom.

The essential signification of this god is best seen from a festival held in his honour on the first of the month Pachons, and which, though not mentioned or represented till the time of the Ramesids of the nineteenth and twentieth dynasty, undoubtedly dates from the time of the Middle Kingdom, and possibly from a time even more ancient. The principal deity of this festival is Chem, the ithyfallic Amun, hence it came about that for centuries, even after Amun-ra had become the chief god, it was in his sacred city Thebes that this festival was celebrated. There occur on the sculptured representation at Medinet-Abu, two images of the deity in the forms usual at Koptos and Chemnis, one uncovered, standing on a litter with a canopy borne by the priests, having beside him the symbols of fertility; the other, inside the sacred chest; but there is no doubt these represent the same god, who, after having received the offerings in his sanctuary, was carried round by the priests in solemn procession. Behind the image on its litter, four priests followed bearing a sacred ark in the same manner as was customary with the Israelites, and out of the ark there sprouted forth a tree with five branches.[1] In two instances the white or yellow bull (Mena), which belonged to Min or Chem, occurs in the festivity; in one the king cuts a bundle of stalks of grain with a golden sickle, and corn is offered to the bull; in the other, incense is offered to him. Another sacred act in the festival is letting fly the sacred geese, who were to tell to the four regions of the four winds that Horos, in the person of the reigning king, had ascended the throne. This would hence seem to have been a coronation festival, which, nevertheless, was celebrated annually. The geese bore the names of the four genii of the dead, Hapi, Amset, Tuau-Mutef, and Kebh-senuf, and were accordingly connected with these; it is however certain that here they are, before all, symbols of fruitfulness. The ideas expressed in this festival are evident enough. It is dedicated to Horos-Chem, the sun-god, as a fertilising nature-power, since the fertility of the land chiefly depends on him. But the guarantee for his blessing and protection is, that his substitute, the king, bear rule in the country, hence the glad tidings of the king's accession are published to the ends of the earth. The fertility of Egypt did, indeed, in a great measure, depend on the king, for only by him could those great public works be carried through, which were such an indispensable means of enabling the whole country to share in the blessings of the Nile. The king is actually for Egypt in a sense the giver of life, the god of fertility. Hence, the cutting of the sheaf is an act of the highest importance in the festival, a solemn reminder

---

[1] An ark of this kind was called *hen*, *i.e.*, the sacred, the consecrated. Upon one like this from which there sprouts an acacia (*schont*), is inscribed (at Thebes), "Osiris sprouts forth." The ark was thus an emblem of eternal life symbolised by the hidden seed which comes to life again in the tree. It is noticeable that the ark of the Israelites likewise was ordered to be made of acacia wood. See Brugsch, Reiseberichte, p. 127.

to the prince of what he is bound to perform, a vow made by himself that he will see to it, that the people do not through his negligence suffer from want of bread.

The eternal interchange of death and life is the principal thought in the theology of the Egyptians: they saw it in the course of the sun, they saw it in the changing seasons, and upon it they based their faith in man's immortality. The same gods often expressed these three conceptions; they were at one and the same time gods of the sun, gods of fruitfulness, and gods of the under world. Some, however, gained a more definite signification, by which they were brought into closer relation with one or other of these conceptions. Thus Osiris, while he is a sun-god, and sometimes god of fertility as well, became almost exclusively the great god of the dead, while Chem on the other hand, although connected with the under world, as for instance in the "Book of the Dead," and though his nature shows that he is a solar deity, became *par excellence* the god of fertility.

This religion is thus, in fact, simply a deification of the fertilising power of nature, the religion of a nation engaged principally in agriculture, for it was not till later, under the warrior kings of the eighteenth and nineteenth dynasties, that Munt assumed his warlike aspect. This peaceful character of the religion corresponds entirely with what we know of the condition of the kingdom during this period. Under the twelfth dynasty especially, the state of Egypt was in the highest degree flourishing, a prosperity due to the diligent pursuit of agriculture, and nourished by the encouragement given to the arts of peace. There was a complete revival of the glory of the Old Kingdom. It was a time of universal prosperity, peace reigned throughout the country, which at that time extended on the north to the sea, on the east to Sinai, on the south to the country of the negroes. Inscriptions of Usertasen I. have been discovered at San, on the Tanaitic branch of the Nile, at Sinai, and at Wady Halfa in Nubia, and others of Usertasen III. have been found in Ethiopia. Numerous monuments bear witness to the power of these kings, their love of grandeur, and the delight they took in building. Some among them preserved their high renown down to a later time. Usertasen I. was so great in the estimation of posterity, that an Ethiopian, or rather Egyptian king (Nektanebos), one of those who took refuge in Ethiopia, and a Greek prince (Ptolemæus, son of Lagus), counted it an honour to bear his regal appellation.[1] Usertasen III., who erected two strongholds at Semneh in Ethiopia, past which no negroes were allowed to go till they had paid tribute to his majesty, was, as is shown by numerous inscriptions, worshipped as a special god of the country throughout all Nubia, and even by so late a monarch as Thutmes I. a temple was erected to him there. Amenemha III. is the famous Mœris, *i.e.*, the inundations-king, whom Egypt has to thank not only for an improved system of canals, but even for an entire new province acquired by peaceful means. I refer to the Fayoom (Mœris), which he artificially made more productive by the excavation of a vast basin. Feeling conscious that this work more than any other was fitted to make his name immortal, he erected there not only a magnificent palace, the so-called Labyrinth, but also his pyramid. He seems to have owed the name Mœris to his regulation of the inundation.

Like the princes of this dynasty, their servants and the great personages of the kingdom erected colossal monuments and lived in princely style. To credit their own assurances, all this grandeur was not, as in the times before them, kept up by means of oppression and extortion. The inscriptions which they caused to be engraved on their tombs breathe a humane spirit and a certain moral earnestness. Work was promoted everywhere.

---

[1] The Egyptian kings at and after this time bore besides their family name three or four others. The regal appellation by which they were mostly called was that which they assumed at their accession.

In years of scarcity careful district governors even took measures beforehand to avert famine. Exact in their collection of tribute for the royal house, and on the watch lest anything should be stolen, they testify upon their tombs with emphasis that they were no men of violence. "No little child," thus says the nomarch Amenj Amenemha at Beni-Hassan, "was vexed by me, no widow was ill-treated, no fisherman disturbed, no herdsman obstructed. There is no pentarch whose men I have forced to do labours. I made the inhabitants live," thus he goes on to testify, "for I offered to them the products of the land, so that there were no famines in the province. I have given equally to the widow and to the married woman; in all that I gave I have shown no preference to the great above the small." Humane feelings like these are very remarkable in such remote antiquity. Saneha, so often before referred to, recounts his own praises in phrases similar to those of Amenj, for modesty does not seem to have been one of the virtues of the Egyptian grandees. "I gave," he says, "water to the thirsty; I put the traveller on his way; I removed the oppressor from the Sakti, and put an end to violence." Utterances like these, by which we are involuntarily reminded of the declarations of Job, give a favourable idea of the moral condition of Egyptian society in those days, and thus also of the influence exercised by religion. It is true, funeral orations, especially when the authors of them are also their subjects, have never been famous for veracity. The reality, no doubt, did not in every case come up to the ideal here sketched to us. In other respects the humanity of the Egyptians, which has frequently been compared to that of the gospel, had limits, and is seen to have diverged widely from that of the New Testament. That very Saneha, who refreshed the thirsty and protected the oppressed, has no difficulty about punishing his conquered enemy pitilessly. He causes the concubines of this enemy, innocent victims of his vengeance, to be devoted to the

I

deity. He appropriates all his enemy's goods, plunders his house, and proceeds in all this upon the maxim that he ought to do to his enemy as his enemy had meant to do to him.

Meanwhile these nobles did not neglect religion, and the morality they advocated does not seem to have been a thing apart from religion. They brought presents to the temples with a liberal hand. Chnumhotep, colleague and successor of Amenj, assures us in his rich and remarkable tomb that he has been beneficent to the sanctuaries, and that he has caused statues of himself to be placed there. "I have given," so he testifies, "offerings and libations to the temples, appointed corn to the priests, and have shown myself beneficent to them." Though people were obliged to work hard, opportunities of relaxation were given by the numerous religious festivals, to the embellishment of which people of distinction did not fail to contribute. The festivals were very numerous. Besides those of the full moon and the half moon there were two new year festivals, one for the civil and one for the fixed year. Other annual holidays were the feast of the great and that of the little warmth; but the feast of the five epagomenoi, or intercalary days, dedicated to the principal gods of the Osirian circle, Osiris, Isis, Set, Nephthys, and Horos, was, above all others, celebrated with extraordinary solemnity and delight.[1]

I have already remarked that the kings of the twelfth dynasty continued to honour the deity of the Thebaid in his three forms just as the kings of the eleventh dynasty had done. He was also invoked by them under the name of Horos (inscription of Usertasen I. at Wady-Halfa). But they nevertheless did not cease to keep up the ancient worships of Egypt, and they considered themselves bound to do this as being rulers over the whole country. Heliopolis was not neglected. The single obelisk of the Old Kingdom that we know of was erected there by Usertasen I. Obelisks like this had a twofold purpose: primarily,

[1] See Brugsch, Histoire d'Egypte, pp. 56, 59.

they symbolised the rays of the sun, and were therefore covered with gilding; their other purpose was to express steadfastness and durability. Or properly, they represented the sun's rays, upon which, as upon glittering pillars, the vault of heaven seemed to rest. They were a stone representation of the props of Shu, upon which Ra walks.[1] Hence at Heliopolis, the town of Shu, they were found in great number. In the inscription of his obelisk, Usertasen calls himself "beloved by the spirits of Heliopolis," whence it is evident that the sacred city still kept its earlier fame.

Not unfrequently there occurs in this period, and especially in the time of the twelfth dynasty, the name of the god Chnum (also Num, formerly read mostly always Kneph). He is, as his name indicates, the architect, the creator of the universe, in whom the two ideas of the cosmic fire and of the breath of life are combined. His worship goes back to very early times. We meet with it, in fact, under the first dynasties; but it was afterwards, especially in the epoch with which we are now concerned, very greatly developed. It is time, therefore, that I should speak of this god, who was worshipped in all periods of the Egyptian kingdom. It is certainly a mistake to place him, as some do, at the head of the whole Egyptian world of gods in the character of "the spirit." There is no doubt, however, that in the estimation of pious Egyptians he took a high rank. Chnum is the local god of the cataracts, and was thus worshipped principally at Elephantine (Ab), on the island Konosso (Kebh). Two goddesses, Sati and Anke, or Anuka, were revered there along with him. It cannot now be ascertained with certainty whether his worship was brought thither from somewhere else, or whether this was his original home; but it is certain that he was worshipped in neighbouring

[1] See F. Chabas, Traduction complète des Inscriptions Hiérogly-phiques de l'Obélisque de Louqsor. Paris, 1868. See also Lauth, Ueber Obelisken und Pyramiden, Sitz. Ber. der Bayer. Akademie, d. Wiss. z. München, 1867, I. i. 93 et seq.

localities also, and that his nature and that of the two goddesses who stood at his side was in itself sufficient to make him local god of the cataracts.. Chnum is the breath of God, in so far as the spirit and the wind were one to the thought of ancient peoples; and in especial he was the breath of God as creative power, not unlike the Hebrew conception of the Ruach Jahveh, who in the beginning brooded over the waters. In this character Chnum was naturally fitted for being god of the cataracts, which are, as it were, the beginning of Egyptian waters, and were called by the Egyptians the source of the waters.[1] On this account he was called the god of the head of the Nomes, because the nomes (districts) of Egypt begin at the cataracts. In the same way Sati, whose emblem is an arrow shot through the skin of a beast, and whose name is derived from throwing, or even signifies "arrow," belongs to the streams of the cataracts that dash down with the swiftness of an arrow. In the same root, moreover, lies the idea of impregnation, which was likewise expressed by Chnum's symbol, the ram. The name of Anka, Chnum's second companion, expresses the idea of "embrace." She is thus the one who conceives, in this case, of course, the goddess of the earth. This is proved beyond question by an inscription in the Sothis-temple at Assouan in Nubia, where it is said, "The divine Sothis, the in love embracing one (*anka-t*), in order to make pregnant the land in this name Anuka";[2] that is, Sothis, the star Sirius, the soul of Isis, and thus the protectress of the earth is named Anuka, as being the embracing one who is impregnated by the god of heaven. In the swift waters, which, being driven on by the breath of the deity, made the ground fertile, the Egyptians saw a divine operation, a representation of the creative spirit. We have here the ancient and universally occurring myth of the heaven, or the soul of the heaven, impregnating the earth by means of the celestial waters

---

[1] Inscription of Amen-meri-nut. Mariette, Rev. Arch., 1865, ii. 163.   [2] Brugsch, Hierogly. dem. W. B., p. 92.

localised in this case in the cataracts, which were to the Egyptians the source of the fertility of their country. Everywhere, too, these celestial waters are personified as goddesses of rivers, at first of heaven, then of earth, like the Ganges, the Sarasvatî, &c. It is noticeable that the Persian name of the river Tigris, and the cuneiform by which it was denoted in Assyria, signify arrow. The same idea may likewise be expressed in solar symbolism, and then Chnum is the sun-god, as being the producer of the wind, Chnum-ra (a combination which, however, is apparently not ancient); Sati is the divine ray of the sun, the means by which the earth is impregnated, and which is sometimes represented as a form of Chnum. Anka alone retains her signification. Here, too, she is the mother-earth as a divine being, and in accordance with this she is called, *e.g.*, at Dakkeh in Nubia, the king's nurse. The names of the principal priest and priestess of Chnum at Elephantine (Abu) correspond to the signification of these deities. The former was named *Tes-ra*, " he who brings near the heaven" (Mariette), or, better perhaps, " he who creates the heaven." The latter bore the name *Senck*, which is, ray of the sun. His sacred bark was named after his common symbol, *chaker-ba*, ornament of the ram, and also simply *chaker-num*. I give these examples in order to show from them the symbolical character of the Egyptian religion. Never was symbolism carried to such a height; never was it so universally applied as in the valley of the Nile.

The mode in which creation by Chnum is represented varies very much.[1] At one time his work is no more than plastic; he is called the great divine former, the first architect who created with his hands the gods and god-

[1] It occurs to me that the god Tetun (or Dudun, as Brugsch reads it), who was worshipped at Semneh with Chnum, but always received a less degree of honour (see Lepsius, Briefe aus Aegyp., p. 259, and Brugsch, Histoire, p. 65), is Chnum himself as *former*, and that this Tetun has some connection with the name of Chnum's northern colleague, Ptah, *tatanen*. Usertasen III., in an inscription at the place just named, is called " son of Chnum and Tetun."

desses, and who stands prepared to form the son of Isis upon the revolving disk, the potter's wheel, a representation irresistibly reminding us of the biblical figure in which Jahveh is called a potter.[1] Then again the description is more exalted, or at least simpler, and he is called "the creator of beings, the first existing, the father of fathers, the mother of mothers." The foundation, however, of all these representations remains always naturalistic, the wind as the breath of God that moves the cosmic waters, and so in the beginning makes the earth fruitful and habitable.

The name of the kings of the twelfth dynasty, which is by turns Sebekhotep and Neferhotep, indicates that during their reigns the god Sebak, with the crocodile's head, enjoyed high honour. The causes that determined this must be looked for so early as in the twelfth dynasty. Sebak appears to have been a native of Ethiopia, and to have been introduced thence into Egypt.[2] Usertasen III. was the first who subdued Ethiopia entirely, and his son Amenemha Mœris appears to have been a devoted worshipper of Sebak, for he imported the worship of this deity into the Fayoom, the new province he had founded, the capital of which the Greeks called Krokodilopolis, and he called his daughter, who, after his son, succeeded him on the throne, and who closes the twelfth dynasty, Sebek-nefru, a name the component parts of which recur in all the kings' names of the thirteenth dynasty. Royal patronage explains the great and speedy spread of this foreign cultus. The Egyptian town where it was introduced is, for reasons easy to understand, said to have been Ombos. Sebak is at least regularly designated " god of Ombos." There, from of old,

---

[1] In the' well-known romance of Anepu and Batau, Ra orders Chnum to form a wife for Batau also. He is thus here a kind of Prometheus.

[2] Later Ethiopian kings are frequently named after him. His name, too, has an Ethiopian sound. The termination *ak* has much affinity with the Ethiopian article, so that Sebak may perhaps be the Kushite Seb or Kronos. This last supposition Champollion adopts, though for quite other reasons, in Wilkinson, M. and C., v. 37.

Set, the Egyptian crocodile god, was worshipped. In other places likewise of the Thebaid, as at Koptos, Silsilis, and Tuphium (Tauut), the worship of Sebak was established, and thence it was transferred to the Fayoom.

Sebak was, there can be no doubt, a god of the Nile, and more particularly of the inundations. There was a widespread belief among the Egyptians that the crocodiles deposited their eggs precisely at the limit to which, each year, the inundation would attain. Hence it was inferred that it was one of those animals who, as king of the river, regulated the height of the overflow. This also led to the worship of Sebak as local god of the Fayoom, a new province created by the muddy deposits of the river.

A feature indicating that Sebak is both a foreign deity and one of the many forms of the great creative god is to be seen in the two goddesses that are usually found beside him. The difficulty of finding him a consort was in general got over simply by assigning to him as companion the goddess of the place where his worship was established;[1] yet not unfrequently, at least from the time of the eighteenth dynasty downwards, he is found coupled with the goddesses Tannit (Tanit) and Anît.[2] Who these goddesses are is not difficult to determine. Tanit and Anît, or Anahid, were two forms of the same widely-spread Mesopotamian goddess who is met with among the Phœnicians, Arabs, Assyrians, Babylonians, Hebrews, and even among the Persians, and in later times also among the Greeks and Romans.[3] They are the two female sides of the deity: Tannit, called simply "the goddess of heaven," is the virgin (Artemis, Athene, Istar of Arbela); Anît, who wears the head-dress of a mother, and is called "the great power," that is, the productive power, is the

---

[1] Thus, among other instances, he occurs once with Anka, and has Anup for his son. Champollion, Monumeus Notice, p. 36.

[2] See Lepsius, Aeltester Götterkreis, Taf., i. 3, ii. 1, &c. Lepsius reads the names there Tennit and Penit, which at this date he would doubtless allow is a mistake.

[3] See my Godsdienst von Zarathustra, p. 180 et seq.

maternal goddess (Demeter, Istar of Nineveh), and corresponds entirely to the Arabic-Persian Anâhita. There can be no doubt that these goddesses have just as little claim to be considered true Egyptian as Sebak. Nor could they have originally belonged to him, even though we accept it as being the case that they were brought to Africa by the Ethiopians, who about this time migrated thither from Arabia, driven out, it would seem, by Phœnicians (Puns). While this may possibly have been the case, it cannot now be proved.

The view has been adopted that Sebak is the darkness of night which triumphs over the sun, and is in its turn overcome by him (Mariette). I think, however, that those who adopt this explanation have allowed themselves to be misled by a later transformation in the part played by this god. He was not, any more than Set, originally a malevolent deity, and, like him, he is often seen on the poop of the bark of the sun, and thus among the number of those who fight by the side of Horos, and not among his adversaries. At Ombos his worship is found associated with that of Horos.

From what has been said above, we come to the conclusion that Sebak was a god of the inundation, and as such was looked upon also as a god who was creator. The principal centres of his worship were, without exception, towns situated at important points of the Nile, e.g., Koptos, Arsinoë, and Athribis, or else on the canals and artificial works by which the fertilising stream was carried to distant places. At Silsilis, where the Nile was worshipped and placed in the rank of chief deities, the place filled by this god was sometimes occupied by Sebak (in the Spéos). What is said by Aelian and Eusebius about the crocodile being a symbol to the Egyptian of the drinking water, and of the fertilising water of the inundations, is in perfect accordance with these attributes.

Certain gods nevertheless, though very different from each other, have the same symbols, and the crocodile, along with some other fierce animals, was also sacred to Set. When this god fell in public estimation, and a war of extermination against the crocodiles was begun in the nomes where the worship of Horos and of Hathor flourished, Sebak suffered equally from this unpopularity, and the interpreters of more modern times forgot that originally he was in any way at all different from Set. But even at a more ancient period Hâpi (who is not to be confounded with Hapi, the bull Apis) appears to have consigned Sebak to a position of obscurity.

Hâpi, or Hapimou, is the god of the Nile. I should not venture to assert that his worship attained a position of importance so early as the time of the Middle Kingdom, but in the period of the New Kingdom he was worshipped with great fervour, especially in the localities touched by the Nile in its course. It has been already noticed that the Nile has, along with Sebak, a place in the higher triad, and therefore among the gods who are creators. This is seen at Silsilis in a temple constructed in a cavity of the rocks, which at this spot leaves to the river only a very confined passage. The Nile god had also temples at Heliopolis and at Memphis. It is to be inferred, from a hymn dedicated to him (Pap. Sall., II., et Anastasi VII., published by M. Maspéro), that the Nile on earth was only one form of the heavenly Nile, source of the fertilising waters of the universe, whose name no one knows, who does not reveal his forms, and of whom consequently it is impossible to make any image. "No abode contains him, people do not offer sacrifices to him, but all the offerings made to the other gods are to be considered as dedicated to him." This god, the date of whose origin is perhaps in the period with which we are now occupied, continued for long to receive great honour. Down to the latest times of the existence of the kingdom of Egypt, and even under Roman rule, Hâpi was still an object of worship.

As we did with the preceding period, we shall now try to review the religious development of this one, the leading facts of which have just been summed up. In doing so, the first thing we may consider established is, that the religion is in perfect accord with the general condition of the kingdom in this period. The worship of 'gods, such as we have described, is precisely what might be expected in a period of great agricultural prosperity, when all the arts of peace flourished and were brought to great perfection, and Egypt was overspread with a regular network of new canals. In other respects, what was said of the Old Kingdom is no less true of the Middle; the kings exercise absolute power not limited or counterbalanced by that of any priestly caste. Yet they are very religious, they support and protect religion, and even go so far as to create new forms of worship and new priesthoods. One of them, Usertasen III., even became the local god commonly worshipped in Nubia. Beneath the kings, the local government was carried out by great officers of state, who were doubtless descendants of ancient local sovereigns, and thus privileged to discharge sacerdotal functions also, yet none the less on that account they were laymen. Their inscriptions testify to their moral sense, and their care for the temples of the gods that were within the districts over which they ruled. The literature of this period is emphatically what would now be called secular literature. This is shown by the maxims of Ptahhotep and the autobiography of Sancha. Nevertheless there are not awanting commentaries on the ancient magical texts which afterwards were incorporated in the "Book of the Dead." The priests seem, however, to have taken only a secondary part in this period.

A study of the sepulchral monuments gives a like result. On the walls of the tombs few images of the gods have as yet been met with, nor have any been discovered even in the monuments dating from the thirteenth dynasty. In the inscriptions, too, with which these paintings are accompanied, the names of the gods are very rarely found. The titles of honour ascribed to the dead have in general a complexion more civil than religious. Especially remarkable in this respect are the famous tombs of Chnumhotep and of Amenj Amenemha at Beni-Hassan. In them the deceased is represented in the exercise of his profession, in the bosom of his family, or taking part in recreations. Nor must we think these paintings were intended to preserve and transmit to posterity the remembrance of the scenes which they represent, for no one was allowed to enter the tombs. It was all done strictly with regard to the dead person. It was the application of an ancient belief of animistic worships, in virtue of which whatever was depicted on behalf of the deceased was actually of use to him in the life to come. These tombs accordingly tell us what the princes and great men of this epoch esteemed most, and wished to retain beyond the grave; they make known to us what was then considered the highest motive for existence, namely, material prosperity, or rather a measure of enjoyment of the good things of life, combined with a benevolent desire for the welfare of all men.

At that time there reigned no dread of the pains of hell or of judgment after death. The life to come was scarcely anything else than a reproduction of life on earth, and no one seems to have thought much about any retribution after death. There is to be found, indeed, the formula destined ultimately to be joined, without alteration, to the name of the dead (like our "the late," or the Fr. feu and bienheureux) *madâcheru*, which signifies "exercising authority" or "speaking truth by the word," in particular, by the magical word.[1] But as yet no idea of justification or

---

[1] Champollion and others following him have translated this, "justified by the word." Devéria (Recueil Vieweg., i. 1, 10), G. Maspéro

of judgment is attached to these phrases, as was once believed. The custom of sepulchral stelæ originated in this period. On these Anubis gives place to Osiris, along with whom numerous other gods are invoked.

(in the German translation of his Histoire Ancienne des peuples de l'Orient, p. 601), and Pietschmann, the translator of the work (*ibidem*), have given a new translation, to which in the main I incline to adhere.

CHAPTER VII.

RELIGION UNDER THE NEW KINGDOM.

LONG centuries of oppression separate the Middle Kingdom from the New. Between them comes the rule of the so-called Hyksôs, or Shepherd Kings. The period of their supremacy is one of the most obscure in Egyptian history. The cause that impelled them to overrun the valley of the Nile in vast hordes can only be guessed at. It seems natural to think that their immigration was occasioned by some movement among the peoples of the middle and west of Asia. Further than the violent usurpation and the rough rule that followed upon it we know hardly anything. The only thing told by later historians is, that in the reign of a certain otherwise unknown king, Timaos or Amuntimaos, an eastern people, of what race cannot easily be determined,[1] made an inroad on Egypt, became masters of the lower portion of the country, and made the whole kingdom tributary to them. The barbarians ravaged and destroyed everything, monuments, temples, towns, but in the end they adopted the Egyptian civilisation, and replaced in new-built temples the monuments of the ancient kings, which at first they had destroyed. They now, however,

---

[1] Josephus calls them Phœnicians or Arabians. Chabas—in Les Pasteurs en Egy., Amst., 1868, p. 27, a masterly treatise, of which I have gratefully made use—is of opinion that their names are not Syro-Aramaic (*i.e.*, Semitic). On this point it is very difficult to come to a decision, as the Greeks have mangled the words so much. Only Bnon or Banon, and Yannas or Annas, especially the latter, have a slight resemblance to common Semitic names. The known proper names of the Cheta or Hethites are totally different. That this people could have been, as Brugsch thinks, Assyrians, is impossible.

inserted on them the names and cartouches of the conquerors. The foreigners became, in fact, Egyptian kings. In the judgment of antiquaries, the artistic merit of the monuments erected by them, especially of those at Tanis, is greater than that of the works of the contemporary, subject Theban dynasty. They had at their side a council of Egyptian scribes and wise men, and one of the latest shepherd-kings, Set-aa-pehti-nubti,[1] even instituted a new chronology, which had not fallen into disuse at Tanis four centuries later. Another, the well-known Apepi (Apophis), probably one of his predecessors, adopted an Egyptian worship and built magnificent temples. But while, on the one hand, civilisation seems to have tamed the rude might of the oppressor, the spirit of the subject-people would seem to have meanwhile revived. Warlike kings in the Thebaid, as yet properly only princes of secondary rank, girt themselves for a war of independence. These were the Ta's or Raskenen's (warlike sun), namely, Ta the great, the very great, and the very victorious, followed by Ahmes (Amosis), who succeeded in driving the foreigners out of their last stronghold, and on this victory laid the foundation of a new dynasty, the eighteenth.[2]

Belonging to the time of Apepi, whose reign is contemporary with that of Raskenen Ta I., we possess a fragmentary, but, for the history of religion, very important account in Papyrus Sallier I. From this it appears that Apepi did not reside, as, according to Manetho, the first Hyksos were in the habit of doing, at Memphis, nor at Tanis, where monuments of theirs have been discovered, but farther to the east at Avaris (Pelusium, Hebr., Zo'ar, Eg., Zar or T'ar, formerly inaccurately supposed to be

---

[1] Mariette reads this name Nubti-Suti. According to him he is the last of the Shepherd Kings Asseth. In the opinion of others he is to be regarded as the very first, Saïtes, which is, however, extremely improbable.

[2] Chabas, *op. cit.*, pp. 33, 39. Lenormant, in his Hist. Ancienne de l'Orient, has devoted a chapter to this period, but he makes wild work in the strangest way with the few historical data.

Tanis or San). His residence there was only occasional, for he is still master of Heliopolis, and it is expressly mentioned that he received tribute, not only from the north, but from the whole country. " He made," so the papyrus informs us, " Sutech (Set) his divine master, and served none of the gods that are in the whole country. He erected a temple to him, of excellent workmanship, for the centuries." In this temple he caused festivals to be celebrated, offerings to be brought daily, erected in it his royal statue, and adorned the approach to the sanctuary with rows of sphinxes confronting each other. This testimony is confirmed by the remains that have been found at Tanis, statues, sphinxes, executed with talent, but in a foreign un-egyptian style. Set was the ancient god of Lower Egypt, whose peculiar unpleasing form has been already met with in the time of the kings of the first Memphitic dynasty. His name was slightly modified by a particle being affixed, which is sometimes used in Egyptian, and is very common in Ethiopian. This was done apparently to make the pronunciation easier for the foreign intruders, for exactly the same deity was meant. The reasons why Apepi selected this god in particular, when he threw over his ancestral religion in favour of that of Egypt, cannot have been that he found Set established at that time as the god of Tanis, for the gods worshipped there up to that time were those of Heliopolis and Memphis, and, most of all, Ptah.[1] The only possible reason for his procedure is, that his own religion may have been a kind of Moloch worship, to which the worship of Set corresponded most nearly.

Nor did Apepi confine himself to taking this step. He

[1] See E. De Rougé, Rev. Arch., 1864, i. 130. Comp. Chabas, *op. cit.* It is utterly incomprehensible to me how any one, in opposition to the indubitable testimony of the Papyrus and the certainty that Set is a genuine Egyptian ancient god, can say, like Lenormant, "They (the Hyksôs) adopted the religion of Egypt, forcibly intruding their god Set or Sutech into its pantheon; and he ended by remaining fixed there, losing only the highest rank which they gave him." *Tot verba, tot errores.*

went further still; he proposed to Sekenen-Ra Ta I., prince of Thebes, who seems by this time to have in a great degree secured the independence of the south, that an agreement should be made between them. The contents of this agreement are not known to us, but one of the conditions it sought to impose was, that from that time forth two gods only should be worshipped in Egypt, Sutech, namely, and Amun-Ra, the god of Thebes. As far as can be made out in the miserable condition of the papyrus, this proposition was indignantly rejected by the Theban prince, and the struggle, destined to end in the emancipation of the whole country, was resumed with unabated fury. Every circumstance gives us the impression that Apepi foresaw the approaching end of his supremacy, and wished to retain what was still in his possession. Up to this time the overbearing Orientals appear to have remained faithful to their own religion, which seems to have been a kind of rude sun-fire worship, and out of religious hatred and zeal for their faith, they destroyed the temples and images of the Egyptian gods. Apepi next made two important concessions. In order to retain the north he offered homage to the god of Lower Egypt; and, that he might arrest the course of his ill fortune in the south, he declared that he was prepared to revere Amun-Ra likewise, but he expressly limits himself to these—he will have besides them no other gods. He cannot prevail upon himself to adopt the manifold and materialistic polytheism of the Egyptians. It was too late, however. The true Egyptians felt their power, and easily divined the object of the foreign tyrant. Accordingly, in the time of his second successor, the sovereignty of the Shepherd Kings, now confined to Avaris alone, came to an end, and throughout the country all the Egyptian gods again received their worship.

This history is characteristic of the great race to the two branches of which the Egyptians and the Menti or Shepherds respectively belong. For this race religion is the one thing of consequence, the centre around which all else revolves. Every war is a religious war. And in this case the struggle is not so much one between two different religions, for we see how the nomad prince is prepared to adopt Egyptian gods; it is rather a struggle between two principles, between that of the rich, varied, polytheistic religion of the sons of Ham, on the one hand, and, on the other, the simple, severe nomad religion of the sons of Shem. It is the ancient strife between Cain, the tiller of the ground, and Abel, the keeper of sheep—a struggle destined to be repeated at a later period, though on Egyptian ground, with the same result.

Meanwhile, though the Shepherds were indeed expelled, the worship of Set was not given up either at Tanis or elsewhere in Egypt. Even in the time of Ramses II., so long as four hundred years after the last of the Hyksôs, the governor of Zar (Avaris) is called Seti, chief prophet of Sutech, and head of the prophets of all gods, a proof that Sutech was no foreign deity, but a genuine Egyptian one, adopted by the barbarians.[1]

A period in which a people's whole strength is put forth in order to achieve freedom and independence, is usually succeeded by a period of prosperity. This fact, in which we may see the operation of a fixed law, may be very naturally accounted for. A struggle of this kind cannot fail to bring into play all the latent powers of a nation, and gives it extraordinary energy. When the object which all its forces had been gathered up to attain is reached, these forces naturally direct themselves into other channels, towards peaceful works, art, or science. The slumbering energy having once been fairly aroused seeks out a way to spend itself. Consequently everything to which the mind can bend it flourishes and develops beneath the shelter of peace at home. This was what now happened

[1] E. de Rougé, Rev. Arch., 1864, i. 138 et seq., and, in opposition to him, Mariette, op. cit., 1865, i. 169 et seq., and again, in reply to that, De Rougé, op. cit., 1865, p. 346.

in Egypt. The struggle for nationality carried on with the foreign tyrants is followed by the most brilliant period of Egyptian history, the glory of which is manifest even at the beginning of the eighteenth dynasty. Nor did the troubles which supervened at the close of that dynasty put an end to this time of prosperity, for under the nineteenth dynasty it immediately revived, and rose to its fullest height, and even in its decline, during the twentieth dynasty, it still continued to be rich and imposing. Industry and trade diffused prosperity throughout the thickly peopled land. Agriculture was pursued with especial care as a sacred task, and the works which in the Nile valley are so indispensable to its success, were kept up or improved. Ancient towns grew in extent and increased in magnificence and wealth of monuments, while new towns were founded. The Egyptian even ventured out upon the sea, the unclean sea, as he always considered it. Fleets were sent out to Arabia to return with rich freights. The wars with northern peoples were partly carried on by sea, and while it is the case that the Phœnicians contributed a chief share to the formation of these Egyptian navies, there is no doubt they were to a considerable extent manned by Egyptians. In these wars Egypt was almost invariably victorious, and her warrior kings extended the empire far into the heart of Asia. In this period, too, art, rising from its long slumber, brought into being the noblest and most beautiful creations, though, it is true, it had lost its early boldness of character, as well as much of its former grandeur and impressiveness. Literature was pursued with especial eagerness by numerous scribes. Tales and proverbs, poems and pœans of victory, as well as hymns of religion, medical and magical papyri belonging to this period, have been preserved in comparatively large numbers. Nor did religious life remain torpid. We notice in this province the most remarkable progress. About this time the naturalistic standpoint is not entirely forsaken, the material husks are still very far from being quite cast away; but the Egyptian spirit becomes more and more conscious of power to rise to the purest conception of deity as an invisible spiritual being, and of ability to perceive under the innumerable forms the one and only God whose names merely were many and diverse.

Under the rule of the Theban royal families—for the three dynasties that reigned in the prosperous days of the New Kingdom were all of Theban origin—Amun, the god of Thebes, is of course the principal god of Egypt. He thus came to be, more than any other deity, the expression of the highest that it is possible to conceive concerning the divine being. He still continues to be the very same god who, in the time of the Middle Kingdom, was reverenced under various names as the god of fertility. He is still named "divine head, who hast power to bring thyself forth again," and "husband of his mother." His temple at Wady-Halfa, erected by Usertasen I. (twelfth dynasty), in which he was worshipped as Chem-Kamut-f, Chem Amun, and as Amun-ra, was adorned by Amenophis II. (eighteenth dynasty), and later by Ramses I. and Seti Merneptah (nineteenth dynasty). At agricultural festivals, and even at the king's coronation, the ithyfallic form of Amun was carried round in procession, and the god was glorified in this character. Even the ancient idea of durability was still attributed to him. It still remained a favourite play of words, " Amun durable (*men*) in all things."

As god of fertility he bears also, like Chnum, one or more rams' heads,[1] and he is even expressly called the great ram.[2] The sphinxes with rams' heads, so common

---

[1] A very common representation of Amun is that of a seated human being with four rams' heads on one neck, and worshipped by the four or eight dog-headed apes, the Hermopolitan gods. See Chabas, Pap. Mag., Harris, p. 90 *et seq.* In the tomb of Seti I., discovered by Belzoni, he occurs as a ram's head in a sun's disk. The same ram's head in a sun's disk, crowned with a ureus adder, is upon the curved sword that Amun holds in his right hand (a sculpture on the triumphal arch of Ramses III. at Medinet-Abu). In the so-called treasure-house he is represented as a ram lying down with the sun's disk between its horns.

[2] Inscription in Brugsch, Reiseberichte, p. 161. Wilkinson con-

at Thebes, are distinctly in connection with his worship. At the well-known oasis of Ammon likewise, into which his Egyptian worship must have been introduced by a Theban colony, he was worshipped under this form.

A sun-god he always was, as is shown by his identity with Horos, Munt, and Chem, and a sun-god he continued to be. In poems dating from the time of the nineteenth dynasty mention is made of how he sends forth rays, and how by them he encircles the earth with brightness until he withdraws himself behind the western hills, and of "his boat that steers past the hidden mountain." Nay more, we find express mention of "the light of his disk." He is named fighter against the darkness, and conqueror of it. It is a less materialistic conception, and shows a transition to the supernatural, when, in that parallelism which the Egyptians alone among the peoples have in common with the Hebrews, who no doubt adopted it from them, we read of "Amun, who hides himself in the apple of his eye, soul that shines in his holy eye;" or when reference is made to his holy transformations of shape, which are known to none, and he is called the mystery of mysteries, hidden in the bosom of the heavenly ocean. The very same expression is, however, elsewhere applied just in the same way to the sun-god Ra.[1]

But a still greater step in advance was taken. This is shown by the name Amun-ra, which came into vogue during the supremacy of the foreign kings, and which was sometimes expanded to Amun-ra-Harmachu. From this it appears that men were beginning to see in Amun something more than the sun-god. Amun-ra is, in fact, a pleonasm, because Amun as well as Ra was a sun-god.

siders the accounts of the ancients about the criocephalous Amun to be a confusion with Chnum; the monuments, however, contradict that assertion.

[1] As sun-god he frequently has, as on the triumphal arch of Ramses III., already referred to, the head of a sparrow-hawk, and a sword with a sparrow-hawk's head on it in his hand. That is his own original form, not exclusively as Amun-ra. Where, too, he occurs, as he mostly always does, with human head, crowned by a high double feather, he bears this latter name.

But now it had ceased to be a pleonasm. Amun was now, and his name also permits the signification, although it cannot have been the original one, regarded as the *hidden* (*Amun*) deity, " of whom even Amun is a form," in the same way as the sun's disk. In this character he is called " the highest power with the mysterious forms," " the mysterious soul that is himself creator of his own dread might;" nay, they even went so far as to call him the spirit, more spiritual than the gods, with whose plans the world is begun, the only, the infinite one.[1]

Let us now try to account for this exaltation of Amunra, by virtue of which he towers above all the more ancient gods of Egypt, and combines in himself all of great and glorious that the Egyptian had personified in his various gods. The close relationship subsisting between the three principal gods of the Thebaid, Amun of Thebes, Munt of Hermonthis, and Chem of Koptos, was, as will be recollected, pointed out in the preceding chapter. Now these three gods are accurate representations of the three kinds of higher gods worshipped in different parts of Egypt: from a mythological point of view they are respectively the god of fire or of the wind, the god of the visible or living sun, and the god of the sun invisible or dead: from a theological point of view again they are the creator, operative and hidden from the sight of men in the uppermost sphere of the heavens; manifesting himself in the air; and hidden in the bosom of the earth or in the under world. Besides Shu of Heliopolis and others, Chnum belongs very specially to the first category. Now, Amun, the god of the town of Thebes, whose name must have signified originally, " He who fertilises," was very frequently represented under the form proper to Chnum, that is, with a ram's head, the symbol of the soul of the world, and sometimes even with four rams' heads, emblems of the four spirits of the heavens, of the air, of the earth, and of the under world;

[1] See Chabas, Pap. Mag., Harris, sec. vi.

that is to say, of the light, of the wind, of fire, and of the Nile. Amun has thus a signification entirely identical with that attributed to Chnum of Mendes in Lower Egypt. The fact of Amun-ra assuming the same form as Chnum is not therefore a mere coincidence, for there is no doubt whatever that he was conceived of as being the creative soul of the world. Not only is it said of him as of Shu, that the winds proceed from his mouth, breath from his nostrils, but moreover in the book of the breathings of life (Shaï an Sinsin [1]), that used to be deposited in the tombs of the priests and priestesses of Amun, he like Shu gives the breath of life to the dead, and the soul lives in him as the body does in Osiris; and in a picture at Karnak (Thebes), Osiris is seen on the funeral litter no longer as a mummy but as a young man, and therefore just at the moment when he is about to resume life; above him floats Amun-generator in the form of a bird, the usual symbol of the soul and of new life. The inscription accompanying this picture is conceived in the following terms, " Amun-ra, the venerable soul of Osiris, lies upon his body in the place of the resurrection." [2]

The principal representative of the gods of the second category is Ra-Harmachis of Heliopolis, between whom and Munt of Hermonthis, sun-god and warrior, there is really no difference. Now, Ra was combined with Amun under the name of Amun-ra, and even this last was named " Lord of An " (Heliopolis), and mention is made of his revered appearing in the house Benben (a mystical place localised in a sanctuary of Heliopolis). In this character, Amun-ra bears, like Ra-Harmachis, a sparrow-

[1] "Records of the Past," iv. 121.

[2] It is true that the head of Amun's ram always carries horns of a different form from those of Chnum, a fact to which Lepsius called attention ("Zeitschrift," 1877, pp. 8, 11); but this only proves that the ram's head was not borrowed by Chnum, but that the symbol was properly his own from the beginning. There is no doubt about the primitive meaning of the symbol, and hence none about the original signification of the two deities.

hawk's head. The principal gods of the third category are above all Atum or Tum and Osiris, and we find Amun-ra identified with both, which has come about through his form as Chem, being that of a hidden god, the same as Osiris. The hidden gods have in general a human head, with which Amun-ra likewise is represented.

It would be quite a mistake to look upon this as an amalgamation of gods, carried through without rule, and on no principle, a thing which has sometimes happened in epochs of transition. This was effected in a way distinctly systematic, and was the fruit of earnest and profound speculation, which has likewise found expression in the cultus. We see, in fact, that one bark only is represented in connection with each of the other gods, while Amun-ra has three quite distinct from each other; the largest, that of the mysterious soul, is adorned with rams' heads, the next, that of the manifested deity, has sparrow-hawk heads; the last, that of the hidden god in the underworld, has human heads.[1]

Amun-ra of the New Kingdom, as worshipped in the time of the Theban dynasties after the re-establishment of independence, is thus in fact the highest hidden deity who reveals himself in the sun. He is the embodiment of the loftiest and purest religious conception ever reached by the Egyptians. In him we see the conception of deity at the moment of its transition from the natural to the supernatural. The power to cast away entirely the materialistic elements, or to change the nature being into a pure transcendant god, was one not possessed by the Egyptians. This decisive step was not taken till much later, and by the Hebrews, who also must have had at first a dualistic idea of the deity. Traces of this may be seen in the case under our notice and likewise in the later Hebrew doctrine; and their conception of God, as we know it from the writings of the eighth century, is a development from such a dualism. In the Theban theology of the

[1] See Mariette, Abydos, Tom. i. 26° et 31° tableau, pp. 63 and 71.

New Kingdom all the germs of monotheism are present, but in Egypt they remain stationary in the first stage of their development, a result which is due mainly to political considerations. The people were not yet ripe for the adoption of the results of priestly speculation, and the reverence felt for the innumerable existing forms of religion, being also a primary condition of the unity and continued existence of the kingdom, would not suffer the worship of one God to supplant their varied polytheism.

This ambiguity is the key to the phenomenon that appears on the monuments of this period, where undeniably mythological representations are found side by side with utterances that would not be misplaced in the psalms and prophecies of Israel. In the famous poem of Pentaüra, in which the victory of Ramses II. over the Cheta is celebrated, the king speaks of Amun-ra just as the kings of Judah speak of Jahveh. " Shouldest thou be my father, O Amun ?" he asks; "and, behold! should a father forget his son ? Have I then put my trust in my own thoughts ? Have I not walked according to the word of thy mouth ? Has thy mouth not directed my marches, and have thy counsels not guided me ? Amun will bring low them that know not God."[1] The king next sums up the proofs of homage and worship paid by him to his divine protector, and goes on to say, " Shame be unto them that resist thy counsels ; blessed is he who comprehends thee, O Amun!" And when, forsaken by all, he finds himself surrounded by the enemy, he boasts that Amun was more to him than millions of his men of war. " The snares of men are nought, Amun will overcome them!" "Amun would be no god if he did not make his face glorious in the sight of the countless legions of the enemy." One of the successors of this king, Ramses III., testifies in the same spirit (inscription at Medinet-abu), " Amun-ra was on my right hand as well as on my left, his spirit inspired my resolves.

---

[1] Comp. W. Pleyte's translation of this hymn in the Theol. Tijds., 1869, p. 221 et seq.

Amun-ra has himself prepared the destruction of my enemies, and has given into my hand the whole world." He, too, in his campaigns followed the commands of Amun's mouth alone. Amun is likewise "the ruler of the circle of the gods, the absolute lord, the revered divine father." At the same time, however, the other sun-gods also, such as Ra, Tum, Harmachis, are invoked, and mention is made of Munt, of the divine sparrow-hawk, and even of Baal.

Another proof that Amun, notwithstanding the lofty character attributed to him, was never entirely disengaged from primitive nature conceptions is, that he continued to be coupled with goddesses as wives. And just as we have seen Amun combine in himself even the very greatest gods, so we find some of the very greatest goddesses conjoined with him. Three especially are mentioned at Thebes. They, it is true, are, properly speaking, only one and the same divinity presented under different aspects, the mother goddess in three forms, corresponding to the three forms of Amun that have just been explained. To the supreme creator in the form of Chnum, Amun *par excellence*, the ancient god of the town of Thebes, corresponds Amunt, a name which is simply the feminine of Amun. To the visible god of the sun, Amun-ra, corresponds the goddess of Thebes, Mat or Mut, the "mother," sometimes united with Neith of Saïs in the form Mat-Net, and more commonly, the Hathor of the Thebaid, the queen of Thebes, "the friend of him who is named with his mysterious name." Lastly, to the hidden god of the sun in the under world corresponds a form of Isis, goddess of the nocturnal heavens, represented in the repulsive shape of a gravid female hippopotamus, and called at Thebes Apé. In the actual worship, however, the place of most importance was taken by the second form, the type of the queen mother, the princess who gave to Egypt its future king.

The most erroneous idea that could possibly be entertained about the religion of Egypt would be to represent it as stationary, and fossilised into unchanging conceptions. There was in reality progress, but by the process of superimposing new and purer ideas on the old foundation, without ever sacrificing the least particle of the beliefs of the past.

The triad of Amun and Mut was completed by Chonsu, the son assigned to them. Like them he, too, lost the marks of his original character as nature-god, so completely, that for long it was a matter of uncertainty whether he was a moon- or a sun-god. But this uncertainty exists no longer. He was a moon-god. His father Amun-ra having combined in himself all the sun-gods, nothing was left for the son but to rule over the moon, and, in fact, he bears on his head the lunar disk, and, like Thot, he has in his hand a palm-branch, the symbol of time and of eternity. There was a temple at Thebes dedicated to Chonsu-Thot, and it is only in the character of a moon-god that he could have borne the name of measurer of time (*heseb hâ*). He bears, moreover, the attributes of royalty, like Osiris, who is also sometimes represented as a moon-god. The fact that Chonsu has been discovered represented with a sparrow-hawk's head is not proof sufficient that he was also a sun-god, for gods of very diverse character have this symbol in common. He is certainly the revealer of the will of the hidden god of night. Very great power was attributed to him; his oracles were consulted, he himself watched over the execution of his commands. One of his surnames is Pa-ar-secher, " he who does what pleases him ; " and in the temple of Chonsu-Thot this may be read, " Whatever comes out of his mouth comes to pass, and if he speaks, what he has ordained happens." He was resorted to for the cure of all diseases, or for the exorcism of all the evil spirits who inflict them.

The request addressed to Ramses XII. by one of his sons-in-law, the king of Buchten in Asia, that the statue of Chonsu might be sent to him to cure his daughter of a malady which the gods and priests of the country had attempted in vain to remove, shows what Chonsu's reputation in this respect was, even though the story itself is probably fictitious. Represented in the form of a mummy he is called Chonsu, the good repose (Neferhotep), a surname which indicates a god who originally reigned over the souls of the dead or the shades, as the moon reigns over the stars, but to whom afterwards a political signification was given. At least, in the time of the twentieth dynasty, in calling him Neferhotep, people thought of the repose of the country, and Chonsu was regarded as the most powerful enemy and destroyer of the rebels.

There is frequent mention made of him, and he was already worshipped under the eighteenth dynasty, but it was not till the time of Ramses III. that he rose to the height of his power as Lord of the Thebaid. This king erected for him a special temple, where he was worshipped under his three principal forms. It was then, too, that his fame spread to foreign parts.

Throughout this period Amun-ra was, there can be no doubt, the principal god of Egypt, although homage neither was exclusively paid to him, nor was he worshipped in common with one rival only in the north in the way suggested to Raskenen Ta by Apepi; for not only did he receive the highest honours as god of the king and of the court, but the other principal gods of the kingdom were, moreover, reformed after his pattern. This is a truly remarkable phenomenon, though it is not an isolated one, being met with elsewhere; in India, for example. All the chief sun-gods and gods of light were now represented and glorified in the same manner as Amun; they all became, in the eyes of their worshippers, the highest deity, and then, like the chief god of Thebes, frequently had Ra added to their names; for instance, Chnum-ra, Ptah-ra, Sebak-ra, and even Munt-ra. "Thy personality," so it is said in a hymn in praise of Shu belonging to this period, "is intermingled with that of Ra." In the same hymn Shu is raised to the position of leader of the gods, and called, exactly in the same way as Osiris and Ptah, the true lord of the double righteousness. He is now called likewise the god who formed his father and the husband of his mother, the well-known mythological mode of expressing that the highest god is uncreated. He is invoked by all the gods, and he is twice as great as they. This is expressed still more strongly in a hymn in honour of Ptah, which has been translated by Pleyte, a Dutch scholar. This hymn could be used equally well in the worship of Amun-ra as in that of Ptah, who also is called in it "the great hidden one whose image is not known," and he assumes sovereignty over the gods. Creator, life-giver, orderer of the portions of the earth and lord of righteousnesses, the eternal and exalted one unto whom there is none like, the living spirit who causes his spiritual being to go forth, lord of the years, who at his pleasure bestows life; he is, in fact, in no respect inferior to Amun-ra. The same thing could be shown in the case of other deities also. This inevitably led to the inference that all the gods did not differ essentially from each other, and were merely revelations, manifestations of the one great god. Accordingly, in this period the gods were confounded with each other, amalgamated and intermixed; the names and attributes of one were ascribed to another, and all were moulded after the same pattern. Upon the sarcophagus of the priest Beken-Chonsu, the living soul of the heavens is called Amun-ra-Tum-Harmachis. In the Magical Papyrus Harris, Shu is named like Ptah, young oldest one, *i.e.*, the eternal unchangeable;[1] like Sekru and Osiris, the two-horned god; and like Horos-Tem, the god who drives away the crocodiles; nay, he is even called "the very great goddess." In the same place Amun-ra likewise has a name applied to him which is usually borne by Ptah, namely, Tatanen, or Totunen.[2] In reality there was no longer any distinc-

---

[1] Records of the Past, viii. 5.
[2] In Wilkinson, Pantheon, p. 36, there is even found an image of Hathor as a sparrow-hawk, with the

tion made. The principal gods became amalgamated, the minor ones sank to the position of servants, or were regarded as forms in which the gods were manifested. Theocrasies of this kind could not have been formed unconsciously. Men knew perfectly that they were taking a great step in advance of their fathers. The absence of progress in Egyptian theology is more apparent than real, because the old forms were so carefully maintained that nothing appeared to change, but, in reality, an altogether new spirit had entered into the forms. The priest Bek-en-Chonsu, just referred to, speaks repeatedly on his sarcophagus of "the development of the doctrine of his gods."[1] This the priests actually accomplished. Already, under the dynasties of which we speak, their highest god was truly what Iamblichus described him, "one, self-existing, eternal, creator of all that is." Egyptologists deserve much credit for having brought this clearly out, though we cannot agree with some of them in regarding it as the surviving remnant of an earlier revelation, which had continued to keep its place in the midst of the deviations of priests and people.[2] We can see in it only the result of a protracted development. This advance Egypt owed to her scribes. They did not, as is generally supposed, keep their new ideas carefully concealed, so as to leave to the multitude nothing but coarse superstitions. The contrary is evident from a number of inscriptions which can be read by anybody, and from books which any one can buy. Whence came it, then, that the new was, as has just been noticed, merely put alongside of the old, which it had not power to supplant, and that a monotheism so plainly expressed did not effect a reform of the

---

legend, "Hathor under the robe (or the disguise) of Ra." De Rougé has directed attention to this in the Rev. Arch., 1867, p. 129, note 2. The representation may possibly be more recent, but it cannot be more ancient than the Theban dynasties of the New Kingdom.

[1] Devéria, in the Rev. Arch., 1861, vi., 102 *et seq.*
[2] Thus De Rougé, Exposé de l'Etat actuel des études Egyptiennes. (Recueil de Rapports, l'Egypte et l'Orient), p. 58.

worship, did not even, so far as is known to us, bring about in it the slightest alteration?

The cause of this I find in policy. If we except the Chinese, the Egyptian nation was more than any other faithful to tradition. If a place, a house, a district was sacred to any particular form of the deity, no alteration, at least externally, could occur. The name of the god and the forms of his worship must of necessity remain the same. Fallen temples might be restored or wholly rebuilt from the foundation, but they were always dedicated to the gods in whose honour they had originally been erected.

This peculiarity of the Egyptian nation, to the existence of which all the monuments testify, was one which the kings were obliged to respect, if they would not endanger their authority. The example of Amenophis IV. gives us an idea of how perilous it was to attempt alterations in religion. Rulers, consequently, who were prudent, carefully upheld all the peculiar sanctuaries and reverenced their usages. In regard to forms of worship they exercised the completest toleration, and allowed each place, each family, perfect freedom to choose and maintain their own deity and mode of worship. Yet, on the whole, the kings standing at the head of the priesthood managed to maintain an essential unity such as has seldom been found in conjunction with diversity so great. The worshippers of the various gods were not so tolerant, and showed often undisguised mutual detestation of each other, and of each other's gods. But the princes who were wise, kept the peace between the different districts precisely by this entire freedom of worship granted to each in his own territory, and by the protection which they extended to every local worship.

The religious policy of the kings of the New Kingdom was thus a policy of balance and of equal rights for all. The four chief gods of the different divisions of the kingdom, Ra, the god of Heliopolis, or properly the national god *par excellence*—the god of the whole country;

Amun, the god of Thebes and patron of the royal house; Ptah, the honoured god of the former capital, Memphis; and almost always also Sutech or Set, the god of the north since the days of king Apepi, worshipped principally at Tanis; these four were constantly united in the worship of the kings, and were honoured equally with gifts and temples. Sanctuaries were erected in Nubia for the three first-named deities so early as the time of Thutmes III. of the eighteenth dynasty, and these were afterwards embellished by Ramses II. Even in Syria, the inscriptions that were graven there in remembrance of his victorious campaigns record the names of these three gods. Nor did he and his father and their successors as well neglect to give a place to Sutech in the catalogue of these highest deities, even though this god was at certain places, as at Dendera and Edfu, regarded as identical with the evil one. Even in the king's names, the Rameside kings sought to maintain this balance; when the father was named Seti, beloved by Ptah (*Seti Merenptah*), the son was named child of Ra, friend of Amun (*Ramessu Meriamun*). If in that of the king the name of one of these chief gods was omitted, he was careful to bestow it on one of his sons. Even the high priests of Amun, when they had driven the kings of the twentieth dynasty from the throne, remained at first faithful to this traditional policy.

Thebes would thus appear to have been turned into a kind of pantheon; at least, there was there a visible token of the unity of the kingdom, a sanctuary dedicated to Ptah annexed to the temple of Amun-ra. This latter became a sort of religious metropolis,—a centre where, around the great god-ruler of them all, the principal gods of the country had their appropriate places. In regard to this, however, it will be necessary to enter somewhat more into detail.

The prince who was the first to introduce this religious policy, and who gave it his powerful support was, Thutmes III. His predecessors, Amenophis I. and Thutmes I., had already erected a stately edifice in place of the remains of the temple of Amun, founded by Usertasen I. The sanctuary of this new temple was surrounded by a number of chambers and a wide fore-court with side towers (pylons) and obelisks. Thutmes II. proceeded to enlarge this temple, adding among other things a hall supported by fifty-six pillars. When he introduced Ptah worship into Thebes for the first time, and founded in that city a special sanctuary for this god, he besides imported this worship into the temple of Amun. Here Ptah was even called Lord of the Thebaid.

At Thebes, too, he was distinguished by his green colour, by the blue beard and diadem of Amun, whose colour was blue; and at Thebes as at Memphis he was called "Lord of the Ell and of righteousness." Also, although his usual spouse Sechet occurs in the sanctuary, Hathor is assigned to him as wife; he retains, however, his son Imhotep, "the eldest child of Ptah, the beneficent god who comes when men call upon him who gives life to men." Thutmes III. likewise gave a place in the temple of Amun to Anubis and Thot. This king showed great zeal in the work of restoring or building up holy places in all parts of the country. His rock-temple in Nubia has been alluded to already. In like manner he founded sanctuaries for Chnum at Elephantine (Abu) and Esneh, for Sebak at Ombos, for Suben at Eileithyia, and for Munt at Hermonthis; and he rebuilt or adorned the temples of Ra at Heliopolis, and of Ptah at Memphis.

To judge from the monuments, it was long before Thutmes IV. showed any zeal like this. He seems to have been specially devoted to the worship of Ra-Harmachis; it was he at least who bestowed great care on the sphinx at Gizeh. A stela between the paws of that symbolical animal contains the following address to the king:—"The majesty of this beautiful god speaks by his own mouth, as a father speaks to his child, saying, Look to me, let thine eye rest on me, my son Thutmes! I, thy father, Harmachu-Chepra-Ra-Tum, I give you the kingdom." His successor, however, Amenophis III., again erected monuments for various gods, and in particular enhanced the glory of the Theban worship of Amun.

Amenophis IV., who succeeded him, acted in a totally different way, for not only did he abandon the policy of his predecessors, he even attempted to bring about an entire reformation, or rather, for so it must be called, a complete revolution in religion by the substitution of the god Aten, the sun's disk, in the place of Amun-ra. This is one of the most remarkable facts ever brought to light by antiquarian research.

It is impossible to fix with certainty the causes that provoked this religious revolution. Was Aten a foreign god introduced into Egypt? That has been conjectured, and from the similarity of name, it has been attempted to identify him with the Phœnician Adonis. Confirmation of this hypothesis has even, it is thought, been found in a story of the reign of Queen Misaphris, or Hatasu, sister of Thutmes III., who reigned some years before Amenophis IV. This queen sent a trading expedition to the country of the Pun or Puns; and the ambassadors of this people conveyed to Egypt in the Egyptian ships asserted that, equally with the queen, they adored Hathor, who is Aten. Was, then, the worship of this deity borrowed from them? Mariette has called attention also to the names of the mother and grandmother of Amenophis IV., Taya, daughter of Yuaa and Tuaa, which assuredly are not Egyptian names, and belong, in his opinion, to the Semitic branch of languages. But, in the first place, it is to be noticed, that Aten is a masculine deity, that the name is derived from a purely Egyptian root, and that mention is made of him in Egypt from time to time down to the reign of the Ptolemies. In the second place, Adonis is not exactly the god of the sun's disk; and lastly, the Puns, who, because of the analogy of name

L

have, till now, been confounded with the Pœni (Punians) or Phœnicians, were probably a people of African race.

The fact, however, that the mother of Amenophis IV., a devoted worshipper of Aten-ra, as the monuments show, was not of pure Egyptian extraction, but had very likely African blood in her veins, and that the principal officers of Amenophis IV. offer testimony in the inscriptions on their tombs—constructed while they were still in life— to their fidelity to the beliefs, to the worship, and to the "piety handed down by the old queen;" all this makes the supposition legitimate that even in her reign attempts were made, either on the part of herself or on that of her family, to change the hitherto received religion.

Before his accession Amenophis IV. had been a priest of Ra. Whether that may have led him to give supremacy to the worship of this god in the form of Aten, the glittering sun's disk, or whether it was owing to the influence of his mother, Ti or Taya, just referred to, I cannot tell; but, in any case, the fact remains that at this period the king forced upon the country the exclusive worship of this deity as a masculine being. Nor did he do this work imperfectly. Everywhere he rooted out the worship of other gods, especially of Amun, causing their names to be chiselled out and the monuments dedicated to them to be destroyed. The names of Ra and of Osiris alone were respected.[1] Out of hatred for Amun, after whom he was named, he changed his name, Amenhotep, into Chu-n-aten, "glitter of the sun's disk," and to the name of his wife, Nefer-Juti, he added besides that of Nefru-aten. He even purified the cartouches containing the kings' names. Where the name of Amun occurred in combination with theirs it was erased, and the reigning appellation of the king substituted, which is thus con-

---

[1] Not of Ra alone, as Brugsch, in his Histoire, p. 119, asserts, but also of Osiris and his circle of gods. This appears from a stela, on which a song in praise of Osiris remains sculptured. In it the name of Amun is erased throughout, but the names of Osiris, Isis, and Horos have been left. See Chabas, Rev. Arch., 1857, p. 67.

stantly found written twice, the one which was added side by side with that originally engraved. In Thebes, the town of Amun, it was impossible for him to live; it seems to have been too polluted for him. He accordingly chose to forsake it, and set up a new residence in Middle Egypt at Tell-el-amarna. The remains of it are still in existence, and show that it must have been of vast extent and magnificence. Traces have also been discovered of the great temple of the sun which he built there, with two forecourts and three pairs of pylons. In the cliffs near by are still to be seen the tombs of his courtiers, who, as their nature is, were humbly subservient to the royal caprice, and bowed low with the king in adoration of "the living sun's disk," although apparently, if he had been a servant of Amun, they would have offered their homage with not a whit less devotedness to that deity. There was no lack of servility among them, as is proved by the slavish attitude they always take on the monuments towards the king and his family, a servility unusual even for Egyptians, certainly in no way infected by the taint of republican ideas. Could it be from an excess of flattery that they allowed themselves to be represented just as ugly, nay, as horrible, as his majesty himself, with his fat paunch and idiotic look? The repulsiveness of the productions of the sculptor's art that have been discovered in Chu-n-aten's residence is at any rate very remarkable. It is scarcely possible in this case to suppose want of skill in the artists, though it might be that practised sculptors refused to lend themselves to the sacrilegious work of the reformer of religion. We are almost obliged to believe that it was designedly produced, though what motive there could be for so strange a whim cannot now be even conjectured. These defective works of the sculptor and painter are in strong contrast with the poetical productions of the worshippers of Aten. Aten-ra himself was represented as a sun's disk with a ureus and four suspended rings, whence shot rays terminating in hands; one of these hands is joined with the right hand of the king, another carries the emblem of life to his mouth.[1] All kinds of offerings were presented to him, flowers being the most frequent of these. A chief part of the service consisted in song, for which certain male and female singers were appointed, and the songs that they raised were distinguished by an elevation and poetic beauty which one would expect least of all in this peculiar court.[2]

In so far as we can judge of the reformation of Chu-n-aten, on which we hope newer discoveries will throw more light, its aim seems distinctly to have been to introduce a kind of monotheism. In this way alone is it possible to find an explanation of his persecution of Amun-worship and the other forms of religion, sun-worship alone excepted. This movement, happening at so early a period, is in the highest degree remarkable. It bore no fruit however. The very next successors of the reformer, though related to his family, being his sons-in-law, for he left no son, forsook the way in which he had walked, and once more offered homage to Amun. This, however, was not enough in the eyes of the orthodox. Every trace of Chu-n-aten's heresy, the very memory of this king and of the rulers who owed their sovereignty to him, must be blotted out. This was the work of King Horemheb (Horos), who, after the third successor to the reformer, gained possession of the supreme authority. He appears to have been of pure royal extraction. He caused the monuments erected by Chu-n-aten at Thebes to be defaced, and made use of the stones for other buildings. The capital in Middle Egypt was razed to the ground. Out of the monuments at Memphis bearing the name of Chu-n-aten, he even made a pavement; and thus this heresy was literally trodden under foot.[3] And not only was the

---

[1] See, as one example, the plate in Wilkinson, M. & C., Sup., Pl. XXX.
[2] Brugsch, Histoire, p. 118 et seq.
[3] That is seen from the accounts of Sir Charles Nicholson "On the Disk Worshippers of Memphis" in The Transactions of the Royal Society of Literature, II. Ser., vol. ix. part ii. p. 197 et seq. Up to this time no monuments of the re-

Theban triad now restored to a position of honour—that had been done at once by Amen-tut-anch, the immediate successor of Chu-n-aten—by Horemheb it was revered with passionate devotion. Accordingly, Amun, in his temple, built up out of the wreck of the defaced sun-temple, promises him a rich blessing. Along with Amun, Thot, god of the scribes, to whom his exaltation seems due, was worshipped.[1] As of old, Horemheb caused himself to be depicted standing between the two patron gods of the north and south of the empire, Set and Horos. The restoration was thus in full progress. Most of Horemheb's monuments are therefore of a religious nature, and he appears to have been what Manetho assures us he was, a kind of fanatic. Nevertheless, at his death the government passed to another dynasty.

The first of the Ramesids ascended the throne; his name and the gods to whose worship he was most devoted, lead us to suppose that he belonged to the north, and that, favoured by the disturbances that must have marked the end of the reign of Horemheb, he rose to be king.

This conjecture is supported by the circumstance that his grandson Ramses II. went afterwards to Memphis to pay homage to his forefathers, and identified himself with Sutech, the god of Lower Egypt.[2] He, it is true, founded a temple in honour of Horos in his ithyfallic former had been found so far to the north. They prove that the whole Pharaonic empire was subject to him. From the circumstance that worship of the deified sun's disk occurs as early as Amenophis IV., and that likewise Seti I. is represented at El Hammamât under that emblem, Nicholson makes out that the hostility to Chu-n-aten proceeded more from dynastic than from religious causes. His proofs do not seem to me sufficient. I myself called attention to Aten-worship under Misaphris; but it is one thing to worship Aten, another and a very different thing to try to make his worship exclusively supreme; which last attempt certainly gave rise to the persecution raised in later times against Chu-n-aten.

[1] Proof of this is afforded by the temple at Djebel-addeh in Nubia. Amun and Horos there take the first place beside Thot. Anka, the goddess of the district, nurses the king. Champollion, Monumens, Pl. II., 1, 2, 3.

[2] See the inscription in Brugsch, Histoire, pp. 150, 154.

form, but the gods principally occurring in his tomb are Tum of Heliopolis, as the "great god, the master of heaven, the first upon earth," and Neith, as "the great mother, the mistress of heaven and the queen of deities," both these being gods belonging to the north.

After his brief reign began the famous government of Seti I. (Ramaa-men Merenptah Seti), who appears to have been not his son but his grandson. His name, too, is purely northern, Ra, Ptah, and Set being gods of Lower Egypt. He accordingly seems to have found it necessary to strengthen his authority by nominating his son Ramses, who, as child of a royal princess, was of pure blood, immediately on his birth to be co-regent.[1] As a wise statesman, he also followed the religious policy of Thutmes III. It has been conjectured that he belonged to the family of the Hyksôs, a supposition based on the Syro-aramaic profile of himself and his son, and an inscription at Tanis.[2] If such was the case, he certainly did all in his power to do away with the offence which such a descent would give to the Egyptians. He paid zealous homage to Amun of Thebes, whose temple (at Karnak) he enriched with its indescribably wonderful hall unequalled in the whole world. It was 164 feet long by 320 feet broad, and supported by 134 immense pillars. In another quarter of Thebes (at Qurna) he caused a sepulchral temple to be erected in honour of his predecessor Ramses I., which, like the others, was sacred to Amun. Even in the temple erected or restored by him in Abydos, the ancient town of Osiris, he offers homage to Amun. The phrases in which this is done are characteristic of the way in which the various forms of religion prevailing at this period were confounded. The relief represents Seti offering the collar *usech* to "his father Amun;" the text that follows does

---

[1] This hypothesis is admirably defended by G. Maspero in his Essai sur l'Inscription Dedicatoire du Temple d'Abydos et la Jeunesse de Sésostris, Paris, 1867, p. 68 et seq.

[2] This conjecture, made by De Rougé, confuted by Mariette, has much to recommend it, but it still remains uncertain. See the passages quoted, p. 174, note I.

not however say one word about this god, but seems to have been adopted from a Heliopolitan writing concerning the duties of kings towards the gods. It is as follows:—" Be gracious, god Tum ! be gracious, god Ra ! thou the creator who rejoicest as often as thou risest in the heavens and as often as thou sendest thy rays out on the obelisks which are on the temple Oer-to at Heliopolis."[1]

The erection of this Osiris temple at Abydos by Seti and his son Ramses testifies to a revival of this very ancient Egyptian worship during the reign and under the patronage of these princes. This worship was, however, apparently not a simple restoration of the ancient system. The god to whom the new sanctuary was dedicated was not the old Osiris, but a combination of the three divine forms, Ptah-Sokar-Osiris. "Come to me," so it is said on an inscription, "Ptah-sekru-asiri, who art enthroned in Ramen-ma (the name of the temple), divine mystery of deities, and I come to thee, whose invocations are the divine mystery of deities." The three cognate divine forms that in the time of the first dynasties are met with separately, are here combined into one. This testifies to a modification in the original Osirian theology, which may well, however, be of earlier date than the reign of Seti. Besides, this temple, just like the temple of Amun at Thebes, was meant to be a metropolis, a pantheon. We have already said that Amun also was worshipped in it. Besides this reference to the god of the under world in his triune form, mention is also made of "the circle of the gods united with him there," which was divided into the great and the little circle of the deities of the north and south, and the sun-god Harmachu was particularly mentioned. Numerous offerings, consisting of four-footed beasts and of birds, were ordained by Seti and Ramses to be presented there. The texts tell of hundreds, thousands, hundreds of thousands, millions of such offerings; and the mode of expression used proves that the Egyptians, in

[1] Mariette, Rev. Arch., 1860, ii. 24.

common with the peoples most nearly akin to them and with the ancient Aryan peoples as well, regarded these offerings as being food for the gods.[1] In connection with this renewal of Osiris-worship, we find that under the nineteenth dynasty it was again regarded as a great privilege and as a pledge of future blessedness to be buried at that Abydos where the god of the under world reigned, and at which the mythic topography of the kingdom of the dead was expressed in the nomenclature of the surrounding places and districts.[2]

While Amun had a place in the temple of Ptah-Sokar-Osiris at Abydos, Ptah and Osiris were in their turn worshipped by Seti in the town of Amun. The so-called Speos Artemidos, the rock temple of the northern goddess Sechet at Beni-hassan in Middle Egypt, likewise owed its origin to Seti. This king accordingly neglected no one form of his country's religion that was of any consequence, and he thereby proves himself to have been as able a ruler as he was a fortunate general; and it would seem as if, by his worship of local gods in districts to which they had not originally belonged, he wished to offer a proof that the local gods were now gods of the Egyptian nation, and worthy of the homage of all.

To the gods of Egypt there were even added in this period foreign deities with whom the Egyptians had become acquainted in the brilliant and victorious campaigns of Seti I. and his successors. Baal, Astarte, Anata, Kedesh, Reshpu,[3] Canaanite and Syrian gods, were now worshipped and had their priesthoods in the valley of the Nile; although, by the mode of their representation, they may still in all cases be distinguished clearly from the Egyptian gods.[4]

---

[1] Mariette, Rev. Arch., 1866, i. p. 76.
[2] Lepsius Zeitschrift, 1868, p. 2.
[3] This name used to be read Ranpu. First, Birch, and independent of him De Vogüé, discovered the true reading, Reshpu. It denotes the Phœnician god of thunder who occurs often on Cyprian monuments. See De Vogüé, Mélanges d'Archéologie Orientale, p. 76 et seq.
[4] Chabas throws doubt on the

Ramses II., Meriamun, the beloved of Amun, whom the Greeks call by one of his surnames Sesostris, shared, as we saw, his father's throne, and at his father's death he carried on the government in the same spirit. With the tale of his wars and much-vaunted heroic deeds, of which the well-known poem of Pentaüra gives so exaggerated a description, and with the question whether he really deserved the epithet "the great," so frequently bestowed upon him, we have not here to concern ourselves. He was not deficient in energy, industry, and personal courage; but neither did he lack vanity, which made him jealous even of the fame of his predecessors, and caused him to put down their achievements to his own account. In matters of religion he carried out in its entirety the policy of his father and of Thutmes III.; and, following their example, he even founded in Nubia four sanctuaries and four towns in connection with them, dedicated to the four principal gods, Ra, Amun, Ptah, and Sutech, or rather to himself under the form of these deities, and especially of the last. It is to be expected that a king, whose thirst for fame surpasses that of all his not too modest predecessors, and who seems to have made self-glorification the end of his life, would have a passion for building; and that, in truth, is the case. As a matter of course, he extended and embellished the great temple of Karnak (Thebes), but the work done there by his orders is far surpassed by what he did to extend the tomb-temple of his father, Seti I., and his grandfather, Ramses I., at Qurna on the west bank of the river at Thebes, and by his erection in the same place of the Rameseum, his own tomb-temple, dedicated to Amun-ra. The ancients extolled especially a cedarwood bark. It was gilt without, and overlaid with silver within, and was dedicated by the king to the chief god of Thebes, and, in fact, the inscrip-

Egyptian Bar or Bal being the same as Baal. Pleyte has, however, rightly contested the opinion of this scholar. Theol. Tijds. 1869, pt. iii. p. 243, note 27.

tions do speak of a sacred boat of this kind in the first-mentioned grave-temple, intended to bear the god Amun on some particular festival, and which had been made for him by Ramses I. With not less laudation do they tell of a colossal image in the tomb of Osymandias, as they called the Rameseum. This must have been the sitting statue of our Ramses, now broken, but which must once, including the pedestal, have been no less than forty-one feet high. To describe this and other monuments does not come within the sphere of a history of religion, and is important in the history of art or of archæology alone. We shall only observe, in passing, that during the long reign of Ramses Meriamun there was a great decay in art. The most ancient monuments bearing his name are to be counted among the best that Egyptian antiquity can show. The last, on the other hand, are of bad and careless workmanship and show a sad declension; and the declension was manifest not only in this but in everything. The most oppressive despotism alone could have maintained peace in an empire which extended far into Asia, and was thus composed of the most heterogeneous elements. Nothing but a power of this kind could raise levies for such exhausting wars, and supply hands for such innumerable public works. With this despotism is connected the apotheosis of the king, which reached a climax in the reign of Ramses II. Not only did he, like the preceding kings, cause himself to be worshipped in temples which he himself had erected; not only did he place himself as their equal beside Amun and Ptah, Ra and Sutech[1]—others, even in the time of the Old Kingdom, had done something of the same kind—but he placed himself at the head of the gods, and called himself their ruler (inscription at Gerf-Hussên in Nubia). It would, however, be a mistake to regard this apotheosis as

---

[1] In agreement with this worship of Amun, Ra, Ptah, and Sutech, in the Nubian temples, and of Ramses II. along with them, is an expression in the Pap. Leid., 380, where this prince is invoked by the names of these deities.

the literal deification of a man, and simply to class it with, for example, the worship offered to the Roman emperors. It was, in fact, a religious-political fiction of the same kind as the Legitimist's "king by the grace of God," and the "king inviolable" of the Constitutionalist. It was not the man Ramses or the man Thutmes himself personally; it was his essence (*ka*), his heavenly type, to which the highest worship was paid, because that was identified with the being of the highest deity. In the case of the Egyptians the fiction was this:—Horos or Ra, the chief sun-god, is, in short, properly the king of Egypt (just as at a later time Jahveh was of Israel); the living king is his manifestation on earth, into whom the fulness of the god has passed. Hence no one saw any sacrilege in thus worshipping the king in his spiritual being as actually God, and it was a totally different thing from vulgar idolatry. It was a deification of the king's office rather than of the king, one of the boldest ways of expressing theocracy. Because of this —and this must on no account be lost sight of in judging a phenomenon which to us is of so unusual a character— because of this the king himself regularly stands on the monuments as worshipper before his own image, and he himself offers incense and other gifts to his own divine being. The living person, the worshipping king, was thus kept quite distinct from the being worshipped.

It was accordingly no wonder that the king should be regarded as the mediator and the all-powerful mediator between men and the deity. An example of this, in the highest degree remarkable, is given by a stela found at Dakkeh, in Nubia. What is related on this stone gives us, besides, a curious parallel to the story in Exodus, of the supply of water miraculously obtained for the children of Israel in their wanderings in the desert. The case was as follows:—The miners in a district of Ethiopia were in great want of drinking water. A well dug by Seti I., 120 cubits deep, was dry, and remained so. It was resolved to apply to Ramses, who at the time was at Memphis.

Help was expected from him. "Thou art as the sun," with this among other phrases the king was approached; "for thou doest all that thy heart desirest, it all comes to pass. If during the night thou hast formed a project, it is realised as soon as there is light upon the earth. Every utterance that proceeds from thy mouth is as the words of the god Harmachis. The balance (of righteousness) is in the midst of thy lips, and the vessel of equipoise is placed there by god Thot; if thou sayest to the water, Come forth from the rock, the heavenly water comes forth to sight at thy word, for thou art Ra, with the members of Choper (the beetle, the creator). Thou art the living image of Ra, and the son of thy father Tum of Heliopolis. The god Hu is in thy mouth, and the god Sau in thy heart;[1] the seat of thy tongue is the sanctuary of truth. A god is settled upon thy lips, and thy words are daily brought to pass. What thy heart has made goes over to god Ptah, who creates all works." (Ptah is thus here, in fact, he who carries out into action the thoughts of the king as of the highest god.) The prince of Kush, *i.e.*, the governor of Ethiopia, presses the request of his subjects, and says in addition, "If thou thyself sayest to thy father, god Nile (Hâpi), the father of the gods, Cause the waters to come forth from the mountain! then will it all come to pass as thou hast spoken and commanded; for although we ourselves should be present, yet would not our prayer be heard; but thou, thou art beloved by thy father and all gods more than any king since God reigned" (after Brugsch's translation). We hardly need to say that on this occasion the trial was perfectly successful, for otherwise the inscription would not have existed, and this success was, of course, ascribed to the miraculous power of

---

[1] Hu is the god of taste, and likewise also of sensible feeling. Sau, the god of intelligence, sometimes also regarded with hearing, sight, and touch, or taste, as one of the four senses. In the sun-bark, Sau is the head of the equipage, and Hu is steersman. In this place Hu appears to be the god of eloquence. In the "Book of the Dead," xvii. 16, a mystic use is made of this. See De Rougé, Rev. Arch., 1860, i. 244.

Ramses.[1] The well-turned phrases provoke a smile, but we should err if we took them to be mere empty formulas such as are in use in the no less bombastic style of government papers in the East in our own day, and it would be equally a mistake to see in them mere barefaced flattery. Such phrases expressed the belief of those times; people were as firmly convinced in regard to the miraculous power of the king as Roman Catholics are now in regard to the infallibility of the Pope.

Ramses II., the great antagonist of the Cheta, who were worshippers of Sutech, was himself fervently devoted to this god. He had dedicated a temple to his service at Thebes in the southern quarter of the town, and in other places, too, he seems to have done the same. A priest of this sanctuary is called "The consecrated of Osiris, the scribe of the temple of Sutech, Nofremen." Two of the king's sons were named after this god, and at Tanis (Sân), in the temple of Set, he caused Seti, governor of the district of T'sar (Avaris, Pelusium), commander of the army and chief prophet of Set, to erect a monument in commemoration of the fourth centenary of the new calendar instituted at that place by Nubti-Suti, or Sutech-aa-pehti-nubti, shepherd-king and worshipper of Sutech. This possibly indicates the ground on which he favoured the northern god, and gives some support to the supposition that he was really a descendant of the king just mentioned. Or it may be that he deemed it a matter of importance from a political point of view that he, as conqueror of Palestine and ally of his former enemies the Cheta, should pay special honour to the religion of these northern regions. It would appear that even at Koptos, where from of old Chem or Min, in whom we recognised the same god as Horos-Munt and Amun, was worshipped, the worship of Set was introduced by Ramses, and combined with that of the local deity.[2]

---

[1] Brugsch, Histoire, p. 150 *et seq.*
[2] At least a stela of this period discovered near Koptos contains the unusual combination Munt-har-Set.

Nor was Memphis forgotten. It was in the reign of Ramses Meriamun that the Apis-worship revived with renewed glory, and that the worship paid to the dead sacred bulls, if it did not then originate, was at least practised with especial devotion. If every justified dead person became Osiris, the same happened in the case of the consecrated Apis at his death, and hence he received the name Asar-hapi, which gave rise to the word Serapeum, applied to the magnificent burial-place of these animals which Mariette discovered in the neighbourhood of Memphis. One of the sons of Ramses, probably the heir-apparent to the throne, who, however, died before his father, Chamûs (Sha-em-Zam, as his name used to be read), had devoted himself wholly to the service of Ptah in this form. It would appear that he caused himself to be entombed in the most beautiful sepulchre of that edifice. At least in one of the chapels, on the outside of which are nothing but inscriptions applying to a dead Apis, there has been discovered the fragment of a mummy in human form, upon which the name of Chamûs may be seen several times repeated. If it is really his corpse that lies buried here, this is one of the most striking examples of how the Egyptians were accustomed to identify themselves completely, both in life and death, with the deity to whom they had chosen to consecrate themselves. Chamûs, governor of Memphis and high-priest (Sem) of Ptah, and the living Apis, thus desired to rest by the side of the adored animals to whom, as manifestations of his favourite god, he had during his life paid homage. It is certain that in this respect the place of Chamûs was filled, even in the lifetime of their father Ramses, by his other son and future successor, Merenptha (Menepthes).

Ebers has drawn from it the same inference as that in the text. The expression, however, may also simply signify, "Munt, lord of Upper and Lower Egypt," which appears to me not unlikely. Even the ancient kings called themselves Horos-Set, as being rulers over both divisions of the country.

The treaty made between Ramses II. and Chetasir, king of the Cheta, the powerful nation that persistently contested with the Egyptians[1] the sovereignty of Western Asia, and whose exact geographical position and race are not yet precisely determined, gives us very valuable insight into the religious ideas of the time and the principal religions of the kingdom. It is represented as the execution of the decrees of the gods, particularly of "Ra and Sutech for the land of Egypt in its relation to the land of Cheta." Ra is here the representative of Egypt, Suti, or Sutech, that of the people of the Cheta; these were accordingly the distinctive national gods of the two countries respectively. In the next place, the following, Amun-ra, Harmachu, Ptah of Memphis, lord of Anchta (the land of life, or the living world), Munt, lady of Acheru (the under world), and thus a goddess of the mother earth, and Chonsu-nefer-hotep, are named as patron gods of Ramses, and he, besides presenting offerings to most of these gods, presents them also to Set, "the great warrior, the son of Nu." As the solemnities of the treaty were transacted in the town named after the king, Pa-Ramses Meriamun, the town at the building or fortification of which Exodus tells us that the oppressed Hebrews were forced to labour, Ramses paid homage expressly to the forms of Amun and Ptah, for which he had in that place erected sanctuaries. Among the Egyptian gods whose blessing was invoked over this treaty there were named, over and above those already mentioned, the hills and the streams, the earth, the winds, nay even, what is very remarkable, thunderstorms, and the great sea. The Cheta likewise, although they worshipped Sutech as their principal god, and his name seems to have acquired among them an appellative

---

[1] Prof. Sayce of Oxford has recently conjectured, on the evidence of the Hethite names and of some words deciphered in the inscriptions of Hamath in Syria, and of Jerabees (Girbâs, the ancient Gargamish), that they were nearest akin to the Sumirs and Accads, the original founders of the Chaldean and Assyrian civilisation.

signification, like that of Baal among the Syro-Phœnicians, were by no means monotheists. Among them, as among the Egyptians, we hear of hundreds of male and female gods, some of whom are referred to. Antarta (Astarte?) is specially named. They likewise looked upon mountains and streams as sacred. From all this it is seen that, as regards religious worship, there was in the main no difference between the two peoples, and that the Egyptians at least found no difficulty in adopting the gods of the Cheta as their own.

It is generally supposed that it was in the reign of Menephta, son and successor of Ramses, that the exodus of the Hebrews from Egypt occurred, for the hypothesis, which was till recently the most favoured, that this event took place in the reign of Ramses III. of the twentieth dynasty, has been completely refuted by Chabas. This distinguished scholar has also proved that Menephta was not, as has hitherto been believed on the authority of Manetho, a feeble and incapable ruler, and the whole tale of the priest of Sebennys about the exodus Chabas regards as being a pure fabrication, an opinion which is likewise my own, and which I published in 1870. Menephta seems to have had his residence at Memphis. If he supported the worship of Amun, his personal devotion was directed with fervour towards Ptah and Set, and the latter he worshipped chiefly in the form assumed by him at Avaris (Pelusium), which was of a character rather foreign than Egyptian. He worshipped him also as Nub, lord of the south; for Set, no doubt on account of his coarse nature, had been adopted as their god by the barbarian negroes of Nubia. This preference for gods of the Hethites may probably be explained in its general principle by the dread of an invasion by that people, and by the wish, if a conflict should occur, to gain for Egypt the favour of the foreign deity; yet in the case of Menephta, as in that of his father, the leaning towards these gods may perhaps have been a natural characteristic, the effect and the mark of the race whence they descended.

With Menephthes (Merenptah) the decline of the southern power begins, which, under the twentieth dynasty, was destined to proceed with increasing rapidity. It is true that a long series of Theban kings still bear rule, and that among them there are some who, like Ramses III., approach the glory of Seti and Sesostris. They, it is true, likewise continue to erect monuments and to announce in bombastic phrases the grandeur of their warlike achievements, but the traces of growing feebleness are unmistakably visible. I shall not follow these Ramesids through the monotonous history of their reigns; they possess little or no originality, and are mere copies, some of them very unsuccessful copies, of their predecessors. The most conspicuous among them is Ramses III., already referred to, who erected the great temple of Amun-ra at Medinet-abu (Thebes). He was the last conqueror of his race. His successors had difficulty in keeping hold of their possessions; only in the love of fame they were not inferior to those before them. They continued to erect monuments and to celebrate their own praises upon them, until at length the priests of Amun succeeded in obtaining for themselves in reality the sovereignty which for long they had practically possessed, and the last of the Ramesids was driven by them from the throne.

Under the twentieth dynasty, religion remained the same outwardly as under the preceding kings. The only difference we can perceive is a more zealous worship of the god Chonsu, who now comes more to the front. Ramses III. erected a special sanctuary in his honour, which is the principal source for the history of this period; and a tale is told of how Chonsu's fame extended even to a foreign land. This seems to be connected with two circumstances which may be observed in this period, namely, the growing power of the priests and the increase

M

of superstition. Chonsu was, it is to be noted, like Amun, but to even a greater degree, god of the priests, and an oracle-god who worked miracles. The first high priest who assumed the crown, Her-hor by name, selected the temple of Chonsu as the place in which to announce his great deeds. Chonsu is also closely connected with Thot, who properly is the god of scholars. We have already frequently cited the hymns translated by Pleyte, and which date from the time of the twentieth dynasty; they are principally dedicated to Ptah, yet in them the form Thot-Chonsu occurs, and Thot is invoked with a great show of affection. The poet forgets that it is Ptah he is celebrating, and all at once breaks out into praises of the god of Hermopolis; and in doing so calls to mind how Thot, the patron of scholars, artistically laid out the garden of the land of Egypt after his plans, and arranged the partition of the fields in beautiful order. "He distributed," so he himself says, and the application is unmistakable, "the powers, he set up the heads, he rooted out faults, he abolished lies, a pleasant breath came forth from him." He then calls to mind what he did in the conflict of the gods—"He, the great arbiter between Set and Horos, the reconciler of powers, the great peacemaker in the conflict. On this account has Ra exalted his spirit, and he, skilled in ruling, governs men and gods." Does not this read like an invitation to have confidence in the image-bearers and representatives of Thot on earth who would remove offences, and prove better sovereigns than the weak kings? All the benefits enjoyed by Egypt proceed in truth properly from them,—the learned class. Ra himself has judged that they are fit to rule. When we recollect that this was written in the reign of the ninth Ramses, the allusion to what was about to happen is evident enough.

A conflict between the authority of priest and king was hardly possible in earlier times, for then the kings themselves, their sons, and their principal officers of state were the chief priests, and the priestly dignities were not dis-severed from nor held to be inconsistent with other and civil functions. There was merely a learned class, not marked off, however, more distinctly than among our-selves, and which men could enter or leave at pleasure. But at the commencement of the twentieth dynasty an alteration appears to have begun. There are high priests of Amun other than the kings. Priesthood and laity are further apart. The temple of Ramses II. at Qurneh is quite open, that of Ramses III. at Medinet-abu (both quarters of Thebes) is closed by a balustrade against the eye of the curious.[1] The office of first prophet or high priest did not, it is true, become hereditary, as seems to have been the case at this time with other offices;[2] but still it passes in several instances from father to son. A thing hitherto unknown in Egypt was now in process of formation there, namely, a separate spiritual caste, a fixed priesthood. The priests, whether nominated by the kings or appointed in some other way, were now suffered to take charge not only of the service of the sanctuary, but of other things as well. To the authority of the kings this concession was fatal. In the reign of Seti II. the high priest Roi had made his influence felt, and under his successors in the priestly office—Roma, Meribast, Ram-ses-necht, Amun-hotep—that influence continued steadily to grow more and more considerable, until at last Herhor exchanged the title of grand vizier or Major-domo for the royal dignity. With that event, however, the power of Thebes was broken for ever, and its influence, which would seem latterly to have been maintained by the glory of the name of Ramses only, now became extinct. There

---

[1] This is noted by Sharpe, His-tory of Egypt, p. 92, a book which must in other respects be used with great caution.

[2] Thus we have a full list of the ancestors of a certain Chnum-het-ra, who, under Amasis (571-527 B.C.), was head architect of North and South Egypt, and who combined that office with the discharge of other functions, some of them re-ligious. All the ancestors, the first of whom goes back certainly to the end of the twentieth dynasty, fill the same office. Brugsch, Histoire, p. 256 et seq.

was, it is true, in Egypt, nothing more common than that the king should be at the head of religion as well as of the state, but a supremacy exercised by the priesthood of one particular deity, even the highest, was entirely contrary to the spirit of the people.

Contemporary with the growth of priestly authority in the south, which still continued to be the seat of empire, was the growth—not unconnected with the first—of superstition. The people of Egypt were already sufficiently inclined to it, and in their religion mysticism and magic took a prominent place. With a symbolism so extensive that at last even the learned failed to decipher it, this was inevitable. But in the period on which our attention is now fixed, this inclination waxed stronger. Sober moral maxims like those of Ptah-hotep of the Old Kingdom, tales of real life like that of Saneha of the Middle Kingdom, are no longer to the taste of this period. Fancy made good her claims. There must be poetry now, and above all, magical books filled with spells, and songs of power, and tales of wonder like that of Anepu and Batau. This change is visible even in the "Book of the Dead." In the chapters that belong to this period the symbols and ceremonial are more intricate, and the formulas longer. The advantage to be gained by the use of particular chapters is brought more forward, and is dilated on at greater length.[1] To such an extent did sorcery increase, that in the reign of Ramses II. it became necessary for the authorities to take measures against it. A certain Hai, or Hui, was condemned to death because he was a conjuror, and had bewitched people "by divine power," for which purpose he had cunningly contrived to get possession of a magical book. Evidently the judges themselves never doubted the reality of this magical power, but they passed sentence of death upon Hai, who was a herdsman, because he carried on the practice of magic in an unauthorised manner.[2] The love of magic

[1] See Lefébure, Hymnes au Soleil, p. 6.
[2] Chabas, Pap. Mag. Harris, p. 170.

must certainly have been great, when people busied themselves with it even at the risk of being capitally punished. About this time, too, great stress began to be laid upon particular days. There are various calendars of the time of the Ramesids which tell the good and the fatal days (*dies fasti et nefasti*), and which contain rules to be followed, in order to prevent disaster. One of these I cite with some examples:—

24. Thot (June—July) was a great day of mourning. On it and on the two following days the great conflict took place between Set and Horos, in which Set was not slain, and Isis was wounded.

9. Paophi (July—August). A propitious day, for on it the gods had slain their enemy.

12. Choiak (September—October). On this day one ought not to go out, because it is the day on which the transformation of Osiris into the Bennu-bird takes place.

14. Toby (October—November). Listen to no voluptuous songs, because Isis and Nephthys on this day bewail their brother Osiris.

17. Toby. Do not bathe, because the goddess Nu, the heavenly water, goes out upon this day.

20. Toby. Barisis takes away the light of the world, where is darkness only. Therefore until sunset do not go out.

3. Mechir (November—December). Do not travel, for on this day Set accomplished one of his journeys.

14. Mechir. Sebak slain upon the deck of the bark of the gods. Do not go out.

29. Mechir. Set in all his fury. Look upon nothing till sunset.

24. Pharmuthi (January—February). Do not pronounce the name of Set in joke, else there will be quarrels and dispeace in the house.

Much fasting is now enjoined. Days without mythological reference, and those on which the gods were victorious, are all propitious. The references are chiefly borrowed from the Osirian mythology.[1] In the opinion of the ancient Egyptians, the day on which a man was born, naturally exercised of necessity a great influence upon his future lot. One born on the 5th Paophi will be killed by a bull, but one whose birthday is kept on the 9th of the same month, is destined to live to a great age. And so on for a great many other days in the year. People also occupied themselves not a little at this period with mystic names and magical formulas that were utterly destitute of meaning. The 162nd chapter of the "Book of the Dead," that must have been written in the time of the New Kingdom, contains invocations of such names as Penhakahakaher-her, Uarauaakarsank-Robiti, and was therefore considered to be very profound. Other texts of the time of Ramses II. comprise invocations of senseless names of the same sort, such as Kamchar-Kamerau-Karchamu, Shatabuta, Artabuhuïa, Anrohakata-Satita, and countless others. Whoever wishes to be convinced how far belief in the miraculous had overstepped, among the Egyptians, all bounds of possibility, has only to read the tale of Batau and Anepu,[2] already referred to, which has so much in common with the history of Joseph, and which, just on that account, offers an admirable opportunity for instituting a comparison between the sound sense of the Hebrew narrator, and the unbridled phantasy that prevailed among Israel's former oppressors. It is comparatively nothing that Batau understands the language of animals, and that there springs into existence between him and his brother who persecutes him a broad stream filled with crocodiles; but he has the power of laying down his heart, his principle of life, in the flower of an acacia, so that when the flower is cut off, his death must of necessity be the result. But if the heart is laid

---

[1] De Rougé, Rev. Arch. 1852, ii. 687-691. Another calendar is contributed by Chabas, Pap. Mag. Harris, p. 157.
[2] The tale is translated by De

Rougé, Rev. Arch., 1852, p. 385 et seq. Brugsch, Aus Dem Orient, p. 7 et seq. Ebers Aeg. u. d. Bucher Moses, p. 311 et seq.; and Chabas treats of it op. cit., p. 164 et seq.

in a certain liquid, it will find its way to its ordinary position, and Batau will rise again. Thus it came to pass. The gods shape a wife for him. The king seizes her from him. She confides the secret of Batau's heart to her new husband. Anepu, however, brings his brother to life again by the aid of the magical liquid. He next changes himself into a bull, a holy Apis. The king having discovered who the bull is, causes him to be killed, but from two blood-drops of the sacred animal two magnificent persea trees arise. These are in turn hewn down, and all would have been over with Batau, had not a splinter of one of these miraculous trees flown into the mouth of the queen, who, by and by, brings her own husband forth into the world again as a son.

The material out of which this tale is woven is not far to seek. Evidently it is nothing but the ancient mythology and theology transferred to the region of humanity. Who does not recognise in Batau the husband of his mother: the god who, when he dies, like Ptah, in the sacred bull, revives, like Osiris, in the sacred acacia, or persea tree: the good being who is persecuted and killed, but who through the care of Anepu (Anubis) rises again from the dead? But the fact that these holy myths are brought down from the world of the gods among the children of men, is a proof that the original signification of these sacred emblems had become lost to many, and that belief in the miraculous had risen to an amazing height.

It would not be fair, however, to judge of the religious development of this period merely from such extravagances. That is only one side and the dark side of the picture. There are poems and hymns which give brighter light, and show that loftiness and beauty were not wanting. Of these, examples have been already given, and it would be quite easy to multiply the number of them very considerably. The religion which was the source of inspiration for such works, was not, we may be sure, lacking in true piety. A sufficient proof of this is to be found in the truly grand conception of Amun-ra, who under the New Kingdom was still celebrated in hymns that recall often the most beautiful passages of the Hebrew psalms. In one hymn he is designated by these names "the greatest in heaven, the oldest upon earth, the Lord who gives to everything existence and duration." "His hands give to those whom he loves, but his enemy he casts down into the fire, for his look annihilates the workers of iniquity, and the ocean engulfs the wicked whom he consumes." "Thou alone existest, thou the creator of being." "He alone has formed all creatures. Men are born from his look, from his word the gods receive their being. He makes the plants for the beasts, and fruit-bearing trees for mortals. He makes the fish live in the water, the birds beneath the vault of heaven; he makes the germ that is in the egg grow, he gives life to the grasshoppers, he feeds all that crawls, and all that flies. He gives their food to the mice in their holes. Blessed be thou, thou who doest these things! Thanks be unto thee, who art one only and alone, and who hast several arms (symbol of Amun-ra's activity, and of the manifoldness of his works). In thy rest thou watchest over men, and considerest what is best for the beasts. . . . As high as heaven, as wide-stretching as the earth, as deep as the sea, the gods fall down before thy majesty extolling the spirit of him who has created all things. . . . Praise to thy spirit because thou hast made us; we are thy creatures, thou hast placed us in the world."

Taking everything into consideration, we may say that at this time religion was much more powerful than in the preceding periods. Its action was upon the whole field of life, so that no single step could be taken, no enterprise could be entered on, no thought could be formed apart from it. That is likewise the result of an examination of the tombs of this period. In them the dead person is no longer represented in his personal and domestic life, but in his political and religious life. While the ancient magical texts, afterwards gathered together in the "Book of the Dead," are rarely found in the tomb temples of the preceding periods, in those of the New Kingdom they cover all the walls; and the images of the gods, vainly sought for in the ancient tombs, here shine everywhere in high relief, side by side with those of the dead. The mortuary stelæ are also covered with religious representations.

As a consequence of this development, we must note an important change in the doctrine of immortality. From this time all who die become Osiris. In place of the ancient faith that the future life was only a continuation of the present, we find now the doctrine of retribution. The resurrection of the god of light continues indeed to be the pledge and guarantee of that of his worshipper, but this new life is believed to depend henceforth on the man's moral conduct and religious zeal. This indicates genuine progress in religion, though on the other hand it must be acknowledged that this eudemonism did not always exercise the most favourable influence on morality. The superstitious practices and magical formulas of which we have just spoken, coupled with the increasing power of the priests, are to be accounted for in a great measure by fear of the judgment.

CHAPTER VIII.

THE EGYPTIAN RELIGION FROM THE FALL OF THE RAMESIDS TO THE PERSIAN CONQUEST.

THE supremacy of the South ended simultaneously with the fall of the Theban sovereignty. If Thebes again recovers once or twice a little of its former greatness, it is indebted for that to northern kings who raise it for a time from its humiliation. The South does not indeed give up the contest. The Theban high priests of Amun who had usurped the throne of the Rameside kings were soon driven out, and found themselves compelled to take refuge in Ethiopia, and in their persons the genuine Egyptian royal line was in fact banished from the country. Yet, constantly, whenever the least opportunity offered, when there was the smallest chance of success, so soon as any division or confusion arose in the North, they come forth from their retreat and bring the whole country into subjection; but they no longer have power enough to maintain their sway. It is from the North that the dynasties arise which now reign and are regarded as legitimate, till foreign conquerors deprive them of their sceptre, at the time when those nations, who were then foremost in the world, contested the sovereignty of it among themselves, Egypt being part of the prize.

A dynasty of Lower Egypt having its seat at Tanis, or belonging originally to that town, took advantage of the strife between the kings and priests at Thebes so as to get the supreme power into their own hands. Were these descendants of the former Shepherd Kings, or at least connected with them in some way? Had they perhaps sprung from the family of the commander Seti, whom we met with in the reign of Ramses II. as governor of the north-eastern districts? As to this we are quite in the dark, as we also are in regard to the history of these kings. This much is certain, under their rule the Tanitic religion, the worship of Sutech, was not the prevalent one, but rather a religion which had its seat at Mendes, another town in the Delta.

The religion of Mendes was very ancient, and existed all along under the kings of the Old Kingdom. Thus early, whether by Kakau (Kaiechos), or by his son Binuter (Binothris), the worship of the sacred he-goat appears to have been instituted at that place (see p. 97). Mendes—for this properly was the name of the he-goat, and it seems to have been the Greeks who transferred the name of the sacred animal to the town—signifies "the he-goat of Ded or Dud," or also, because the he-goat is its symbol, "the spirit, the soul of Ded." Ded was the name of the town, and it also has a mythological meaning. *Ded*—or as the various readings give it, *dudu* or *dad*—is the familiar pillar with the four cross-beams or tables on the top, commonly called the tat-pillar, and believed by Champollion to be a nilometer. The pillar expresses the idea of durability, stability,—an idea which from the most remote antiquity takes such a prominent place in all Mesopotamian religions. To me it appears that the pillar is an image of the universe itself, of which the cross-beams represent the four heavens arching above each other, as they are frequently to be seen represented in the vignettes of the "Book of the Dead."[1]

[1] In Hebrew the word signifying *world* is likewise, as is well known, derived from a root signifying "to be durable." That the dad-pillar has some connection with Osiris, and also with Ptah, is evident from the fact that they are themselves often represented in this form, as we have already noticed. At Busiris, too, a place which takes its name from Osiris, a festival was celebrated, called, "The erection of the dad-pillar." The name of the priest Pe-nehem-isis, upon whose tomb-monument the name of King Ban-ded, the first of this dynasty, oc-

Ba-n-ded would then signify the spirit of the universe, and was no other than Chnum himself, in his highest and most comprehensive form. Chnum, represented at Mendes as the god with the four ram's heads, to whom reference has before been made, was worshipped there as the creating or life-giving spirit of the four worlds of Ra (the upper heaven), of Shu (the air, or heaven of clouds), of Set (the earth), and of Osiris (the under-world), and these worlds are precisely those which are symbolised by the pillar Ded or Dud. These four spirits were represented separately in various places : in the highest conception of Chnum they are united together, and form a quaternity. It is probable that each of the four gods had also his own special temple at Mendes.

In spite of great divergence, and a more or less differing conception of the deity, Mendes and Thinis-Abydos continued always in relation with each other, and priests were even transferred from the one town to the other. Transference from Mendes to Abydos seems to have been considered promotion. A certain scribe in the time of Ramses VIII. tells how he was a servant of the king in the fortification Mendes, in Lower Egypt, while his father was singer and servant of the Pharaoh in Abydos, and he himself was soon transferred thither by command of the king to fill the important post of messenger or courier. His account is introduced by an address to Osiris of Abydos in company with the deities worshipped along with him in that town, and to Osiris of Mendes.[1] We can at the same time see from this inscription that so early as under the Rameside kings, the revival of Osiris worship had begun.

The first Tanitic kings were succeeded on the throne by

curs, indicates likewise the worship of Osiris. The Greeks called this king Smendes. To explain this transformation we need not with Brugsch accept a syllable, -nes, prefixed to the name Banded, for the Greeks were pretty much in the habit of prefixing such an *s* to foreign names, as Smerdes, which was their form of Bardiya. See Brugsch, Histoire, p. 213.

[1] See the inscription in Brugsch, Histoire, p. 204.

a dynasty that must in all likelihood have originated in Bubastis, the town of Lower Egypt more to the south than Mendes and Tanis, situated however on the Tanaitic branch of the Nile. The names of this dynasty are mostly very un-Egyptian, and sound like pure Babylonian-Assyrian, Takelut (Tiglath), Nimrut, Sargin, Nabonesha, Shashank; yet these were by no means foreign conquerors who now took the government into their hands. For many years their ancestors had been quietly settled in Egypt. Their origin was indicated by the names they continued to give to their children, but so completely had they adopted the Egyptian manner of life that they even fulfilled priestly offices. They had allied themselves by marriage with the immediately preceding Tanitic dynasty, and were even, previous to that, connected with the priest-kings of Thebes. It was by virtue, no doubt, of this blood-relationship that they attained the sovereignty.

Nor was it a foreign religion they introduced; rather they reverted to the Theban Amun worship which they held in high esteem. Shashank I. is familiar to us through his patronage of Jeroboam, when the latter was obliged to flee from the wrath of Solomon and of Hadad the Edomite prince; and likewise on account of his campaign against Judah, he having, as we know, been hostile to Solomon and Rehoboam. As he himself testifies, he was a high priest of Amun-ra, the king of the gods. On the whole, these kings did not depart from the religious tradition handed down by the rulers of the eighteenth and nineteenth dynasties. The same gods who were then most reverenced are now also found at the head of the official pantheon. Shashank I. serves Amun and Mut, Harmachis and Tum, Ptah (in the form of Ptah-nun); thus the same triad that in the time of the eighteenth dynasty represented the religion of the whole empire. Sutech alone, whom the Rameside kings, or rather the descendants of Seti I., placed alongside of this triad, is awanting. He began to fall a little into the background and to lose favour, though his name still occurs frequently. The day of his greatest glory is over, but, as yet, the days of his utter humiliation have not arrived, when he is destined to be thrust as an evil and repulsive being out of the company of his brothers and sisters and from the ranks of the great gods. He appears to have been indebted to the Persians and Greeks for this furious persecution. As in the good old times Shashank made his son Shuput (Shofet?) at once high priest of Amun and commander of the cavalry; and to another high priest of the same god, who discharged the function of architect, he issued an order to restore the temple of the Theban chief god in full magnificence, a command carried out, if we may trust the inscriptions, with great zeal. From this it would appear that the service of Amun had fallen into decay along with its principal seat. But it is said of Shashank that he caused Thebes to revive. Nor were his favours confined to Thebes, both at Hermonthis and at Heliopolis (the two Ans) he erected monuments (Inscription in the temple of Amun at Thebes). His intention was thus clearly to restore the brilliant Theban theocracy to its former glory.

All his successors followed the same course. Osorkon I., his son, is mentioned at Thebes as a worshipper of Amun, Hathor, and Chnum. Under Osorkon II. the worship of Apis was restored at Memphis, and just as in the time of Ramses II. it was his son Chamûs who brought about a similar reformation, so now it was the son and heir-apparent of King Shashank to whom the restoration was intrusted.' Another of his sons was appointed as high priest of Amun, commander-in-chief of the troops belonging to the temple of this god, and governor of the South. Hence in every particular the pattern set by the ancient kings was followed. The restoration was thorough, and until the end of this dynasty Amun and Ptah continued to be the principal gods.

But meanwhile, according to the usage of reigning Egyptian dynasties, they by no means forsook the local religion of their former place of abode, although now they were settled at Thebes. What they did in this respect cannot be defined with certainty, for Bubastis is now a mere heap of rubbish; but it is evident that they, as well as the three Tanitic kings of the twenty-eighth dynasty who succeeded them, remained faithful to the worship of Bast, for a number of names of both families are combined with that of Bast, and among other instances proving this, there occurs the name Pachi, the cat, the sacred animal of the goddess of Bubastis.

Bubastis appears to be very ancient, and its name (Pa-Bast, abode of Bast) indicates that it was called after the goddess Bast, and that homage had always been paid to her there.[1] It must certainly, however, have been to these kings, to their supremacy, and to their royal patronage, that the worship of this goddess is indebted for its wide extension, and for the height of splendour to which it attained at the time when Herodotus visited it five centuries later. The father of history wrote a vivid account of the beautiful temple sacred to Bast, and of the joyous celebration of the festival in her honour. The temple, he tells us, is surrounded on all sides by water, except at the entrance, for two canals that lead from the Nile to the entrance of the temple meet behind it, thus shutting in the whole edifice both to right and left. The sacred wall encircling the whole sanctuary extends 600 feet in length and the same in breadth, and, like other parts of the temple, is covered with numerous drawings. The holy of holies is surrounded by a sacred grove of very lofty trees. From the entrance a broad well-paved road, planted on both sides with trees, leads to another temple dedicated to Hermes, who seemingly is Thot. As the ground on which the town was built had been perceptibly

---

[1] Brugsch, Histoire, p. 33, infers the antiquity of Bubastis from the fact that the town is mentioned by Manetho so early as in the reign of a king of the second dynasty (Boe- thos). This is but slight proof, still the goddess occurs in very early times on the monuments, and among other instances in the "Book of the Dead."

raised, and the temple alone remained standing on its old foundations, it was easy to overlook the whole sacred enclosure, situated as it was in the middle of the town. Such is an outline of the chief features of the temple at Bubastis, as given by Herodotus, who had seen it himself (ii. 138). Elsewhere (ii. 59 *et seq.*) he says that no festival was celebrated with such magnificence and such unconstrained, nay, even such wanton delight, nor did any other awaken such universal sympathy as that held in honour of Bast. The pilgrimage to Bubastis was made in boats filled with people of all ages and of both sexes. Music and song beguiled their journey. At every town to which they came in passing, a halt was made, the inhabitants hurried out to look at the pilgrims, but had to submit to being scolded by the women of the party, and were obliged to dance when they heard the music. On such occasions the Egyptian ladies appear to have been absolved from the natural laws of chastity. If we believe Herodotus, this festival alone was attended by no less than 700,000 persons, which is not very probable; and not only were a vast number of sacrifices offered on this occasion, but more wine was drunk than in the whole year besides.

Who then, let us ask, was the deity to whom homage was paid in so merry a fashion?

She is called Pacht, "the devouring one," a name which she has in common with the lion, and still oftener Sechet, "she that kindles the fire." There is no doubt she was a goddess of the heavenly fire, whether of the thunderbolt, or, what is more likely in Egypt, of the scorching rays of the sun. She vomits out flames against the wicked to consume them, and the torture of the wicked in the under-world is under her direction. She is represented as a lioness *couchant*, or sometimes *rampant*, vomiting forth flames, and likewise as a woman with the head of a cat,[1] and is nearly akin to Tafnu the Heliopolitan goddess,

---

[1] She is named, which is remarkable, after the animal under whose form she is usually represented. In this, so far as I am aware, she alone

who is represented in the same form. As goddess of fire, especially of the scorching sun-heat, she is goddess of war. Enough light has not been thrown on the subject to enable us to explain how she came to be also patroness of works of peace, of libraries for instance, and "mistress of the thoughts." We find the same combination, warrior goddess, and "mistress of thoughts," in Athena and Minerva. Possibly the reason why power over the thoughts was ascribed to the dread Sechet is simply to be found in the belief of the people in the great inherent virtue of magical songs and spells, as a means of conquering and annihilating the wicked and all enemies. She may thus be goddess of the violent destructive power of words. This explanation, however, I do not bring forward, except as a pure hypothesis.

It will be remembered that most of the goddesses who by their origin belong to Western Asia, as Sechet seems to have done,[1] had a double form, and a double manifestation (see p. 135); on the one side as maiden-goddesses, warlike, severe, violent (Astaroth, Tanît), on the other as mother-goddesses, benevolent, beneficent. Their worship in the latter form, out of opposition to the strictness of the former, generally ran into the greatest licence (Ashera, Anahit). In like manner, in opposition to the raging Sechet, we find here the mild Bast, "the mistress of life in the two tracts" (Ins. at Aradus), and mother of Nofre-tum, the good sun-god. She is represented equally with Sechet as having the head of a lion or a cat,[2] and she is a fire-goddess, for her name is connected with *best* = "flame,"

among all the gods of the Egyptian pantheon is in agreement with Sebak the crocodile god, who was imported from Nubia, or Ethiopia, and this is an argument for her being of foreign origin. The Egyptians, like all the peoples of antiquity, gave significant names to their own gods, and distinguished clearly between the god and his representation.

[1] See Pap. Mag. 825, Br. Mus. Birch's trans. in Rev. Arch., 1863, vii. 125. Comp. ibid. viii., 429 *et seq.*, and 438. She is there described as "Pacht who presides at the scaffold, fire breaking forth against her enemies."

[2] See Wilkinson, M. and C. Supplement, Pl. LI., No. 4.

and also corresponds to the word signifying "to embalm." But she represents fire in its beneficent functions, not as devastating, but as conserving and fertilising; nature's immanent power of growth, and also the fire of the passion of love. In ancient times, and in the reigns of the kings of the Bubastic dynasty, she was no doubt an independent divine being, but, like all the mother-goddesses of Egypt, she afterwards became identified with Isis or with Hathor. With the latter especially, whose worship was likewise accompanied with song and dance, and consisted in joyful festivals, she had much in common; and Hathor, in her temple at Edfu, which had become the metropolis of the worship of all mother-goddesses, is also called Bast.

Meanwhile, the warlike Sechet, as if vexed by the preference given to her rival, let loose the miseries of war upon the land. Under the latter kings of the twenty-second, and seemingly also under those of the twenty-third dynasty (a Tanitic one), the unity of Egypt was broken up. Various princes struggled with each other for supremacy. The country was split up into different little kingdoms, to the number of twelve or thirteen. This, of course, had the effect of weakening the nation. And now the descendants of the Theban high priests saw an opportunity offered them of again bringing the country entirely under their sovereignty. Of this opportunity they at once proceeded to take advantage. For the Ethiopian conquerors, who now in succession make Egypt bow to the might of their sword, and some of whom even reign for a time and form an Ethiopic dynasty, are, in truth, no other than the priests of the Theban Amun, who had not been able to maintain the royal authority they usurped, and had fled as refugees to the south. In Ethiopia they had founded an independent kingdom, the capital of which was Napata (at Djebel Barkal), which bore the name of Meröe, Meru, Merua.[1] The form of government there

---

[1] The Meröe referred to by Strabo lay, as is well known, more to the south; but the name of the village Meraui, in the Barkal, thus close to

was, as might be expected, purely theocratic, like that of Egypt, but with a preponderance of the priestly element. The king himself was first priest of Amun; his son, the heir-apparent to the throne, was second in rank.[1] But although the successor seems to have been thus already indicated during the life of his father, he was obliged nevertheless to submit to the oracle. The king was nominated by the word of God, equivalent in this case to the pleasure of the priests, though as a rule the choice seems to have fallen upon the son of the king who had died.[2] Religious laws seem to have been enforced with great strictness. A careful watch was at least kept lest any unclean foot should tread the temple of Amun. A certain tribe or sect (the obscurity of the inscription which gives the account leaves us in uncertainty on this point) was excluded from the temple of Amun, because they taught that there was nothing wrong in committing murder. On this account it is said they must be cast into the fire of Suti, in order that all the priests and prophets who approach to the exalted god (Amun) may be reverenced. We see that even Suti is named here as the god of avenging righteousness. The gods worshipped in this Ethiopian kingdom were purely Egyptian, Amun-ra in the first place, then Num, the god of the waterfalls, though he is perhaps only the ram's-headed form of Amun mistaken for Num.[3]

At a somewhat more recent period festivals were instituted in honour of Horos, Ra, Osiris, and Isis. That the Amun-worship of the Ethiopian dynasties was of the

---

the site of Napata, justifies us in extending the name Meru also to the older Ethiopian kingdom, which lay more to the north.

[1] Lepsius, Briefe, p. 217.
[2] The Greeks (Herodotus, Diodorus, and Strabo) assure us that the election of the Ethiopian kings was by oracle. This is confirmed by a stela at Djebel Barkal, on which it is related how Asran, son of the deceased king, was chosen in this way.

See Mariette in the Rev. Arch., 1865, ii. 171 seq.
[3] Wilkinson, M. and C., Pl. II., i. 241, calls the god of Ethiopia Num, apparently because he will not hear of a ram-headed Amun. It is certain that on the Ethiopian monuments, on the later ones at al. events, no distinction is made between Amun and Num with a ram's or he-goat's head.

purified Theban sort, no longer at the stage of nature-worship, is evident from a saying of the conqueror Amun-meri-nut, that above all gods he adores him whose name is hidden.[1] The deeper signification of the Egyptian religion, transported to Ethiopia, fell, no doubt, in course of time into oblivion; but the forms continued to exist for centuries just as they had been. For in Ethiopia, long after the place of the descendants of the Theban priests had been taken by natives, and the Egyptian language supplanted by that of Ethiopia, Egyptian hieroglyphics were still used in writing, and the gods of Egypt were still invoked.[2]

So early as in the reign of the first kings of the dynasty of Bubastis, an Ethiopian prince, Azachr-amun, had ventured to attempt the conquest of Egypt, but he appears to have been unable to maintain it. One of his successors was more fortunate. This was Pianchi Meriamun, namesake and apparently descendant of one of the high priests of Amun, who still under the last of the Rameside kings lived at Thebes. The help of this king was sought by the Thebans against a certain Saïtic conqueror, Tafnecht, father of King Bochoris (Bok-en-ranf), and giving a ready response to this request he at once flew to arms. Thebes seems thus to have borne the supremacy of the north with no good will, and preferred to be under the sceptre of its former chief priests rather than subject to a warrior of Lower Egypt. To describe the campaign is beyond my province, it must suffice to tell that Pianchi met with a joyful reception at Thebes; that Memphis, after an obstinate resistance, was at last conquered; and that, along with all the princes, whether these were petty kings or Libyan commanders, Tafnecht was compelled to submit to the warlike priest-king, who granted them pardon and received their homage. None,

---

[1] Mariette, *op. cit.* 163, considers this god to be Osiris. But in the continuation it is said that the priests in the temple of Amun-ra at Thebes bring to him the flower *anch* (the life) of that one whose name is hidden. This can only refer to Amun.

[2] Birch, in Lepsius' Zeits., p. 61, June 1868.

however, of the conspirators, on the ground of their being unclean—and in this we notice a trait characteristic of the priest-king—were allowed access to his palace. One only, Nimrut of Bubastis, related to the kings of the twenty-second dynasty, who had fully adopted the Egyptian civilisation and religion, was permitted to approach Pianchi, because he, in common with all orthodox Egyptians, abstained from sea-fish.[1] Pianchi having invoked the blessings of Amun at his installation, and having likewise testified his devotion to all true Egyptian deities, proceeded forthwith to declare himself ruler of the North, by assuming, as one of his titles, the name of the goddess whose worship was at that time the prevailing one in Lower Egypt. He accordingly took the designation, Pianchi Meriamun Se-Bast, son of Bast. He paid homage to Thot, lord of Hermopolis, and his eight gods, and next allowed himself to be solemnly consecrated as king at Memphis and Heliopolis, just as had without doubt been done previously at Thebes.

The stela from which all this information is derived, and which was discovered in the ruins of Napata, describes the consecration in detail. The solemnities were very elaborate. They commenced with an offering made to Tum, the god of Heliopolis, at a place near the town, and this was followed by offerings to other gods, and amongst them to the god of Memphis. After the king had returned to *Cher*, the place where the first offerings were made, and after he had there purified himself in the Nile, the latter portion of the ceremonies was proceeded with. These were all performed in the neighbourhood of An (Heliopolis). Upon a sort of sand hill (*Shai-ka-em-an*, the high sand at Heliopolis), white cows, milk, incense, and other burnt-offerings were made to the rising sun, and there-

---

[1] The eating of fish is frequently forbidden in the "Book of the Dead." River fish might, however, be eaten by any one except priests, but sea-fish was considered as unclean for all. Yet there is no doubt the mixed population of the Delta, consisting mostly of Asiatics, paid no attention to this prohibition, and even made offerings of fish to the gods.

after, within the great temple itself, two acts of worship took place. The chief singer, the Her-heb, now sang his hymn to the deity. Thus the king was duly prepared and sanctified for the crowning function of his consecration. This took place in the temple Ha-ben-ben (see p. 74, note 1), "the place of the two pyramids." There, was the holy of holies, *seshet ur*, "the great niche," where Ra himself dwelt, and where the two sacred barks of the sun were placed. Before entering, the king purified himself with incense and "living" blood. He then, like the high-priest of Israel, entered alone to behold the great mystery. "He stood alone there, drew the bolts, opened the door, and looked upon his father Ra in Ha-ben-ben, with the two sacred barks of Ra and Tum."[1] The coronation ceremony was thus, in reality, an act of initiation into the highest religious mysteries, a high-priestly act. In no sense could it be described as the consecration of a secular prince by the priests to the office of theocratic king, for the king himself, as head of the priesthood, goes alone within the innermost sanctuary, and no priest is allowed to accompany him.

I have entered into the particulars of Pianchi's campaign more fully than would otherwise have been called for, because in its character it is religious rather than political. Thus, Pianchi affirms that it is Amun who commanded him to undertake it. He gave instructions to his soldiers, whom he did not accompany from the beginning of the expedition, that so soon as they arrived at Thebes they were to submit themselves to a religious purification, and to have their arms blessed by the divinity, "for no victory comes to men without the knowledge of Amun." And having been once sprinkled with water from the altar of Amun, they ought, with foreheads bowed in the dust before his majesty, to repeat the following prayer: "Cover for us the war-path with the shadow of thy scimitar; multiply the strength of the youths whom thou

[1] De Rougé, Rev. Arch., viii. 103 *seq.*, 1863.

hast called; make them myriads." When Pianchi arrives to take part personally in the struggle, his first care is to celebrate at Thebes a panegyric in honour of Amun. Wherever he comes his attention is taken up with temples and sanctuaries, and in all the towns conquered by him he levies sums from the revenues of the priests, which were destined to be given as offerings to the Theban god. Amun-meri-nut likewise causes statues of gods and temples to be set up again everywhere. Their restoration to their proper power in the mother country was, with the Ethiopian kings, synonymous with the re-establishment of the power of Amun, and, as they believed, with the overthrow of the plots of the blasphemers of Amun. With the reign of Pianchi there began a brief renewal of the supremacy of the south. He apparently did not reign over Egypt to the end of his life; at least his sway in the country of the Delta very soon ceased; but his inroad was the precursor of a somewhat prolonged Ethiopian supremacy.

It is inaccurate to represent this as a foreign supremacy. Sabaka, Sabataka, and Tahalka (Taharka) have indeed Ethiopian names, but they are without doubt of pure Egyptian extraction; and genuine Egyptians regarded them rather as deliverers from a foreign yoke than as conquerors. The struggle between North and South was now one between Saïs and Ethiopia. It was against Tafnecht of Saïs that Pianchi had fought. The son of Tafnecht, Bok-en-ranf (Bokchoris), who had now become king, was involved in a war with Sabaka, the king familiar to us in Israelitish history, and was killed. When, at a later period, the Assyrian king, Assurbanipal, chastised the petty kingdoms of Lower Egypt, which his predecessor had brought into subjection, and which had since then revolted, and when he brought all Egypt into subjection to himself, he appointed the great antagonist of the Ethiopians, Necho, prince of Saïs, as his viceroy, who accordingly, as soon as the Assyrians had withdrawn to their own country, experienced the vengeance of Taharka. It was a struggle for life or death that went on between the African Mesopotamians, who continued to be forced southwards, and the Asiatic Mesopotamians, who had now for long had a firm footing in Egypt. The latter found their most powerful allies in the Assyrians, who a second time conquered Taharka, and forced him to retire on Napata, where he seems to have consoled himself by erecting a temple in honour of Amun. He was again victor on one occasion when, being called in by his former enemies the Asiatic princes to help them against the Assyrians, he was so fortunate as to accomplish their overthrow and to regain the throne. But he died very soon after, and his son, Rutmen, who succeeded, soon found himself obliged to leave Egypt for good.

If Herodotus is to be believed, the Ethiopian kings, like all priest-kings, were mild in their government. Sabaka is said to have transmuted capital punishment to forced labour, and to have executed many useful works, especially canals. It need hardly be added that they restored and favoured the Theban worship, and proof of this is afforded by the monuments in the ancient city of Amun.

They made one other attempt to regain what was lost. Amun-meri-nut (read also Amun-rut, and believed to be the same as Urdamani of the Assyrian inscriptions[1]) dreamed a dream in which the sovereignty of Egypt and Kush (Ethiopia) was assigned to him. Like a good Egyptian, he perceives in this a hint of the deity himself, and at once sets to work. It is not clear whether they were Assyrians or native princes with whom he fought, but he too was joyfully welcomed at Thebes, and in the temple of Amun went through those sacred ceremonies which it was lawful for the king alone to perform. After an obstinate struggle he made a victorious entry into Memphis likewise, but he was unable to hold his ground. His son Pianchi II. reigned in succession to him in the

[1] See Haigh, in Lepsius, Zeits., p. 3, January 1869.

Thebaid, but it was not long before the whole country had to bow to other masters. Since that time Egypt was independent no more, unless in appearance. The people had become superannuated and their proper nationality was lost. It is true that the Saïtic kings who came next in succession, although foreigners, did as much as they could to reinstate the ancient Egyptian civilisation, nevertheless unconsciously they became the means of making their country the common property of the world by opening it up to the Greeks.

After the retreat of Amun-meri-nut, the kings of Saïs had their hands free, and lost no time in seizing upon the sovereignty. The reigns of these Nechos and Psamtiks, whose dynasty ended by being overthrown, or rather continued by the lucky conqueror, the genial soldier of fortune, Amasis, has been not inappropriately called the period of the Egyptian *renaissance*. At least it was the beginning of the *renaissance*, which was not arrested by their fall, but still went on in the time of the Ptolemies. Its initiatory stage dates as far back as the time of the kings of Bubastis, who were not of purely Egyptian extraction. Nor were the kings of Saïs purely Egyptian; they seem to have belonged to a Libyan race settled long before on the north-west of the Delta, but like the Takeluts and Osorkons of Bubastis they had so completely adopted the civilisation of Egypt, that the period of their reigns may be characterised as a revival of it, and, under their patronage, even art attained a relatively high degree of splendour. Along with its civilisation they adopted as their own the entire religious system of Egypt. Psamtik I. dedicates gifts to Tum of Heliopolis (Ins. discovered at Pompeii), and promotes the worship of Ptah at Memphis, without at the same time forgetting Thebes and Philak. The Apis worship was his peculiar care. It is no sooner made known to him that the temple of "his father Osiris-apis," the Serapeum, is in a ruinous condition, than he issues orders to have it fully restored without delay. He also commands the divine body of the sacred bull that had died not long before, to be consigned to the grave with royal state. During the reign of this dynasty, the worship of this dead god, whether as Ptah-sekru-asiri, or as Asiri-hapi, was everywhere zealously practised. Amasis followed their example : when an apis died in his reign, he likewise caused him to be interred with unheard-of magnificence. The sarcophagus was of rose-coloured granite, more beautiful and larger than former ones, and all the adornments and sacred amulets were of gold and precious stones. All the chiefs of the towns in Upper and Lower Egypt were invited to come, bringing their presents to the dead god, and to take part in the homage paid to him (Ins. of Amasis, commander of the Bowmen). The temple of Ptah at Memphis was not overlooked, for it was enriched by Amasis with the most magnificent monuments. The gods of the Osirian family were still held in honour, as appears from a sarcophagus of the wife of Amasis (Brit. Mus.), on which she is represented as Hathor, with the sceptres of Osiris in her hand. Another indication is, that the king founded a temple at Memphis in honour of Isis; and lastly, on a relief at Silsilis, Amasis is depicted with his wife Anchnes making offerings to Amun, Mut, and Chonsu-nefer-hotep, the well-known gods of the now decayed Thebes. Egypt surpasses all other countries in conservatism. Dynasties pass and change; wars and revolutions threaten to bring everything into confusion; conquerors, soldiers without birth or breeding, possess themselves of the supreme power; foreign intruders reign for centuries in succession; new forms of religion and new names come to light, and even religious views pass through many a change and development, but the ancient and unchangeable comes always up again to the surface, or at all events continues to exist side by side with what is new, even though it be in actual conflict with it.

The worship of Neith, the goddess of Saïs, which became, under the princes of this dynasty, a prevailing one, was not new either. She had been worshipped in the time of the first dynasties. Princesses of the blood-royal, or at least women of high station, held the office of high priestess of Neith in the time of Chafra, Sahura, and others. Even at that early time Neith had the surname "of the northern wall," *Mehit Sebti*, in contradistinction to Ptah "of the southern wall."[1] Since then she for a time fell into the background, until the Saïtic kings brought her into prominence once more. The Libyans, from whom these kings were descended, had always been worshippers of Neith. On the monuments of the earliest times, in which they are found depicted, there is to be seen on their garments the emblem peculiar to Neith.[2] In Mesopotamia, likewise, her name sometimes occurs as a constituent part of the names of the queens (Nitokris Nit-aker), though possibly these queens may have been of Egyptian descent. The combined questions, whether the Libyans already worshipped Neith previous to their arrival in Egypt, or adopted her worship from the Egyptians, and whether we ought not to seek the origin of Neith worship in Assur or Babel rather than in Egypt, cannot as yet be answered satisfactorily.

I cannot prove that she was a deity of the Libyans, who certainly belonged to the Hamitic race; they may have adopted her from the Egyptians, in accordance with a strongly-marked tendency of theirs. Amun, another certainly Egyptian and perhaps at the same time

---

[1] See De Rougé, VI. Prem. Dynasties, pp. 63, 97, 109. Among these princesses occurs also a certain Anta, an Asiatic name. Does this prove that the worship of Neith was not a native one? But then Anta was a priestess of Hathor as well.

[2] See Ebers, Ægypten u. d. BB. Mos., p. 108. The emblem of Neith was apparently a shuttle. Can the gigantic shuttles brought with them by the Amu under Abisa, when they migrated into Egypt in the time of the twelfth dynasty, have anything to do with the worship of Neith? The manner in which one of these is placed on the back of an ass would lead one to think so. It is to be noted that under the Old Kingdom the symbol of Neith is two arrows crossed, corresponding to the emblem of Seti.

Asiatic Mesopotamian god, had become their chief god. Another Berber god, Gurzil, betrays his Mesopotamian origin by the termination of his name, which recals the Hebrew el = god.[1] In some of the sculptures on their rude monuments it has likewise been thought possible to discern traces of Egyptian influence.[2] And so there would be nothing wonderful in their having adopted the worship of Neith also, who, so far as I can see just now, can be regarded only as a true Egyptian goddess, though related to other Mesopotamian forms of religion.

The proper signification of Neith is not easy to define. There is no doubt she is a mother goddess, for she is frequently called mother of the gods and divine mother. Sometimes too she is united with Anka, who, as we saw (p. 132), signifies the fruitful mother-earth. She is closely related likewise to the Theban mother of the gods, Mat or Mut, and not unfrequently is confounded with her; but at the same time Neith is distinguished from Anka and Mut by being a virgin goddess. This is expressed in the words inscribed on her temple, "My garment no one has lifted up," which is immediately followed by, "The fruit that I have borne is the sun."[3] She is thus the virgin mother of the sun, and combines in herself what is usually among the Egyptians, as well as among the Phœnicians, Assyrians, and other kindred peoples, separated into two persons. The sun here signifies the highest sun-god, as

---

[1] Prof. M. de Goeje, De Berbers in De Gids, Juli 1867, p. 30 et seq.

[2] Barth, Discoveries and Travels, i. 174, describes a relief which shows a considerable amount of artistic skill. Upon it are represented two warriors, apparently gods in human form, but with heads of beasts. One of these heads is much like an ibis, the other is very like the head of Set. Like the Egyptians, the Berber youths wore the single lock of hair depending from the right side. Barth, op. cit. iii. 243. According to F. de Rougemont, L'âge du bronze, p. 271, all the symbols met with in North Africa are of Semitic origin. This author has, however, a habit of regarding facts always in the light of his own theories.

[3] The whole inscription as given by Proclus who is more accurate than Plutarch, is as follows:—Τὰ ὄντα, καὶ τὰ ἐσόμενα, καὶ τὰ γεγονότα ἐγώ εἰμι. Τὸν ἐμὸν χιτῶνα οὐδεὶς ἀπεκάλυψεν, ὃν ἐγὼ καρπὸν ἔτεκον, ἥλιος ἐγένετο. (Comp. De Rougé, Rev. Arch., 1851, i. 58-60.)

the Creator who also has created himself without a father. These are all so many attempts of the symbolic mysticism to personify the ever-productive but always pure nature-power whence everything derives its origin. Hence at the commencement of the same inscription it is said, "I am what is, what shall be, and what has been," and still more clearly as follows: "The great productive mother of Ra, who is a first-born child, and who is not begotten but brought forth" (Ins. of Uza-hor-penres, son of Pefanit, priest of Neith at Saïs). What Neith represents is not nature as such, not inert matter, as some have asserted;[1] for I cannot regard this as other than the transference to Egyptian ground of the later pantheistic speculations of foreigners; but she is the eternal deepest ground of all things symbolised as the divine mother-maid. Only when regarded in this light is it possible to say that she is "Commandress of all gods," and that there is "no second beside her" (Ins. on the tomb of Titi at Thebes).

In reality there is no one of the Egyptian gods quite like her. Her attributes are transferred to other goddesses, but they all reproduce only one side of the double being that we find in Neith. With all its mystic awkwardness this conception is still one of the highest and most exalted in Egyptian theology. Neith was also originally, no doubt, like all the other deities of Northern Egypt, a personification of the heavenly fire. She represented the cosmic fire, hidden, mysterious, to which all that is owes its existence. She is the same goddess as the virgin mother of Western Asia whom the Greeks, not without reason, compared to their Athena.

Mysticism found in all this, wide scope for its fantastic play. I shall cite only one example. In a magic papyrus[2]

---

[1] This idea owes its origin to the Egyptian view in which the female principle was purely passive. Maury, in other respects distinguished for his knowledge of ancient religions, holds Neith, after Mariette, as the *matière inerte, le milieu sans vie au sein duquel la génération s'était operée*, Revue des deux Mondes, i. 189, Sept. 1867.

[2] Pap. Mag. 825, Brit. Mus., transl. by Birch, p. 15.

the house of Osiris is found on a pedestal, which is the emblem of truth. Beneath it is an oval, bearing the name of Neith as goddess of foreign peoples. In front of the house stands, "O thou who daily art hidden!" on the sides, "Very hidden, very secret." At the corners are placed the names of Hor, Thot, Isis, and Nephthys. Then follows the description, "I have opened the heaven and the earth." The house is thus the universe—"I am the seat of Neith, hidden in the hidden, covered in the covered, barred into the barred, unknown I am knowledge. . . . I am the one who is hid in the flame that never ceases to burn; heaven is shut up and the waters are enclosed: where the waters rage, there the flame is still . . . the abode of Neith is on the throat of Nunhur, the god of Tenu (Thinis)." The last reference is sufficiently obscure, but it is clear that Neith is called the very hidden one because she is the deepest ground of things, and the legend of her veiled statue, so finely reproduced by Schiller, is true to her essential character. She hence became goddess of the most profound science and wisdom, usually with the epithet of *aker*, "the wise, the learned;" and thus the Greeks could very well compare her to Athena, whose very name has indeed been regarded as a transposition of hers. Like Athena, Neith was also a warlike goddess; it was she always who kept the land of Egypt safe from the barbarians by means of her northern wall. The name which she derived from this wall was in more modern times still so usual that we find it even at Tyre (Ins. discovered by Renan). This likewise would account for her being often combined with Ptah, the god of the southern wall, though Sechet was his proper consort. Her worship was closely connected with that of Osiris, and the tomb of this beneficent god was shown in her temple. To connect thus the hidden deity of the under-world and the hidden deepest ground of all things, is evidently natural enough. She was represented either in human shape or in that of a cow lying down, and in both forms has a disk of gold between horns, and her head and neck adorned with gold, and draped with a mantle of purple. As to this, however, she does not differ in any way from Isis, Hathor, and the other Egyptian mother-goddesses.

In the time of the Ptolemies and Cæsars, the attributes of Neith were imputed to Isis, the Isis whom the Roman ladies and even the young girls worshipped with a zeal which the law forbidding foreign superstitions was powerless to check.

So great is the attraction which the mysterious and inexplicable has for the religious spirit, that we find these ancient nature myths reviving in the form of legends and of dogmas in religions with whose spirit they harmonise least, and this long after the character of the nature gods has been forgotten, and the religions to which they belong are fallen into oblivion. This is especially the case when such myths appeal to sentiment, and when they combine in offering to the contemplation of humanity the two objects which are the most graceful and touching in nature, but which in nature are never united in one—a happy mother and a pure young maiden.

The town and temple of Saïs were extolled by foreigners like Herodotus on account of their great magnificence. The fragments of that magnificence are now scattered far and wide. The splendid naos (the holy of holies), hewn from a single stone, and dedicated as a gift by Amasis, is now at Paris. On the monuments two sacred spots at Saïs are principally referred to. One is "the great distinguished," or "double great" (*aa ur*), apparently the large fish-pond mentioned also by the Greek historian, and which served as the arena for the spectacle of the great mysteries of the Osiris myth; the other is the *chen*, the innermost or hidden, apparently the tomb of Osiris, the site of which was on the back of the wall adjoining the sanctuary of Neith. Her offerings consisted principally of sheep. In the usual representation of the goddess, she has a human form, and the crown of Lower Egypt on her head. If, however, we accept the sarcophagus described by Herodotus as that of the daughter of Mycerinus, as being an image of Neith, she bore in her temple at Saïs the form of a cow, ornamented in the way already described. In front of this image there always stood an altar with an offering of incense, and a lamp kept perpetually alight. Such a representation corresponds well with the nature of the goddess, for the immaculate conception of the Hapi Bull, living image of the sun-god, was likewise among the dogmas of Egyptian theology. On one particular night of the year, the festival of lamps was celebrated in honour of Neith. On this occasion all Egypt was lighted with lamps filled with oil and salt and having a floating wick, and these burnt the whole night through. A number of pilgrims resorted then also to Saïs, to be present at and take part in the great solemnity. The festival had reference to the never-dying light of the sun. The temple at Saïs, like most of the principal Egyptian ones, had become a pantheon. There, in addition to the worship of Neith in two forms, corresponding to her double nature, homage was paid to Selk the scorpion goddess, Ma the goddess of truth, Isis, Seti, Nephthys, and Suben the goddess of fertility and of victory, and to the masculine gods, Thot, lord of Sesennu, Seb, the father of the gods, Osiris, with the crown of Upper Egypt, Chem, with the double crown, Anubis and Horos, each in two different forms, and finally, Chepra the sun-god, as creator. These are all gods belonging to the Osirian circle, or who express one aspect of the goddess's nature.

Neith retained her supremacy longer than the kings who paid her such high honours, for in the time of the Persian conquest she was still one of the most celebrated deities, and her fame was afterwards spread far beyond the confines of Egypt.

The great catastrophe that brought Egypt into subjection to an altogether foreign race brought about at first no alteration in the religion of the country. This was owing principally to a high officer of state who was a zealous worshipper of Neith. This was Uza-hor-penres, son of Pefanit, priest of that goddess, and apparently also himself one of her priests. In the calamity that had befallen the country, this man bestirred himself to save what it was still possible to keep. He managed to gain the confidence of Cambyses, the Persian conqueror, who assumed the Egyptian name Ramesut, and obtained for himself the appointment of principal counsellor to the king. The first thing he did was to give the king an idea of the great importance attaching to the worship of the Saïtic goddess.[1] He complained that the temple was desecrated by having foreign troops quartered in it. Cambyses gave ear to the counsels and complaints of his Egyptian minister. He ordered the temple to be purified, and another place of encampment to be selected for the troops, whose dwellings within the temple were to be destroyed. Moreover, he caused the ranks of the priesthood to be filled up, and issued orders that offerings should be made regularly, and the festivals celebrated at their proper time; and he did all this "because he had charged Uza-hor-penres to make known to him the greatness of Saïs." It would thus appear that Cambyses himself had made inquiry about the chief religion of his new province. He went still further; for when he came to Saïs he had himself initiated into the mysteries of the goddess, and performed in her temple all the ceremonies gone through there in former times by all the Egyptian kings—all the good ones, innocently adds the zealous priest of Neith. Following their example, Cambyses instituted a litany for the lord of eternity (Osiris), in the innermost sanctuary of the temple of the goddess.

[1] The theological lessons given to the king by Uza-hor-penres took in more ground, and dealt not only with the service in the various temples of Neith, but also with all the gods and goddesses worshipped at Saïs, and the four divine abodes in the four quarters of heaven, "which are the abyss where the gods settle," of which last particular the warlike Achemenide had very likely no clearer conception than any of us at this moment.

Very soon, however, there came a change. Cambyses, who at first had ruled Egypt with such moderation, and had even publicly displayed his reverence for the national religion, became a desecrator of temples and a tyrant. This change is not to be ascribed to any violent religious bias, but must simply have resulted from the disappointments brought upon himself by the monarch's own folly and imprudence. Three hostile expeditions which he had simultaneously planned were totally unsuccessful. The first, against the Carthaginians, had to be abandoned because the Phœnicians refused to fight against people of their own race. The other two were actually attempted. Without any knowledge of the districts to be traversed, without sufficient provision for the long journey, he set out in person with an army against the Ethiopians; and another army was despatched by him to the oasis of Ammon, to bring its inhabitants into subjection to his authority. Cambyses was obliged to return without effecting anything, and the troops sent to the oasis were completely buried beneath the sand. After this the fury of Cambyses knew no bounds. Immediately on his return to Thebes he destroyed many monuments. At Memphis it was worse still; for there, rejoicings happened to be going on on account of the birth of a new Apis, and in his madness Cambyses imagined that the subject of their celebration was his defeat. He accordingly had the governors of the town put to death, and he wounded the sacred Apis. Having penetrated into the sanctuary of Ptah, he mocked the dwarfish image of the god, and burnt the statues of the Kabirs. The grief and horror that now filled the whole of Egypt may be imagined. Such sacrilege was unheard of. Uza-hor bears witness that a calamity like this had never before happened. His own painful experience made the learned scribe forget that in the religious history of his people there were pages darker still. Saïs seems to have escaped the fury of the tyrant; and if it really did, it was indebted for its immunity to its distinguished citizen Uza-hor, who could testify, " I was a good citizen of my town; I saved the inhabitants in the great calamity that fell upon the whole country."

But happier days were in store. No sooner had the great Darius ascended the throne than he proved to be, in regard to Egypt, a mild and intelligent ruler. He commanded Uza-hor-penres, who again brought the religious interest of his fellow-subjects under the king's consideration, to regulate everything throughout the country, and to restore the order (the signification of the original word is doubtful) of scribes, and " the names of all gods, their temples, their offerings, the celebration of their festivals for all time coming." In the oasis of Thebes (Wah-el-Kardjeh) he caused a temple to be built in honour of Amun, the god by whose name he had called himself in his character of Egyptian prince (Ra-amun-meri or Meri-amun-ra). And when the Egyptians had risen in revolt against his arbitrary viceroy Aryandes or Oryandros (Ariyârâmna?) he restored peace again, and won their hearts by offering a hundred talents for a new Apis, the old one having just died. This incident is very characteristic of the Egyptian people, to whom their religion was all in all. Despotism had driven them to the extremity of revolt, and they had taken up arms to cast off the foreign yoke; but the gift of a new sacred animal suffices to bring them to reason, and to make them willingly place upon their necks again the yoke they had wished to break off. Simple as we may be tempted to think them, a people that could be held in check by such means stands higher than the people of Rome, who were willing to bear every extreme of tyranny so long as they were kept supplied with food and sports (*panem et circenses*).

This is the proper place to say a few words about the temple of Amun in the oasis Sivah, to which Cambyses had despatched his fruitless expedition, and which, world-famous as it had long been, appears now for the first time distinctly in Egyptian history.[1] This sanctuary, whose oracle was consulted far and wide, lay deep in the wilderness, eight days' journey from the Cyrenean coast and twelve from Memphis. Its seclusion and mysteriousness gave it a great reputation for sanctity, although in ambiguity it differed in no respect from other oracles. The "Ammonite crookedness" (ἀμμωνιακὴ ἀπάτη) was sportively said to be derived from the twisted horns that ornamented the ram-headed god. As to the foundation of the oracle, we have nothing but myths and legends. The Theban priests of Amun told Herodotus a tale about two prophetesses stolen by the Phœnicians, one of whom was sold into Libya and the other into Hellas; the former founded the oracle of Amun, the latter that at Dodona. The Greeks relate the same tale of two black doves. This much is evident, that the colony in the oasis of Amun was an Egyptian one and went thither from Thebes. According to Diodorus (iii. 71 *et seq.*), Dionysus is said to have founded the oracle of his father Ammon, when the latter was "expelled from the kingdom," and had foretold to his son that he would be victorious. This would lead one to infer that the colony consisted of people who had been banished; and, if so, it could have happened only at one of two periods in Egyptian history,—either at the time of Chunaten's (Amenophis IV.) persecution of the worshippers of Amun, or at the time when the Theban priests of Amun took

---

[1] The account of Bokchoris (24th dynasty), who is said to have consulted this oracle in the 8th century B.C., is part of the apocryphal system which makes the exodus of the Jews take place in his reign (Lysim. in Joseph. c. Ap., i. 34; Tacit. Hist., v. 3), and is consequently worth as little as this fable itself. There is a better foundation for the story, that one of the opponents of Psamtik I., called Tementhes (Tafnecht?), consulted the oracle of Amun and received a warning to beware of cocks; after which he is accordingly said to have been defeated by Carian soldiers wearing cocks' feathers on their helmets. Var. Hist., 7, 3, quoted by Parthey, Das Orakel und die Oase des Ammon. Abhandl. der Phil. Hist. Kl. der Berl. Akademie, 1862, p. 158. The oracle may quite well have existed in the reign of Bokchoris. In Greece and Asia Minor, it was already very famous. It is well known to have been consulted by Crœsus, and it is celebrated in Pindar's song.

FALL OF THEBES TO THE PERSIAN CONQUEST. 213

refuge in Ethiopia. The former would be the more probable. These, however, are no more than conjectures. The deciphering of the hieroglyphic inscriptions, and especially of the royal cartouches observed in the temple Omm-beidah, one of the sanctuaries of the oasis, would be more likely to throw light on the subject. In any case, these inscriptions and cartouches prove that the temple and colony were purely Egyptian, and always remained in connection with that kingdom; although, according to Herodotus, the oasis formed an independent state under its own rulers. The fact of the language now spoken there being no longer Egyptian but a Berber dialect, is not a strong argument against the Egyptian origin of the colony, for we see nearly the same thing in the case of Meröe; and in the time of Herodotus the language of the oasis of Ammon was, according to him, midway between Egyptian and Ethiopian.[1]

The god worshipped in the temple of the oasis was the same who was worshipped in Ethiopia, Amun with the ram's head. His image is found in the temple of Omm-beidah. Thus Alexander, when he clothed himself as Amun, wore horns on his head (Dhu-l-karnaïn). Mention is made, however, of another image, namely, a cone (*umbilicus*) set with gems, one of those representations that are found most frequently in Phœnician temples. This may have been the local Libyan way of representing the god whom the Libyans worshipped in common with the Egyptians.[2] Within this temple, as in that of Saïs, a lamp was kept perpetually burning, as emblem of the never-dying light. The oracle was given not in words

---

[1] Parthey, *op. cit.*, p. 149 *et seq.*

[2] In the opinion of Parthey, *op. cit.*, p. 137, the Greeks gave the name of Amun to the god of the oasis by mistake, because images of Amun have never a ram's head, and it must have been in reality Chnum. To this we cannot assent. Parthey's idea arises from Wilkinson's opinion that Chnum alone is depicted with a ram's head, but it has long been proved that this was one of Amun's symbols as well. In the same way Hathor, Isis, Neith, all had a cow's head; Osiris and Ptah both had the dud-symbol; Horos Ra and Munt, the sparrow-hawk's head; and the crocodile is the sacred animal of Sebak as well as of Set.

but in genuine Egyptian fashion, by signs and emblems, which, however, were duly translated into words by the priests. Very renowned too, in ancient times, was the fountain dedicated to the sun, or perhaps merely called after the sun by reason of its varying temperature.

We have now come to the end of the history of the Egyptian religion in so far as it is comprised within the limits I have laid down for myself. Egypt managed for a short while to evade the dominion of Persia, continuing for half a century longer to be ruled by its own kings, who, as the monuments they left behind them show, followed in everything the former national kings, protecting and paying homage to the national religion of Memphis, Hermopolis, and Thebes. The Persians then became masters of the land, to be succeeded in turn by the Greeks. In the time of the Ptolemies, Egypt was, it is true, independent, but its development was arrested. In spite of the magnificent and, in some respects, beautiful temples that were founded or restored, a decline is very evident. The period is indeed one of the highest importance in the history of religion, but it is so because it belongs to the new era that was just dawning, the era of universalism. The beginning of the formation of this great era is visible at the period to which we have now come, not in Egypt only but everywhere. Religions begin to melt into each other. Not only do peoples adopt from each other gods and customs, which then take their place in the system of their national religion, becoming in the process entirely modified, but foreign religions are introduced simply and without alteration. The oasis of Amun became the means of spreading the worship of the Theban god through the whole of Africa and Greece, and it therefore is very appropriately placed at the end of my historical review; for it was precisely the worship of the ram-headed god in the Libyan wilderness that paved the way to the new era. Amun, who does not seem to have penetrated as far as to the Romans, was followed by Isis, with Harpokrates and Serapis, whose worship, especially in Italy, was prosecuted with a zeal amounting to fanaticism. But not only did forms of religion extend, the religions themselves were intermingled. Egypt was, for the West, the true home of this intermixture, and Alexandria was its centre. There Hellenic, Jewish, and Egyptian elements fermented through each other. That which resulted from this fermentation exercised afterwards, when the gospel of Jesus began to spread abroad from Palestine, a deciding influence on the doctrine and institutions of the new world-religion, and traces of this are still in existence. Interesting, however, as this period is, and attractive as the study of it would be, it belongs not to the ancient but in reality already to the history of the new religion, to which it forms the introduction, and consequently lies outside my sphere. It only remains for me now, to give, in some general remarks on the character of the Egyptian religion and its relation to morality, the state, and art, a summary of our investigations.

CHAPTER IX.

CHARACTER AND MORAL RESULTS OF THE EGYPTIAN RELIGION.

To grasp aright the character of the Egyptian religion, we must first of all seek an explanation of the two great phenomena which it at once presents to the observation of the student. These phenomena consist of two great contrasts, which to the superficial observer appear enigmatical, though in reality they are not so difficult of explanation. In the Egyptian religion we find characteristic qualities conjoined, apparently mutually exclusive, but yet, as a matter of fact, seeming to be not irreconcilable, while they may also be shown to be logically capable of co-existing in the same system. In all that the monuments tell us about the beliefs of the ancient Egyptians, two things may be clearly observed: first, a vivid consciousness of the spiritual nature of the deity combined with coarsely sensuous representations of the various gods; secondly, a no less vivid consciousness of the oneness of God conjoined with the greatest diversity of divine persons.[1]

---

[1] This is very truly brought out by Chabas (Rev. Arch., 1862, v. p. 273) as follows : "In contemplating the doctrines of ancient Egypt, we are seized with a kind of giddiness like one on the verge of a fathomless abyss. No mythology has ever possessed so great a store of fantastical and complex myths engrafted on a simple principle like that of monotheism. In this system it would appear as if man and the shades of the dead were imperceptibly bound by one immense chain to innumerable deities representing the special modes of being, the forms and the will of the universal being in whom the whole centres. As a whole it constitutes a special kind of pantheism, to define which exactly would require a science more advanced than ours." I do not hold myself responsible for this author's expression, "pantheism," which, it

The explanation of these phenomena has been sought in the supposition of a double theology among the Egyptians, an esoteric and an exoteric,—the one being intended for the learned, and known to them alone and to a chosen few, but kept carefully concealed from the multitude; the other being intended for the people, who thus had the husk given to them while the kernel was kept out of their reach. Or, in plain words, the priests allowed the ignorant multitude to persevere in their superstitions, while they themselves knew better, and attached not the slightest value to all the sensuous representations and usages. This is, however, an utterly baseless opinion,—a mere fancy of modern times. In Egypt, as everywhere else and in all periods, there were cultured and uncultured, educated and uneducated, people. The latter never got beyond the visible symbol, and were, as a rule, satisfied with the external form ; the former penetrated deeper, and followed up the thoughts that were latent in the symbols. Yet they, too, attached a certain value to the visible emblems, to the forms of religion, to its ceremonies and customs. They valued the forms because of the ideas to which they gave outward expression, but they were not in a condition to emancipate themselves from these forms. There is no trace of their having designedly kept their deeper interpretations hidden. The contrary is the case. The hieroglyphic writing, though not so plain as the Roman alphabet, was not a mode of secret writing. All the pictures with which the walls of their public buildings were covered were accompanied by texts explanatory of the subjects depicted. The books in which they published their religious speculations could be obtained by any

seems to me, ought not to be applied to the Egyptian system but with great reserve. And while I venture upon an explanation where he has shrunk from attempting to give one, I do so not because I can boast of more advanced knowledge than his, but because I think that the mere observation of the principal phenomena, and attention to the leading thoughts everywhere expressed, put us at once in possession of the desired explanation.

one, and it was even considered a necessary condition of future blessedness that one should know the sacred texts by heart. In short, the only limit set to the spread of their teaching was the believers' intellectual capacity. Even towards foreigners they showed no reserve in the communications they made with regard to religious subjects. Greeks in search of information like Herodotus, and philosophers like Plato, enjoyed the benefit of their instructions, and were even initiated into their most profound science. The only subjects as to which they felt obliged to maintain silence were those which a feeling of reverence forbade them to make common; as, for instance, the name of the highest god, from the utterance of which the Israelites shrank in like manner. But every person who showed any real interest could be initiated, and even slaves were not excluded. Among the initiated, however, we find in every case the spiritual conception and the rude sensuous form combined together. Chamûs, the son of Ramses II., who would unquestionably be familiar with the deepest mysteries, was at the same time zealously devoted to the Memphitic bull-worship. Accordingly the problem, how two things apparently so irreconcilable could go together remains intact thus far, and cannot be solved by accepting the supposition of an esoteric and exoteric doctrine.[1]

For it is indeed very remarkable how men could express themselves so clearly and emphatically about the nature of the deity as unseen and hidden, as we have seen them so often do in the preceding chapters; how they could name him the "soul of souls," "the spirit more spiritual than all spirits," and the self-existent one, uncreated, un-

---

[1] Lepsius, Die Götter der vier Elementen, p. 198, says truly, "In as far as religious representations admit of being clothed in image or word symbolism at all, just to the same extent they, for that very reason, become exoteric, accessible to every well-educated person. But the deeper speculative interpretation or *rationale* must, up to a certain point (it is easy to understand), be reserved for the initiated priests, and must be to that extent their secret."

begotten, eternal, and yet at the same time represent him in the monstrous shape of a man with the head of a beast, or actually in that of a beast, or in the form of a tree, of a pillar with cross beams, of a winged disk, and even in the disgusting form in which the god Chem-Min is usually depicted.

The most obvious cause of this phenomenon lies, I think, in the symbolic-mystical tendency of the Egyptian religion, which is a development from the mythological principle. A symbol is a simple or complex thought clothed in a sensuous form. A myth is a phenomenon of nature represented as the act of a person. Usually symbols originate in myths, and in every case mythology is antecedent to symbolism. To the formation of mythology there is needful, not only capacity for poetry, but also the condition of a roving life, of conflict, of conquest; a, so to speak, epic condition; a state of coming into being and taking shape; not fixity and order, not a settled and peaceful life. If this condition of struggle preceding the establishment of order and the regular institution of church and state is of long duration; and if, in addition, this is the case with a people rich in imagination and in poetic faculty, the mythology of such a people will likewise be rich and multiform: it will, after having at length attained a settled life, proceed to transmute its mythology into poetry and history, to glorify it by art, and to make it the groundwork of philosophical speculation. If, on the contrary, the epic period of a people or of a religion is only of brief duration, and if, under favouring circumstances, such a people passes early from the wandering hunter or shepherd life to the settled agricultural condition, in that case the faculty of forming myths is soon lost, the myths become symbols, and symbolism asserts itself, while the mythology is cast into the shade. The latter process is what we see in the case of the Egyptian people. On good grounds it has been supposed that it, like the Aryan peoples, migrated once upon a time from

Asia to the West. It had thus its heroic age, its period of struggle and wandering, "of struggle for life." This does not, however, seem to have lasted long. Mesopotamia is not far distant from Africa, and the tribes with whom a contention had to be waged for possession of the valley of the Nile were, there can be no doubt, neither numerous nor powerful. When a settled life, an ordered government, and art along with it, began for the Egyptians, their mythology had as yet scarcely had time to grow. It is possible that the speculative powers of the scholar, the imagination of the poet and artist found but one single myth, the Osirian sun myth, which under other names is everywhere the same; and, besides this, they may have found a wealth of mythic representations that were still rude and had not passed into anthropomorphism. The anthropomorphic human element is chiefly represented by Osiris and by the northern Atum-Ra, who is Osiris in another guise. In addition to this, the Egyptian, like the other peoples most nearly akin to him, seems to have had a certain hesitation about representing deity in human form, and considered some symbol, some monstrous representation, more in keeping with the reverence due to the deity. A profound feeling of God's exaltation above mankind is characteristic of the Mesopotamian religions in general; while, on the other hand, it is a characteristic of the Aryan to give a more prominent place to the relationship between gods and men. In Egypt we find both these characteristics, as might be expected in the case of a people who are proved by their language to have been related on the one side to the Aryans, on the other to the Semites.

And now the first contrast referred to can be explained. It proceeds from the symbolic tendency of the Egyptian religion which was fostered by the circumstances we have just mentioned. When symbols are not rightly understood—as usually they are not by the ignorant multitude —they naturally lead to far greater deviations than mythological (in the sense of anthropomorphic) representations.

If the symbol is worshipped for its own sake, if the animal, the tree, the stone is regarded as the deity himself, such a worship ranks lower than the adoration of a god like the Olympian Zeus, the Attic Athena, the Delphic Apollo, in the case of whom the whole symbolism is combined with, and it must be added, concealed in a human being, the highest being of whom we have any actual experience. If, however, the symbol is understood, if the emblematic form is distinguished from the thought latent in it, a much easier task with symbols than with myths, then in that case men reach a spiritual conception much more quickly, and are not offended by the coarseness and hideousness of the emblem. On the contrary, a certain attraction is felt in the element of mystery, and fresh symbols continue to be employed as the means of conveying new thoughts. It could easily happen that men might in this way become entangled in a wilderness of mysticism, but they could not so easily lose the consciousness that a deeper meaning was latent under all the forms, and they would be in no danger of seeing the whole doctrines of their faith degenerate into a mere collection of meaningless fables whose only attraction lies in their poetic beauty. Thus, Christians have never had entire satisfaction in any representation of the Heavenly Father in human shape, even though traced by the pencil of a Rafael or a Michael Angelo; yet not one, not even the strictest Protestant, is offended by the emblematic representation of God in the form of an (all-seeing) eye, or of the operation of his Spirit in the form of a dove. These figures, in fact, under which the Egyptians represented divine beings, unfamiliar as they are to our taste, are more reconcilable with a purely spiritual and exalted conception of deity than are the beautiful and noble divine forms of Hellas.

The case is in no way different with the second contrast I referred to, the lively consciousness of the unity of God conjoined with the greatest multiplicity, the most extravagant diversity of divine persons. Monotheism is, in fact, expressed in the clearest terms in many an Egyptian treatise, yet it would not be easy to discover a richer polytheism than that which flourished on the banks of the Nile. The explanation of this contrast is, in part, the same as that of the other. If uncultivated people did not take offence at the coarsely sensual symbols, because they had the idea that a deep sense lay hidden behind them, and that the monstrous representations were in this way holy, and also because they were not yet raised to a high enough point of development to feel these offensive; if the learned, on their part, did not object to these representations because they comprehended their meaning, and simply did what was done originally, transferred their reverence for the mystery to that which veiled it,—the same applies to the polytheism which had increased in proportion as monotheism became clearer to the consciousness of the more advanced. As yet the people had certainly no conception of monotheism, and saw nothing to offend them in the multiplicity of gods; each, however, chose his own god, and, as a rule, worshipped him as if he were the one only god. The learned regarded the many divine persons only in the light of revelations, manifestations; not, as some would have us believe, as emanations of the one immortal, uncreated, hidden god. The gods were his creatures. Ra himself creates his members, and his members are the gods. The hidden god by whom, in the beginning, all things came into existence (Tum in the Book of the Dead), is a being who is one only, but afterwards he revealed himself, and he reveals himself continually in innumerable forms. It was on this account that people were so tolerant of all forms, of every conception of deity, provided it was confined to the locality of its home; and it was on this account also that foreign forms of religion were so easily adopted. Thus, although the thought— God is one—was expressed ever more and more emphatically, polytheism was nevertheless quietly allowed to propagate itself. This was because, to the mind of the Egyptians, the proposition, God is one, was bound up with this other, his manifestations are numberless. It was, however, just because of this that, on the other hand, they were so intolerant of every form of religion which laid claim to being the only true one. Thus Apepi failed in his attempt to reduce the pantheon to two gods, Amun-ra and Sutech; and Chunaten was equally unsuccessful in his attempt to obtain for his god, Aten-ra, a life longer than the duration of his reign. Such a claim was, in truth, a heresy, against which the learned, and the priests in particular, felt obliged to rise in revolt. It was the substitution of one single revelation of god for the one Most High over all. It is indeed the case that, for example, Amun, Ra, Ptah, and Sutech, and likewise Osiris, Chnum, and Atum, and occasionally Thot, were each in particular represented as the Most High, the only god. Men had, however, been accustomed for long to regard these various divinities as nothing more than different names for the same god. This is plainly seen from combinations like Amun-ra-tum-harmachis, Ptah-sokar-osiris, Ptah-chnum, &c., and also from the fact that invocations of the one were placed in inscriptions below the image of the other. Moreover, political motives forbade the extinction of any one of the forms, and especially of any of the local worships attached to considerable towns or to important districts.

We are now in a position to understand the main idea of the Egyptian religion. According to the form of its doctrine, it is to be classed with those in which symbolism preponderates; according to the form of its organisation, or, if it is preferred, its ecclesiastical structure, it belongs to the category theocratic. In these respects it betrays its close relationship to the Mesopotamian (Semitic) religions, which likewise are all symbolical and theocratic. In its development it belongs, not to the exclusively monotheistic, nor to those in which polytheism preponderates, but stands just at the point at which men try to reconcile the unity and spirituality of God with the multiplicity of his manifestations.

Regarded from the other side, it is equally akin to the Aryan religions by its tendency to pantheism, its rich mythology, and especially, if I may be allowed the expression, its theanthropism, that is, the king being not only god living on earth, but every believer being destined to become at his death Osiris himself in the realm of the under world, and one of the genii of light who accompany the god Ra in his triumphant course. The Egyptian religion is thus actually quite as much pre-Semitic as pre-Aryan, for it is the representation of an epoch when Semitic and Aryan had not as yet become distinct.

Every religion has its own peculiar character, a character not defined by the form in which it is manifested and the degree of development it may have reached, but by the leading idea it expresses, although that too is in intimate connection with its form and development. The leading thought of the Egyptian religion, that which had on the whole most struck the Egyptian, and which he accordingly reproduced most prominently in his theology, is: life in its eternal unchangeable foundation, and its innumerable modes of manifestation. "Life, health, well-being" (*anch uza seneb*) is his motto, the sum of all his wishes. The indestructibleness of life, in spite of the hostile powers of death and of destruction, was what constituted his whole faith and all his hope. This was his great dogma, and all his innumerable symbols were called in to aid him in giving it expression.

The gods and the kings in their character of divine persons have always the emblem of life in their hand. The divine triads, likewise—father, mother, and son—give expression to the same thought. In everything; in the shining phenomena of the heavens; above all, in the course of the sun, which daily died and rose again; in the course of the seasons, regulated for him by the periodical rising and falling of the Nile; in the inexhaustible fertility of the earth;—in all these changing phenomena the Egyptian saw the traces of eternal life, of persistency in the midst of change, and he made an application of it to human life. Hence it is that his highest deity is in all cases at once both sun-god and god of fertility, and in most cases water or Nile god as well, and a type of man himself. Hence it is that his one myth, the best representation of which is the Osiris myth, may be correctly explained from any of these considerations. It is at once a myth of the year, a Nile myth, and a myth of immortality. Hence it comes that the doctrine of immortality takes the chief place in his theology. Hence, lastly, it is that the word by which he renders the abstract idea, God (*nuter* or *neter*), literally signifies "the one ever renewing his youth, the imperishable one." [1]

The same leading thought which forms the basis of Egyptian theology is reflected likewise in the Egyptian state. There too the greatest variety and freedom of forms found a centre of unity in the absolute divine office of king. The king is "the lifegiver like the sun." His kingdom is eternal, and his ideal is "to reign for millions of years upon the throne of Horos."

Even taking into account all the difference in special points, the forms of government, in spite of the great revolutions that took place repeatedly, remained wonderfully uniform and essentially unaltered all through the long succession of centuries during which the Egyptian kingdom existed. Each new period, even after long-con-

---

[1] Brugsch, Hierogl. dem. W.B., *in voce*. De Rougé also gives this explanation. He holds *nuter* is derived from the verb *nuter* = to renew, and says (Rev. Arch., 1860, i. p. 351), "I think the idea which has given rise to the choice of this word for God is eternal youth periodically renewed." "The lord of centuries" is a very usual name for the highest god. Since that time, M. le Page Renouf, in the Hibbert Lectures, 1879, Lon., Williams & Norgate, 1880, p. 93 *et seq.*, has endeavoured to prove that the explanation of the word *nuter* by M. de Rougé, although generally accepted by Egyptologists, ought to be rejected, and that the word originally signified the strong, the powerful. It would then be entirely synonymous with El, Ilu, the strong, the powerful, the appellation of God among Semitic peoples.

P

tinued confusion, is in reality a renewal, a repetition of what had been before.

The same thing may be observed in regard to art. In harmony with the serious and mysterious symbolism, its products are rather grand and impressive than pleasing and attractive. In connection with the erection of monuments likewise, " for millions of eras," "for centuries," is a very common and favourite expression. Massiveness, durability, is a principal characteristic of Egyptian art.

And although art too had its period of splendour and its time of decline, although an attentive observer with a knowledge of the subject can see the unmistakable difference between the productions of the different periods, the principal types nevertheless remain unaltered from Chufu to Amasis, nay, even down to the time of the Ptolemies, and to a certain extent on even into the period of the Roman emperors.

In still closer connection than religion and art are religion and morality. Between these two there is always mutual action and reaction; and in Egypt, likewise, it is evident that both religion and morality are mutually dependent on each other.

The purity of Egyptian morality has caused some astonishment. It must not be forgotten, however, that it remained stationary at the elementary stage, and its moral maxims never rose to the rank of principles. The maxims are, at all events, very beautiful, and in part they are found recurring in the Mosaic law and even in the Gospel. Some of these have been already cited (p. 129 *et seq.*) The virtues praised and celebrated in these are again and again piety, loving-kindness and pity, mildness, moderation in deeds and words, chastity, protection of the weak, kindly dispositions towards inferiors, reverence to superiors, and also respect of property to the very smallest iota. If we inquire what testimony the deceased must be able to bring forward in their favour at the day of judgment, we find it is partly negative. "I have been guilty of no sins against men; I have not oppressed the miserable; I have not imposed work beyond his powers on any officer; I have allowed no master to maltreat his slave; I have done injury to nobody; nor have I caused any to weep or to perish with hunger. I have not told lies, or stolen, or committed murder; I have not even ordered anybody to be treacherously put to death. I have not prayed that it might be said I had done so; I have not committed adultery; I have not been a hypocrite, or licentious, or a drunkard. I have not falsified weights or measures; I have not appropriated the animals of the divine offerings, or stolen anything belonging to the deity. I have not taken the milk from the mouth of the nurslings. I have blasphemed neither the king nor my father, nor have I mocked God, or despised God in my heart."[1] But, on the other hand, we find positive duties, too, which the deceased must be able to declare that he fulfilled when he appears before the Judge in the hall of double righteousness. "I have given bread to him that was hungry, water to him that was thirsty, clothes to the naked, and shelter to the wanderer;" whence we see that, in the eyes of the Egyptian moralist, it was not enough to cease to do evil. Such assurances are very frequent. The ideal prince or nobleman (*erpa ha*) is described as being one faithful to his mother, zealous for his mistress, with a pleasant tongue, sweet of speech, courteous towards great and small. Very beautiful is the eulogy upon an illustrious personage of this sort. "His love was the food of the poor, the blessing of the weak, the riches of him who had nothing." A kindly spirit seems to breathe upon us from these precepts, and it is not without a show of reason that it has been asserted that such pure moral principles could not be the fruit of a religion the forms of which were still so imperfect, and, in some instances, so

---

[1] The so-called ancient canon is found in Pleyte, Etudes Egyptologiques, pt. vi. p. 168 *et seq.*; the more modern one, translated by Birch, in Bunsen : Egypt's Place in Universal History, pt. v. p. 253 *et seq.*

unchaste, and that, therefore, morality must have been totally independent of the religion.

The truth is, that with the Egyptians, moral teaching was not at all divorced from theology, but that they both belonged to and corresponded to each other. The rude and, to our ideas, offensive symbols did not prevent the religious conceptions of the Egyptian from being amongst the purest in all antiquity. We have already noticed his belief in the oneness and spirituality of God. And besides this, we have to take into account the utterances of the Egyptian poets or scribes which refer to the being of God in his relation to humanity, which are in no respect inferior to those of the psalmists and prophets of Israel. The feeling of dependence on the deity is nowhere more profound. The kings describe all their mighty deeds as being due to the assistance of the deity. It is his god who guides the king, who imbues his limbs with strength, who spreads his spirit and the dread of him through all lands, and grants him victory and might over all nations; who communicates to him where he must go, and who deprives the nostrils of his enemies of the breath of life. On the other hand, the king, or man in general, is pledged on his part to glorify the deity by his works (Ins. of Shashank I. at Silsilis). Everything is from God. The calamities brought upon the country by Cambyses are referred to on the so-called *statuette naophore*. " Great calamity over the whole country, the like of which never was, great trials sent by God." And P'tah-hotep says to his pupil, " When you cultivate *terh* (?) upon your land, it is God who bestows it upon you; the great provider for the satisfying of your mouth."[1] In the same book a good son is called a gift of God. Another lesson taught there is, that "God lives through that which is good and pure."

In this last expression the idea of the holiness of God is latent.

[1] See Chabas, Rev. Arch., 1851, i. 23, 715, 723.

Such religious conceptions are not only not inconsistent with a pure morality, they are distinctly favourable to it. A religious teaching that includes conceptions such as these of the deity and his relation to mankind, ranks higher than a collection of myths, more or less intelligible, but for the most part unpractical; and it also ranks higher than a set of prescriptions concerning ceremonies and customs. Such religious teaching does not occupy itself with that which is outside of life, but goes into and takes hold of life, and must hence have exercised influence over it. When man feels himself so entirely dependent on God, and is conscious of owing everything to Him, and when in his mind he connects all that is good and pure with God, when he feels himself called to live to the glory of God; or, as it is expressed in chap. cxxvii. of the "Book of the Dead," when he feels it incumbent on him to do God's good pleasure, and through his love to bind God to himself, man's moral consciousness rests not merely on the feeling of his responsibility towards his fellow-men, it is likewise due to his feeling of responsibility to a higher superhuman power.

The Egyptian gods accordingly became, for the most part—certainly the principal gods became—moral beings. Thus Ptah is called Lord of the Ell, or, what is the same thing, of righteousness; and consequently law and also property is under his divine protection, and transgression in respect of them is an offence against God. The prominent part taken by Ma, the goddess of truth and of righteousness itself, in the whole symbolism and mythology deserves notice in this connection. When the Egyptian wished to give assurance of his honesty and good faith, he called Thot to witness, the advocate in the heavenly court of justice, without whose justification no soul could stand in the day of judgment. The entire symbolism, as it sprang from the great myth of the Egyptians, depicts the struggle between light and darkness, fertility and barrenness, life and death; and in that idea there is a moral power already latent. But the moral significance was given to it by the people themselves. Osiris was not simply the sun-god; this signification was even completely thrown into the background by the later conception of him. He is the good being (Unnefer), in opposition to the evil power by whom he is persecuted, Apepi the serpent, or, at a later period, Set, his brother. And, to crown all, we have that striking feature in the religious views of the sons of Ham, the judgment of the dead, with its great tribunal of forty-two judges, who each institute an inquiry as to one particular transgression; and presiding there we see the Great God, the Lord of Ages, Osiris himself with his unerring balance and his sure retribution. All this shows us that a moral life, a life of holiness and beneficence, was conceived of as being a matter of solemn obligation towards the deity himself. To become like god Osiris, a benefactor, a good being, persecuted but justified, judged but pronounced innocent, was looked upon as the ideal of every pious man, and as the condition on which alone eternal life could be obtained and the means by which it could be continued.

THE END.

www.ingramcontent.com/pod-product-compliance
Lightning Source LLC
Chambersburg PA
CBHW020800230426
43666CB00007B/783